Improvisation and *Inventio*
in the Performance of Medieval Music

Improvisation and *Inventio* in the Performance of Medieval Music
A Practical Approach

Angela Mariani

OXFORD
UNIVERSITY PRESS

Oxford University Press is a department of the University of Oxford. It furthers
the University's objective of excellence in research, scholarship, and education
by publishing worldwide. Oxford is a registered trade mark of Oxford University
Press in the UK and certain other countries.

Published in the United States of America by Oxford University Press
198 Madison Avenue, New York, NY 10016, United States of America.

© Oxford University Press 2017

All rights reserved. No part of this publication may be reproduced, stored in
a retrieval system, or transmitted, in any form or by any means, without the
prior permission in writing of Oxford University Press, or as expressly permitted
by law, by license, or under terms agreed with the appropriate reproduction
rights organization. Inquiries concerning reproduction outside the scope of the
above should be sent to the Rights Department, Oxford University Press, at the
address above.

You must not circulate this work in any other form
and you must impose this same condition on any acquirer.

Library of Congress Cataloging-in-Publication Data
Names: Mariani, Angela (Mariani Smith) author.
Title: Improvisation and inventio in the performance of medieval music :
a practical approach / Angela Mariani.
Description: New York, NY : Oxford University Press, [2017] |
Includes bibliographical references.
Identifiers: LCCN 2016052897| ISBN 9780190631185 (pbk. : alk. paper) |
ISBN 9780190631178 (hardcover : alk. paper)
Subjects: LCSH: Music—Performance—History—500–1400. |
Improvisation (Music)—History—500–1400.
Classification: LCC ML172 .M366 2017 | DDC 781.3/60902—dc23
LC record available at https://lccn.loc.gov/2016052897

for Leo and Betty Ann

for Tom, Barbara, and Ben

. . . and most of all for Chris

CONTENTS

List of Figures   ix
List of Tables   xi
List of Examples   xiii
List of Practices   xv
Preface and Acknowledgments   xvii

1. The Process of *Inventio*   1
2. Living and "Imagined" Models: A New Oral Tradition   15
3. Notation and *Memoria*: What's Not on the Page   28
4. Mode: The Vocabulary of Melody   56
5. Inventing Melody: Old Instruments, New Voices   88
6. Inventing Organum: *Memoria* and Formula   134
7. Playing Poetry: The Rhetoric of Invention   157
8. The Long Memory: A Reflection on Teaching Medieval Music   191

Appendix: Mode Models   197
Selected Bibliography   215
Index   221

LIST OF FIGURES

2.1 Living models and mode of transmission   24
3.1 D to F, various neume shapes   32
3.2 Hildegard von Bingen, "Spiritus sanctus vivificans vita" (reproduced with permission, Hochschul- und Landesbibliothek RheinMain, Riesencodex, Hs 2, 466v)   35
3.3 Non-liquescent descending major second   36
3.4 Liquescent descending major second   36
3.5 Quilisma   37
3.6 Martin Codax, "Ondas do mar de Vigo" (reproduced with permission, Morgan Library and Museum)   39
3.7 "Viderunt" from the *Liber Usualis* with St. Gallen neumes   46
3.8 "Spiritus Sanctus" with noteheads and neumes   46
3.9 "Spiritus Sanctus" with text and neumes   46
3.10 "Spiritus Sanctus," Thornton transcription   47
3.11 The medieval hexachord system   51
3.12 Hexachord placement, modeled after the Guidonian hand   52
3.13 The "Ondas do mar" building   53
6.1 VOT mnemonic model   147

LIST OF TABLES

3.1	Applying Practice 3.1 to Hildegard's "Spiritus sanctus"	42
3.2	Applying Practice 3.1 to Martin Codax's "Ondas do mar"	44
4.1	Mode names (modern usage)	57
4.2	Modes as "altered scales"	58
4.3	Dorian "diatonic" triads	58
4.4	The *Protus*/Dorian modes	65
4.5	The *Deuterus*/Phrygian modes	66
4.6	The *Tritus*/Lydian modes	67
4.7	The *Tetrardus*/Mixolydian modes	67
5.1	Comparative structures of the French and Italian *Estampie/Istampitta*	119
5.2	Melodic material from *Ordo Virtutum* used in a composed *Estampie*	128
6.1	Immel's model of the thirty-one VOT progressions, from Immel, "Vatican Organum Treatise Re-Examined"	142
6.2	The rhythmic modes	152
7.1	*Planctus cygni*	164
7.2	Sequence form	166
7.3	"Cum polo Phoebus"	179

LIST OF EXAMPLES

3.1   D to F   *32*
4.1   Dorian melody (final transposed to A)   *59*
4.2   *Protus* authentic/Dorian formulaic melody (mode 1)   *65*
4.3   *Protus* plagal/Hypodorian formulaic melody (mode 2)   *65*
4.4   *Deuterus* authentic/Phrygian formulaic melody (mode 3)   *66*
4.5   *Deuterus* plagal/Hypophrygian formulaic melody (mode 4)   *66*
4.6   *Tritus* authentic/Lydian formulaic melody (mode 5)   *67*
4.7   *Tritus* plagal/Hypolydian formulaic melody (mode 6)   *67*
4.8   *Tetrardus* authentic/Mixolydian formulaic melody (mode 7)   *67*
4.9   *Tetrardus* plagal/Hypomixolydian formulaic melody (mode 8)   *68*
4.10 Psalm tone for mode 5   *70*
4.11 Intonation, mode 5   *71*
4.12 Mode 1 psalm tone with terminations   *73*
4.13 Intonation formulas   *74*
4.14 Variants of the intonation formula for mode 1   *75*
4.15 *Neumae*   *77*
4.16 Latin formulas   *78*
5.1   "Reis glorios"   *99*
5.2   "Reis glorios" refrain with drone   *99*
5.3   Bernard de Ventadorn, "Can vei la lauzeta mover," three variants   *105*
5.4a Machaut-style melodic figure, alone and with *repetitio*   *111*
5.4b Machaut-style melodic figure, with *amplificatio*   *111*
5.5   Faenza Codex, "Kyrie cunctipotens genitor," after Richard Taruskin, *The Earliest Notations to the Sixteenth Century* (New York: Oxford University Press, 2005); with permission   *114*

5.6	"La Septime Estampie Real"	120
5.7	"Istampitta Ghaetta"	121
5.8	The *Ordo* dance	130
6.1	Parallel organum from *Musica enchiriadis*	136
6.2	Parallel organum, "Lux aeterna"	137
6.3	Tritone in 6.2 avoided through the use of oblique motion	137
6.4	"Rex caeli domine," from *Musica enchiriadis*	138
6.5	Diagram representing rule no. 1, Vatican Organum Treatise	142
6.6	Musical examples pertaining to rule no. 1, Vatican Organum Treatise	144
6.7	First phrase of "Viderunt omnes"	149
6.8	Opening phrase, "Viderunt omnes," with upper voice following VOT rules	150
6.9	"Viderunt," with organum	150
6.10	The "Omnes" melisma from "Viderunt omnes"	151
6.11	"Omnes" melisma as tenor, with rhythmic mode 5 applied	153
6.12	Discant on "Omnes" melisma from "Viderunt omnes"	154
7.1	*Planctus cygni*	162
7.2	"Clangam" and "Ploratione" motives	166
7.3	*Planctus cygni*, strophe 3b, first line	166
7.4	Rhetorical treatment of "Clangam filii" figure	167
7.5	*Amplificatio* on "filii"	168
7.6	"Ploratione" motive	169
7.7	*Planctus cygni*, verse 9	170
7.8	*Planctus cygni*, verse 10	171
7.9	*Planctus cygni*, sample arrangement of first three verses	174
7.10	Rhetorical variations of "Alitis cygni" motive	175
7.11	Mode 2 formulas	185
7.12	"Cum polo Phoebus," incipit	186
7.13	"Cum polo Phoebus," verse 1	186
7.14	"Cum polo Phoebus," refrain	187
7.15	"Cum polo Phoebus," score	188

LIST OF PRACTICES

2.1	Using models from vernacular and world music traditions	23
2.2	What is your musical lineage?	25
2.3	Listening for "invention."	25
2.4	Discerning layers of modeling	26
3.1	What is and is not on the page	42
3.2	Using "placement" as a memory technique	54
4.1	Using Bailey's intonation formulas	80
4.2	Using the *Liber Usualis* as a source for modal models	81
4.3	Using the mode models (see appendix)	82
4.4	Exploring mode in secular or vernacular repertoire	85
4.5	Modal improvisation	86
5.1	What does the instrument "want" to play?	92
5.2	Preludes, interludes, postludes	97
5.3	Melodic variants as "invitations" to improvisation	109
5.4	Working with repertoire-specific patterns and gestures	112
5.5	A model of improvisatory practice: The Faenza Codex	116
5.6	Inventing a new section for an extant medieval dance	126
5.7	Options for varying the sections of an extant medieval dance	127
5.8	Creating an estampie	132
6.1	Adding a *vox organalis*, using a medieval source as a model	139
6.2	An improvised organum "relay"	148
6.3	Creating organum on a plainchant tenor, using VOT rules	151

6.4	Creating discant on a plainchant tenor, using VOT rules	154
7.1	Rhetorical analysis	175
7.2a	Playing poetry (1)	179
7.2b	Playing poetry (2)	180
7.2c	Playing poetry (3)	181
7.2d	Playing poetry (4)	182
7.2e	Playing poetry (5)	184

PREFACE AND ACKNOWLEDGMENTS

On a mild August day in Vancouver many years ago, I sat in a circle with about a half dozen other medieval music students and Benjamin Bagby of Sequentia. Before us were bits of photocopied chant from the *Liber Usualis*, each representing a different church mode. Having sung them all together a few times and discussed the characteristics of the modes as they were exemplified in the chant, we were invited to choose a mode and sing a spontaneous improvisation. I vividly remember choosing mode 5. Ben Bagby's encouragement of a deep and contemplative internalization of musical and poetic material, of the meeting of theory and practice, and of the creation of a safe space to improvise and invent was transformative for me as both a performer and teacher. During that same week at Early Music Vancouver's Mediaeval Programme, Barbara Thornton helped each of us choose a troubadour song to perform. The prospect of performing five verses of Occitan text was daunting, but she guided us as we learned the notes, studied the translation of the poems, and looked up each word so that we knew what each word meant as we were singing it. We listened to Barbara as she instructed the instrumentalists to "play the poem," a revelatory exercise in what one might call rhetorical improvisation. We followed her suggestions to put the translation into our own words, to adjust those words so that they matched the syllable count of the original, to invent mnemonic images that corresponded to the lines that gave us trouble, and to imagine the entire text plastered onto different locations on the façade of our childhood homes. She told us that "memory was not a function of the mind but of the soul." I turned that statement over and over in my mind, and I am still doing so. At the end of those two weeks, I had not only memorized my troubadour song and a variety of other pieces, but fragments of songs that I had "forgotten" kept surfacing in my consciousness, bubbling up, I suppose, from this thing we call a soul.

 A couple of years before that, Thomas Binkley had sent the students in his Medieval Literature and Performance Practice class home with crisp new copies of Geoffrey of Vinsauf's rhetorical treatise *Poetria nova* and told us to come back to the next class with a rhetorical analysis of the music of the Latin *Planctus cygni*. I was a first-year graduate student at the Indiana University

Jacobs School of Music, recently arrived from the world of rock and roll to attend what is now called the Historical Performance Institute. To say that I was puzzled would be an understatement. As I did the exercise, however, to my astonishment and excitement I felt as though I had discovered a new room in my brain. It would take a couple of decades for me to actually complete the assignment to my own satisfaction, but the link between rhetoric and music that can occur in the process of *inventio* had been forever forged in my musical experience.

I could not have written this book had I not been on the receiving end of the pedagogical techniques described above, nor could I perform and teach as I do today. When I sing the first verse of that troubadour song for my music history class, I usually accompany myself on the harp, incorporating bits of the mode 1 melody of the song and some of the melodic gestures that make up the vocabulary of mode 1. I do not plan a single harp pluck in advance. Improvisation and invention are part of the process that is medieval music performance practice, and in order to do that, one must have a storehouse of memorized musical vocabulary, techniques, and repertoire on which to draw.

One might argue that I learned from living models, and that it is perhaps a fool's errand to attempt to document in writing what is essentially an orally transmitted art. To this I would offer the *confutatio* that we live in a literate age, and our teachers do not always live in our village. While it is undeniable that most of the contents of this book were learned as a result of one-on-one interactions with a teacher or a vastly more experienced performer, it is my conviction that there is a place for a pedagogical text that will present medieval music in the context of the process involved in its invention and performance; that will offer the student an organized explanation of the vocabulary, rhetoric, technique, and practices involved in that process; and that will then figuratively hand the lyre back to the student and say, *Now you do it*.

As a longtime performer of rock music and folk music in the Anglo-Celtic tradition, invention and improvisation were comfortable territory for me when I entered the world of medieval music. For others, however, a single line of melody with an ancient foreign text and no musical directive may seem like those ancient maps with vast blank spaces on which a wary cartographer has written "Here be dragons." But if musicians are invited to explore the processes of medieval music's invention and performance and encouraged to build and accumulate a memory storehouse of material related to the content of medieval repertoire, then they may claim mastery of these dragons, producing substantive and satisfying performances and forever changing the way both they and their audiences experience medieval music.

This book will be useful to musicians whose primary teaching and performing activities are both inside and outside the area of medieval music. It is also intended to be useful to advanced students who want to tackle medieval music performance practice but desire guidance when it comes to providing all the musical content that is not on the page but is still necessary in order to create a convincing performance. It provides usable models for performance while offering sufficient historical and theoretical information to enable the reader to understand the models. A certain amount of individual volition and proactive energy is also assumed; in many areas the content of the book points the way down the path but does not hold the hand of the walker.

It is also my intention that this book should juggle the practical and the theoretical; that it will be challenging to a student but accessible enough that one could require it for students taking a workshop in medieval music improvisation. I imagine it also as a helpful tool to use in conjunction with a course in medieval music performance practice, perhaps along with a more traditional medieval music textbook and scores, so that one might engage the performers in the class and remind them that medieval music is not some opaque collection of musical arcana, but rather a vehicle for their own performance and invention.

Taking all of that into consideration, it is still important to state that no written pedagogical treatise can take the place of learning by imitating a living model. I would encourage any student who uses this book to do so in conjunction with actual teachers of medieval music. In turn, I hope that it might be of use to those who teach medieval music in the contexts of applied performance, music history and musicology classes, and ensembles. I hope that it may also provide an approach to understanding medieval music through the process of its creation and transmission, and inspire us to teach it accordingly.

There are many people without whom this book could not have come to fruition: teachers, colleagues, students, family, and friends. I was fortunate to be born into a family of musicians; my parents, Betty Ann and Leo Mariani, a church musician and a jazz musician respectively, encouraged musical invention in both me and my sister, Deva, a gifted jazz singer and instrumentalist. I am grateful that after putting up with the loud rock and roll in the basement and, years later, with the Irish traditional tunes, they did not appear to think it was insane to become a practitioner of medieval music. I only regret that Leo is not here to read this book on improvisation and invention.

It is nearly impossible to express the extent of my gratitude to Benjamin Bagby and Barbara Thornton. Many of the techniques, approaches, and exercises described in this book were transmitted to me directly from them or inspired by their teaching methods. Both Ben and Barbara, when she was still with us, communicated in their teaching the process of medieval music performance, bringing the same intensity to the classroom that they always put into their transcendent performances. For me and for many other students of medieval music, they were the "living models" that we strove to emulate. I thank them for their mentoring, kindness, friendship, and support.

And then, of course, there is Tom Binkley. I can still hear his voice saying, "What do you need to know to be able to play this piece?" He left us over twenty years ago, and yet I find when I read this book some part of him is still present. From the first time he opened a medieval song manuscript and asked us to tell him "what was not on the page," to his admonition to "play what the instrument wants to play," to his mind-boggling demand to know "why you played an F#" in that particular spot in your improvised prelude, he was the ultimate advocate for *inventio*.

I would also like to express my gratitude to all the faculty of the Historical Performance Institute, formerly the Early Music Institute, at the Indiana University Jacobs School of Music, especially to Wendy Gillespie, who has been a deeply appreciated and admired teacher, mentor, and musical model to me for many years; to Paul Elliott, who through his skill, support, and patience, taught this rock and roller to sing early music; to Elisabeth Wright, whose fluent and spirited performance and teaching skill showed me a completely new way to love and experience Baroque music; and to Thomas J. Mathiesen, for his encyclopedic knowledge, support, and mentorship. I am also endlessly grateful to J. Peter Burkholder, who spent many hours reading and editing the original version of this book, for his encouragement; his insightful comments, criticisms, and suggestions, which improved the book by several orders of magnitude; and for his friendship.

My work on the book was also facilitated by my Texas Tech School of Music faculty colleagues and our director, William Ballenger, all of whom were unendingly helpful and encouraging. I am indeed extraordinarily fortunate to work in such a collegial environment. That good fortune has also manifested in the opportunity to know and work with the numerous students in the Texas Tech Collegium Musicum, who for many years have patiently and enthusiastically allowed themselves to be on the receiving end of many of the pedagogical approaches enumerated in these pages.

Many friends and colleagues contributed to the musical examples, images, and artwork. I would especially like to thank three alumni of the Texas Tech Collegium Musicum, all professionals in their own realms of performance, cognition, composition, church music, and early music, who helped me inestimably with the manuscript. Ryan Best digitized all of the first draft's musical examples from my scribble. Rob DeVet creatively employed the Gregorio software to produce the beautiful chant and psalm tone examples. I am especially indebted to Benjamin Robinette, who worked tirelessly to create the final polished versions of dozens of musical examples, figures, and tables; his creative suggestions and solutions were invaluable, and his generosity with his time, labor, skill, and spirit are deeply appreciated. I am also grateful to photographer extraordinaire Tif Holmes for the creative, beautiful, and evocative photos of my medieval instruments that grace the cover. All the stringed instruments were built by Timothy G. Johnson; the organetto originally belonged to Sequentia and might be recognized from a couple of photos from their early recordings. Thanks and credit also must go to the Morgan Library and Museum in New York for the Martin Codax *cantiga* image from the Vindal manuscript; to Martin Mayer at the Hochschul- und Landesbibliotek RheinMain in Wiesbaden for the image from the Riesencodex; and to Benjamin Bagby for permission to use an image from one of Barbara Thornton's Hildegard transcriptions.

I would also like to express my gratitude to Oxford University Press and to editor Suzanne Ryan for her encouragement, patience, support, and assistance; to Oxford's editorial team, including Victoria Kouznetsov, Andrew Maillet, and Denise Phillip Grant; to the production team at Newgen Knowledge Works; to copyeditor Ben Sadock, for his detailed and insightful suggestions and comments; and to the outside readers whose thoughtful scrutiny and excellent suggestions greatly enhanced and improved the final product.

Much of this book is ultimately about performance, and I would be remiss if I did not also acknowledge and celebrate the friendship, camaraderie, and musical inspiration afforded to me through many years by my fellow travelers in Altramar Medieval Music Ensemble, originally founded back in 1991 at Indiana University by Jann Cosart, David Stattelman, Allison Zelles Lloyd, myself, and, of course, Chris Smith. That leads me to my last and most heartfelt acknowledgement, for there are not enough words in the world to express sufficient thanks, love, and appreciation to Chris, my musical partner, academic colleague, husband, and best friend. His encouragement; exchange of artistic and intellectual ideas; emotional, financial, and spiritual support; marital and musical companionship; thousands of home-cooked meals; and deep and abiding friendship have enriched my life for thirty-five years. This book is for him.

Improvisation and *Inventio*
in the Performance of Medieval Music

CHAPTER 1

The Process of *Inventio*

Part of the art of both actors and musicians is to skillfully provide those elements of performance that exist outside the script or the notation. While this is true of music in any period or style, some types of notation are more prescriptive than others. The extant notation of medieval music is in many ways non-prescriptive; it leaves a lot more room for performer interpretation than most modern notation. The fact that some examples of pre-fifteenth-century music were preserved in notation does not unlock the mystery of how the music actually sounded in performance. In many cases, it omits important bits of musical information altogether, such as rhythm and meter, instrumentation, or even specific pitch. At the same time, it may also contain information that is missing from modern notation, like the vocal inflection represented by a "liquescent" neume, or the enigmatic *quilisma*. Some medieval notation appears to have been intended only as a mnemonic device, hinting at content that had been more fully committed to memory, as with unheightened neumes. If musicians from diverse regions in medieval Europe both composed and improvised "outside" the notation, then performers who claim to be proponents of historical performance practice must engage with that process as well, if we wish to create a living performance that is more than a snapshot of accurately carbon-dated bones.

While we may study the musical objects that survived the centuries, diligently read the theoretical treatises, learn innumerable details about medieval performance practice, and strive to incorporate all of that knowledge into our performances, it is not possible to recreate a performance of medieval music exactly "as it would have been done." The elusive element of *inventio*, as the medieval rhetoricians would have called it, must always be provided by the performer in the present. The modern performer, therefore, is better served to try to understand and replicate processes: how musicians of a particular time and region learned, how they memorized the vast language of mode and lyric, what they valued in music and poetry, and how they passed the music on to other performers.

This book is an attempt to examine aspects of the process of *inventio* manifest in medieval music, so that we may continue to employ it in our own performances of historical repertoire and teach others how to do so as well.

INVENTIO AND *MEMORIA*

In medieval texts, the act of *inventio* is most often described using the language of rhetoric. As Mary Carruthers points out in *The Craft of Thought*, "In antiquity and through the Middle Ages, invention or 'creative thinking' received the most detailed attention in the domain of rhetoric, rather than of psychology or what we would now call the philosophy of mind." *Inventio* was inextricably related to *memoria*, and inventive skill was completely tied to the possession of well-organized reserves of memory from which the speaker (writer, artist, or musician) could draw:

> The Latin word *inventio* gave rise to two separate words in modern English. One is our word "invention," meaning the "creation of something new" (or at least different). These creations can be either ideas or material objects, including of course works of art, music, and literature. We also speak of people having "inventive minds," by which we mean that they have many "creative" ideas, and they are generally good at "making," to use the Middle English synonym of "composition." ... The other modern English word derived from Latin *inventio* is "inventory." ... This observation points to a fundamental assumption about the nature of "creativity" in classical culture. Having "inventory" is a requirement for "invention." Not only does this statement assume that one cannot create ("invent") without a memory store ("inventory") to invent from and with, but it also assumes that one's memory-store is effectively "inventoried," that its matters are in readily recoverable "locations."[1]

Carruthers also refers to this inventory in her significant and influential *Book of Memory*, explaining that the development of a "structured memory" was a very important tool in medieval learning. Medieval rhetoricians and educators encouraged their students to think in terms of consciously designed memory, for memory "without conscious design is like an uncatalogued library. ... Memory is most like a library of texts, made accessible and useful through

---

1. Mary Carruthers, *The Craft of Thought: Meditation, Rhetoric, and the Making of Images, 400–1200* (Cambridge, UK: Cambridge University Press, 1998), 10–12.

various consciously-applied heuristic schemes." Carruthers also points out that a commonly used metaphor for the "educated memory" was the Latin word *thesaurus*, which translates as "storage room," and that "the image of the memorial storehouse is a rich model of pre-modern mnemonic practice."[2]

Most of us born in this technological age do not exercise our memory muscles anymore, and although we may be intrigued by Sherlock Holmes's "memory palace," we do not spend time constructing memory storehouses with containers, bins, and rooms.

Listening to music has become an almost completely passive process; you do not have to leave your house to hear it, much less take part in its creation or memorize it. This passivity sometimes extends to more general learning processes as well; students often ask why they are asked to memorize facts and find it difficult to understand why they are required to memorize data when the facts can be had from the Internet in seconds. The answer is that a storehouse of memorized content enables us to integrate different aspects of that content. In terms of the medieval "seven liberal arts," memory facilitates integration not just in the practice of the language arts of the trivium but also in the practice of the scientific and musical disciplines of the quadrivium. It is quite difficult to generate critical thought or formulate a hypothesis if you have to google the facts every thirty seconds, and it is difficult to improvise Notre Dame organum if you have not internalized the rules of interval progression and you cannot recall the tenor line. A model will not be effective if the demonstration offered by the model is not held in the memory.

The process of improvisation and composition, therefore, depends upon a synthesis of multiple skills and resources that requires a certain amount of information to be stored in the memory:

1. Knowledge of the musical expectations and vocabulary (melodic, motivic, rhythmic, timbral, dynamic, harmonic, etc.) specific to that particular idiom
2. The internalization in memory, through study, practice, and experiment, of the specifics of that musical vocabulary, which in turn permits spontaneous musical invention
3. The technical ability to compose musical material spontaneously, not captured in notation, that fits within the structural, melodic, and/or harmonic framework of a particular idiom
4. Availability of models suitable for emulation.

For performers in the Middle Ages, we must add a fifth memorized resource—their entire storehouse of repertoire. It should be noted that this is also true

---

2. Mary Carruthers, *The Book of Memory: A Study of Memory in Medieval Culture* (Cambridge, UK: Cambridge University Press, 1990), 33–34.

of modern performers in most vernacular musics such as rock, folk, jazz, and so on, and many performers in those genres have a remarkable thesaurus of repertoire, techniques, melodic and harmonic patterns, and other memorized idiomatic musical data at their disposal. But for musicians who have been dependent on learning music from scores, and in many cases have been accustomed to playing from score even in performance, one's own storehouse of memory is unfamiliar territory, and techniques designed to increase the contents can be both a revelation and a challenge.

IMPROVISATION VERSUS COMPOSITION

In addition to acknowledging that skill at *inventio* requires a good storehouse of memory, we must also explore the distinction between improvisation and composition if we are to try and understand the processes by which various musicians in the Middle Ages performed beyond or outside of notation. That distinction is not always clearly articulated, and improvisation is sometimes thought of as a kind of "sped-up composition," a view that is eloquently disputed by jazz musician and educator Ed Sarath in *Improvisation, Creativity, and Consciousness*:

> Improvisation may be defined as spontaneous creativity with little or nothing planned in advance. It is perhaps best understood in relationship to compositional creativity, which is essentially an ongoing planning endeavor. Whereas composition occurs in a series of discontinuous episodes that can span days, weeks, or months in the completion of a work, improvisation occurs in a single, continuous creative episode. Whereas composers usually work alone, improvisation—which can certainly happen in solitude—often occurs collectively. Whereas compositions are created at times and places that are different from when they are presented to audiences, improvisation involves simultaneous creation and performance/presentation.[3]

The two processes also represent different experiences of creative activity in time:

> The moment the composer stops, steps outside the creative flow to reflect upon, capture, and structure as part of a larger work a moment that had just passed, a new kind of temporal consciousness begins to take shape that is the basis for a very different line of creative expression than that whereby the artist sustains a moment-to-moment flow throughout a single creative episode.[4]

---

3. Edward W. Sarath, *Improvisation, Creativity, and Consciousness: Jazz as Integral Template for Music, Education, and Society* (Albany: State University of New York Press, 2013), Kindle ed., locations 870–73.
4. Sarath, *Improvisation*, Kindle location 3367–69.

The difference in process that distinguishes composition and improvisation does not, however, mean that they may not be represented in the same performance. A composed piece can include a section allowing for material that will be improvised; this may have temporal restrictions or be open-ended. A musical performance that is largely improvised may have predetermined structural or harmonic limitations (improvising over chord changes, for example), or the performer may include phrases that consciously allude to, quote, or otherwise reference pre-existing material.

Another dangerous but common misunderstanding is the identification of improvisation with oral processes only, and of composition with only written or literate processes. Variations can be improvised, for example, on the basis of a pre-written phrase or theme. There is some evidence that polyphonic organum and discant may have grown from an improvised practice, and eventually came to be "composed in the mind" and then ultimately written down.[5] Richard Taruskin describes a phenomenon he calls "composition within an oral context," chiding musicians who confuse it with improvisation:

> Improvisation—making things up as you go along in "real time"—is a performance art. It implies an ephemeral, impermanent product. But while some forms of orally transmitted music (jazz, for example) do enlist the spontaneous creative faculty in real time, there have always been musicians (today's rock bands, for example) who work out compositions without notation yet meticulously in detail, and in advance. They fix their work in memory in the very act of creating it, so that it will be permanent. Every performance is expected to resemble every other one (which of course need not preclude retouching or improvement over time, or even spontaneously). Their work, while "oral," is not improvisatory. The creative and re-creative acts have been differentiated.[6]

---

5. One of the most important works regarding the role of memory and transmission in medieval repertoire is Anna Maria Busse Berger's *Medieval Music and the Art of Memory*, in which Berger suggests that even polyphonic repertoires such as organum and discant may have been composed "in the mind" by a process that resulted from a lifelong familiarity with mnemonic patterns and other techniques of memory described at length in rhetorical as well as musical sources. See Anna Maria Busse Berger, *Medieval Music and the Art of Memory* (Berkeley: University of California Press, 2005). Berger's work has greatly increased our understanding of the role of memory in the process of medieval pedagogy, the transmission of repertoire and formulas, and the act of improvisation and oral composition.

6. Richard Taruskin, *The Earliest Notations to the Sixteenth Century* (Oxford: Oxford University Press, 2005), 17, the first volume in Taruskin's multivolume *Oxford History*

Evidence suggests that many medieval musicians also employed both the "spontaneous creative faculty in real time" (in dance music, song accompaniment, or even the trouvères' spontaneous-song-creation competitions) and the "fixing of their work in memory in the very act of creating it" (in the invention and performance of organum).

Quite different from Taruskin's "composition within an oral context" is composition in the context of an oral tradition utilizing memorized themes and formulas. Leo Treitler describes this as "oral composition":

> Oral composition is composition done in the act of performing. The basis of an oral composition is a framework that is described in terms of two kinds of elements: themes and formulas. . . . If the singer has accumulated a repertory of standard formulas, each serves him when his knowledge of theme and formulaic system calls for a phrase of its characteristics. They belong to the complex of habits and associations that enable the singer to compose at high speed.[7]

This "composition at high speed" is part of an oral process, but the formulas themselves are not improvised; this is an important distinction (although the combining of the formulas may indeed be an extempore process).

The act of improvisation can also include some elements of preplanning. In a 2008 article on improvisation versus composition, music theorist Steve Larson pointed out that separating the process of improvisation from the

---

of Western Music. While "composition within an oral context" is not utilized by all rock bands, there are indeed rock bands whose concert performances, played entirely from memory, reproduce their recordings down to the last eighth note.

7. Leo Treitler, "Homer and Gregory: The Transmission of Epic Poetry and Plainchant," in *With Voice and Pen: Coming to Know Medieval Song and How It Was Made* (Oxford: Oxford University Press, 2007), 170. *With Voice and Pen* gathers several decades' worth of Treitler's articles and essays into one volume covering the topics of the oral process, orality vs. literacy, formulaic memory processes, and the relationship of music to poetry. "Homer and Gregory," originally published in *Musical Quarterly* 60 (1974): 333–72, was a groundbreaking study of orality in medieval music, particularly as identified in plainchant and medieval epic, and was influenced to some degree by Albert Lord and his seminal work *The Singer of Tales* (Cambridge, MA: Harvard University Press, 1960), which dealt with the formulaic memorization and transmission of epic poetry. (Treitler and other scholars of musicology and ethnomusicology have since questioned Lord's rejection of the notion that rote memory also plays a part in oral transmission.) Other scholars have also demonstrated that both memorization and the internalization of formulaic patterns played a role in the transmission and invention of medieval repertoire, from plainchant to secular song and even polyphony; two notable examples are Berger's *Medieval Music and the Art of Memory*, and Peter Jeffreys's *Re-envisioning Past Musical Cultures: Ethnomusicology in the Study of Gregorian Chant* (Chicago: University of Chicago Press, 1995).

process of composition because of the supposed "instantaneous" aspect of improvisation is misleading. While Sarath describes the distinction between composition and improvisation in terms of temporal discontinuity, Larson articulates the difference in terms of "storage" and the potential for revision:

> I now understand improvisation as the *real-time yet preheard—and even practiced—choice among possible paths that elaborate a preexisting structure* [italics mine], using familiar patterns and their familiar combinations and embellishments. And I now understand composition as putting together musical elements and storing them—whether in memory, notation, or sound-recording media—in a way that allows, but does not require, revision. ... These definitions are not mutually exclusive. Music can be either, neither, or both of these things. Some improvisations are best regarded as compositions. Other improvisations are not. Some compositions are best regarded as recorded improvisations. Other compositions are not. Some aleatoric music, often cited as an example of music that is both composed and improvised, may be neither. And I suspect that all enduring music is created by improvisation, whether or not it is recorded in notation.[8]

The utilization of processes drawn from both composition and improvisation also occurs when a basic structure or musical framework of a piece or an accompaniment to a melody is sketched out in advance of performance but then routinely altered or varied during the course of performance according to the expressive desire or inspiration of the performer in the moment. I identify this as *fluid composition*, a term to which I will refer throughout this book. Fluid composition is used a great deal in the performance of folk music and some varieties of traditional music, and can be a very useful approach for certain kinds of medieval repertoire such as monophonic song.

THE WAY IT WAS, AND THE WAY IT IS

Because of the nature of the transmission of medieval music, some degree of improvisation, fluid composition, or any other manifestation of *inventio* is necessary to create and deliver a performance, including performances intended to reflect historical practices and processes. Any performance we create—of any music—will also unavoidably contain ourselves: our background of musical experience, our training, and our "storehouse of memory," which contains nearly a millennium of musical repertoire and practice unavailable to our

---

8. Steve Larson, "Composition versus Improvisation?" *Journal of Music Theory* 49 (Fall 2005): 272–75.

medieval forebears. Even the staunchest adherents of "solo a cappella only" performance of medieval song must invent text underlay and make decisions about phrasing, tempo, dynamics, articulations, ornamentation, and other unwritten factors. They must also make choices about vocal production, and those choices are by necessity based on information that is not definitive or is to some degree conjectural.

Daniel Leech-Wilkinson, in his important book *The Modern Invention of Medieval Music*, declares candidly that most "medieval music" currently being performed is in effect "new music." Whether or not this statement was intended to be provocative, it is welcome, and in a sense it frees us from the tiresome expectation that we must have a historical justification for every note and nuance in our performances. In a repertoire with nonprescriptive notation and no living composers, how could our performances not contain "new music"?

Leech-Wilkinson also states that "the modern performance of medieval music absolutely requires that one believe both incompatible things together: we try to do it the way it was, and we know we cannot, and we argue for both."[9] Historical performance practice is indeed often defined by both its practitioners and its enthusiasts as "trying to do it the way it was," and in his statement Leech-Wilkinson challenges us to clarify, refine, or even question this assumed intention. While the "authenticity wars" of the 1980s have cooled considerably among early music practitioners and musicologists, the activities of both "early music" and historical performance are still, for better or for worse, associated with the intention of providing an "authentic" rendition of music "the way it was done," and audiences still come expecting to hear something that in actual fact could only be experienced with the assistance of a time machine.[10] Margaret Bent suggests an alternative:

> Instead of pretending to recover the irrecoverable actual sounds of medieval music, we ought to be devoting more effort to informing aural judgement by reconstructing their—at least partly recoverable—technical priorities; trying to learn the musical language in its own terms must be a first step towards internalizing aesthetic premises that are largely opaque to us. It is dangerous to assume that the notation means what it appears to mean, without understanding the training which complements it.[11]

---

9. Daniel Leech-Wilkinson, *The Modern Invention of Medieval Music* (Cambridge, UK: Cambridge University Press, 2007), 55.
10. An example of this debate can be found in "The Limits of Authenticity: A Discussion," *Early Music* 12, no. 1 (February 1984): 3–26.
11. Margaret Bent, "Grammar and Rhetoric in Late Medieval Polyphony," in *Rhetoric Beyond Words*, ed. Mary Carruthers (Cambridge, UK: Cambridge University Press, 2010), 65.

To discover what might be recoverable of the repertoire, practices, and processes of musical performance in the medieval era and to engage with those aspects of the music as modern performers, it is necessary to release our preoccupation with, and our audiences' expectation of, an "authentic sound." If, indeed, we describe our research into medieval performance practice as "recovery," we are in turn tacitly acknowledging that, as Bent stated, some aspects of early performance are not recoverable. It is in the unrecoverable space, particularly cavernous in the case of medieval music, that we must employ *inventio* if we are to make a convincing and effective performance. A thoughtful application of *inventio*, informed by process and historical practice, will result in a performance that frames and foregrounds the beauty, relevance, and value of that which was recovered. Ultimately, if we do not engage with both recovery and *inventio*, then our alternative is either to avoid performing medieval music at all, leaving a thousand years' worth of Western music's cultural history to molder in a drawer, or to present it in a way that is completely removed from the process by which it was generated in the first place.

Performers of medieval music must, therefore, reclaim the process of *inventio* without becoming hamstrung by the fear that they might take a step beyond an elusive boundary that defines "the way it was done." Even music that has somehow survived on a piece of vellum for eight hundred years only becomes alive when musicians make it their own and perform the music "the way it is," right now in this moment, and even, perhaps, "the way we want to hear it." Ultimately, Leech-Wilkinson's argument supports the notion that there is a difference between the snipe hunt that is the quest for total "authenticity" and the employment of a scholarly, historically informed, and creative approach that allows for invention.

MODELS AND PROCESSES

Approaches to the theory and practice of improvisation and invention in medieval music have tended to fall into one or more of the following categories:

1. *Descriptive*: descriptions or editions of medieval treatises containing information relevant to the art of improvisation, such as the Vatican Organum Treatise, Jerome of Moravia's descriptions of ornaments such as the *longa florata* and "reverberation," manuscripts containing modal intonations and formulas, and so on
2. *Text-driven*: material dependent upon the study of manuscript notations, including interpretation of neumatic notation, comparisons of manuscript variants, examination of relationships between musical and poetic structures, invention of new instrumental dances based on structures found in extant notated dances, and so on

3. *Comparative*: borrowing methodology and/or musical language from extant world music traditions in order to provide improvisational models, including the observation of and possibly adoption of the "other" traditions' instrumentation, orchestration, and arrangement methods, pedagogical styles, approaches to modal improvisation, vocal and instrumental techniques, and so on
4. *Lineage-driven*: using techniques and musical language learned directly from the interpretations of previous modern performers of medieval music, including direct contact with other performers through classes, individual lessons, and workshops and the imitation of performances heard in concert or via audio recordings and videos.

The above approaches each contain abstraction and concrete data and practice in differing proportions, but all of them involve to some degree the imitation of a model, whether that model is a text or a living musician. In this regard, historical performance practitioners are in the same territory as any musician learning a traditional song aurally from another singer or watching a violin teacher's bow hold. It is more complicated in the case of medieval performance practice, where the process of internalizing data acquired through a combination of the descriptive and text-driven approaches contributes to the construction of an "imagined" model where no living models are available. We internalize data that is "certifiably" medieval (repertoire, medieval languages, literature, iconography, music theory, rhetoric, performance context), but in order to actually create a living performance in the absence of living models, we must externalize that data by imagining what it might have sounded like. In accepting the fact that the sound of the model must still be created in the imagination regardless of its basis on historical data, we embrace the freedom that comes with the futility of claiming that we are performing the music exactly "as it was done" in the Middle Ages.

To add another layer of complication to the process of medieval performance practice, the imagined models then come to be employed in combination with the imitation of contemporary living models (the "lineage-driven" category above)—in other words, of modern teachers and performers of early music and live and recorded performances. This was less true for the groundbreaking performers of the 1950s and 1960s, who had no living models. Some of them turned to the approach I refer to above as "comparative," in which various non-Western traditional musics are explored in the hope that they may provide improvisational or inventive models. These comparative approaches can be problematic, as we will see, but they can also be very valuable, because they may introduce the player or singer to an improvisatory process that operates within a modal system of delineated musical scales, patterns, and gestures, as medieval music does, or to develop familiarity with a musical language that, like medieval music, does not follow the conventions of Western functional harmony.

Complicated issues can arise, however, with the comparative approach. Leaving aside issues of cultural appropriation and accusations of Orientalism that go far beyond the scope of the current discussion, the layers of musical transmission can also become difficult to distinguish.[12] If a medieval music practitioner decides to follow the model of another performer who incorporates non-Western music into performances of medieval European repertoire, she runs the risk of misunderstanding which aspects of the modern living model's performances come from the imagined model described above and which come from the non-Western source. It is important for students of historical performance practice to see clearly whether they are incorporating some aspect of performance practice because an influential generation of performers did so or because they understand and agree with the reason *why* the previous performers did so. Is this "what medieval music sounded like," or was the argument for this particular practice convincing and the model therefore worth emulating?

The comparative approach is perhaps best utilized in conjunction with the descriptive and text-driven content of the first two approaches. It can be very enlightening to discover ways in which the functions and processes of a particular world music can inform our performance of medieval music; however, if we abandon the idiomatic repertoire, language, vocabulary, patterns, and structures of medieval music, we run the risk of creating what Ben Bagby once described as "superficial imitations of non-European traditions [that] are hailed as 'innovative research.'"[13] The skillful combination of descriptive, text-driven, comparative, and lineage-driven approaches to the performance of medieval music is a basic premise of this book. Our model for performing medieval music must itself be a process of invention woven of a complex interaction of historical, text-analytical, and ethnographic analysis that generates a language of "medieval" performance practice.[14]

---

12. See John Haines, "The Arabic Style of Performing Medieval Music," *Early Music* 29, no. 3 (August 2001): 369–80, and Kirsten Yri, "Thomas Binkley and the Studio der Frühen Musik: Challenging 'the Myth of Westernness,'" *Early Music* 38, no. 2 (May 2010): 273–80.

13. Benjamin Bagby, "Imagining the Early Medieval Harp," in *A Performer's Guide to Medieval Music,* ed. Ross Duffin (Bloomington: Indiana University Press, 2000), 336.

14. The importance of understanding the role of process in applying improvisation to early music performance practice has been addressed by other performers of medieval music, particularly those who also teach. See Kenneth Zuckerman, "Improvisation in Medieval Music," in *Improvisation II: Internationale Tagung für Improvisation*, ed. Walter Fähndrich (Lucerne, Switzerland: Amadeus, 1993), 134–42; Tina Chancey, "Contextual Improvisation, or Why Swat Flies with a Frisbee," *Early Music America Magazine* 17, no. 2 (Summer 2011): 32–35 and 58–59; Margriet Tindemans, "Improvisation and Accompaniment before 1300," in Duffin, *Performer's*

OVERVIEW: CONTENT, STRUCTURE, AND INTENTION

Improvisation and Inventio *in the Performance of Medieval Music* presents a series of models and processes in a format that is primarily practical and pedagogical. Theoretical and historical evidence for invention in medieval music is combined with practical methodologies designed to help the reader internalize the abstract concepts and use them to formulate processes that function as models for invention. Those processes are then externalized through the use of a series of concrete, repeatable, and productive practice exercises included in the course of each chapter. The practices range from contemplation to active performance and are designed to develop facility with both the expressive goals and the practical processes of musical invention, improvisation, and composition.

Chapters 2 through 7 follow a consistent internal organization, articulating an area of essential knowledge or practice, drawing on existing scholarship on the historical sources of that practice, and describing practical skills and perspectives that must be added to abstract knowledge of these sources. At relevant points in each chapter there will be examples of specific practices intended to facilitate a performer's ability to render these arcane areas of knowledge into compelling, accessible, skillful, and ultimately contemporary performances.

Chapter 2, "Living and 'Imagined' Models: A New Oral Tradition," expands upon the discussion of models outlined above, inviting a contemplative inquiry into models, musical lineage, and the process of *inventio* and the ways in which all three of those elements manifest in our own musical experience. Because many accomplished musicians come to medieval music with almost no experience in improvisation, the chapter also includes some "deep listening" practices intended to demystify playing without notation and to encourage discernment between notated content and invention in other musicians' performances.

Chapter 3, "Notation and *Memoria*: What's Not on the Page," examines ways in which medieval notation itself reveals the importance of a highly developed memory to the medieval musician's process. While it does not offer a primer in medieval notation, specific examples are provided and explained in order to demonstrate the lack of prescriptive information present in much medieval notation. Using two specific pieces as examples (an antiphon by Hildegard von Bingen and one of the Martin Codax *cantigas de amigo*), we find that we can identify areas where musical invention may be utilized by determining, in addition to the original performance context, what information is not

---

Guide to Medieval Music, 454–69; and Ralf Mattes, "Improvisation and Accompaniment after 1300," in Duffin, *Performer's Guide to Medieval Music*, 470–81.

included in the medieval notation. Considered next is the topic of the storehouse of memory, which contains the internalized idiomatic material from which to draw the performative content that will fill the space left open by the non-prescriptive notation. The discussion of memory leads to the presentation of medieval techniques of placement and visualization that were used to enhance the memory capacity, thus providing some tools that can be applied to the internalization of the data in the subsequent chapters.

Chapter 4, "Mode: The Vocabulary of Melody," begins by clarifying that the "church modes" of medieval music are used and understood differently from modes in jazz or popular music, where they occur in the context of functional harmony. Mode is then considered through the didactic tools of *noeane* intonations, melismatic *neumae*, Latin formulas, and psalm tones, all used in the Middle Ages in a systematic way to teach mode as a system of melodic patterns and gestures residing in the memory storehouse. Practices include suggested procedures for internalizing the modal patterns and characteristics and the use of a series of eight "mode models," located in their entirety in the appendix, that juxtapose the formulas associated with a particular mode with actual pieces of plainchant or monophonic song in that same mode.

Chapter 5, "Inventing Melody: Old Instruments, New Voices," examines the process of melodic *inventio* in the modern performance of medieval music. Topics and practices cover practical decisions regarding historical instrumentation, the issue of adding invented material to an extant medieval instrumental piece (preludes, interludes, postludes, drones, etc.), issues regarding ornamentation, and the use of extant medieval dances as models for the invention of instrumental music "in the style of" the original. (Providing an instrumental accompaniment to a monophonic song is a related but different topic, addressed in chapter 7.) While chapter 5 focuses on the role of instruments, it is also relevant to singers; they must collaborate and communicate effectively with instrumentalists, and the discussion of ornamentation applies equally to both singers and players.

Chapter 6, "Inventing Organum: *Memoria* and Formula," begins with the earliest written evidence of parallel polyphony, followed by a practical inquiry into improvised practice in early polyphony and the possibilities for incorporating processes of improvisation and fluid composition into our own performances. Special attention is given to the Vatican Organum Treatise, including the degree to which the treatise may reflect an improvisatory practice, with suggestions for committing its rules of intervallic progression to memory, and exercises that encourage musicians to put the rules into practice by creating their own improvised organum lines alone or in groups.

Chapter 7, "Playing Poetry: The Rhetoric of Invention," begins with a discussion of medieval rhetoric and its connection to musical practice. Rhetoric was taught in an extremely systematic way that lends itself very well to the memory storehouse; however, its application to music can seem somewhat abstract. To illustrate, I offer a step-by-step rhetorical analysis of the Latin *Planctus cygni*. The analysis itself is followed by a discussion via notated examples of the realization of this analytical process in actual arrangement and performance. The process is then taken a step further with a demonstration of the way in which a medieval lyric with no extant melody—*Cum polo Phoebus*, from Boethius's *Consolation of Philosophy*, one of the few *metra* to which neumes have not been applied—can be set to music using elements of rhetoric, mode, structure, and text rhythm characteristic of medieval music—in other words, inventing new music from medieval building blocks.

I conclude in chapter 8, "The Long Memory: A Reflection on Teaching Medieval Music," with a reconsideration of medieval music's role in the narrative that comprises the "long memory" of Western music history. This revision rejects the marginalizing idea that medieval music represents an interrupted continuum of musical practice or the beginning of an evolutionary musical process leading to the canon of Western classical music. Medieval music's processes of transmission and invention and its emphasis on performer agency have more in common with the processes and practices of the uninterrupted continuum of vernacular and popular music than with the processes and practices of eighteenth- through early twentieth-century classical music, which, while glorious in its own right, has dominated both music education and classical music programming. Finally, I challenge those who teach medieval music in academic classrooms and ensembles to change the way it is taught and to incorporate invention, improvisation, fluid composition, and oral transmission into the process, as some have been doing in private lessons and small workshops for the past three decades. In doing so, we will alter the perception of the performance of medieval music as an impossible foray into a misty and impenetrable world of ancient Other-ness. Instead, we will facilitate the forging of a vibrant musical connection with a thousand-year continuum of musical transmission and *inventio*, a community of singers and players who passed the ownership of this music directly to us.

CHAPTER 2

Living and "Imagined" Models

A New Oral Tradition

Music is passed orally from one person to another through a tripartite process of *demonstration, imitation,* and *critique*.[1] The master plays, the student imitates, and the master offers the student constructive critique. Even today, when a musician learns a piece "by ear" from a recording, she is still imitating a model, and in most cases will receive critique through her own ears, from other listeners, or from another musician whose license to critique is based on a more advanced ability to imitate. In most of the world's musical traditions, singers and instrumentalists learn to create music, and in some cases improvise, by acquiring through demonstration and imitation the language of melodic, rhythmic, and harmonic patterns, gestures, and idioms that characterize a particular repertoire and therefore provide tools for invention.

Modern performers of medieval music, however, are in a unique situation because they are attempting to learn a music characterized by a substantial oral element while the line of direct transmission essentially has been broken. The performers have compensated for this absence of living models by using historiographic detective work in an attempt to create credible "imagined" models and in some cases have supplemented that approach by seeking models from other musical traditions. This chapter begins with an examination of this use of living and imagined models, followed by a set of questions for performers to discuss or contemplate: How do we identify relevant models

---

1. Christopher J. Smith, "Homeland of the Mind: Learning and Teaching with the Old Ways," talk at TEDxLubbock, September 2012, available on YouTube at https://www.youtube.com/watch?v=gpcEGA0WQH0.

from other music traditions? How do we develop an awareness of our own performing lineages? In addition, since performers of medieval music do not always come to the table with experience in orally transmitted musics, I offer several practical listening exercises and some suggestions for taking the first step toward recognizing where our models have employed invention.

"GETTING THE MODEL"

In Kenneth Zuckerman's article "Improvisation in Medieval Music," he points out the importance of a living model:

> The transmission of music in unwritten, improvised traditions is completely dependent on a close and long-term relationship between the teacher and student. The teacher's role is not only to instruct in technique, interpretation, composition, and improvisation, but also to literally pass on an entire repertoire to the student, without relying on written materials. Thus it is not uncommon in a tradition like classical Indian music for an apprenticeship to last for over 20 years![2]

The transmission of medieval music relied heavily on memory, and its notation contains a very limited amount of performance information (see chapter 3). The less prescriptive the notation of a particular musical idiom, the more critical it is for the person learning the idiom to be able to imitate a living model.

The first musicians to undertake performances of medieval music in the twentieth century, however, had no living "medieval" models. With no living medieval "master" or recorded sound to imitate, musicians had to make both practical and imaginative use of data that had been uncovered by scholarly detective work. Since they were interested in the processes used by medieval performers as well as the artifacts left by them, their search for data included not just repertoire but languages, literature, iconography, music theory, rhetoric, performance context, and the methods by which musicians themselves may have implemented the demonstration-imitation-critique model—in other words, any information that could contribute to the construction of an "imagined" model where no living models were available. This model is heard only in the imagination and emulated using skills obtained from the modern musicians' own memory storehouses of past musical education and experience. In this situation, the demonstration-imitation-critique paradigm breaks down, since the imitator has essentially created the demonstration. Thus a link in the chain of oral tradition is broken; no matter how authentically

---

2. Zuckerman, "Improvisation in Medieval Music," 135.

"medieval" the construction materials might be, the resulting creation can never be examined against or critiqued by an actual, living medieval model.

Some early music pioneers sought to address this by finding living models from musical traditions outside the world of Western classical music. Both Western and non-Western vernacular musics contain many examples of musical procedures, processes, and even forms that are analogous to what we know of medieval music practice. Here are a few examples:

1. The singing/intoning of epic poetry
2. The use of memorized formulas associated with certain varieties of sacred chant
3. The use of heterophony in the performance of instrumental melody, with or without vocals, as can be heard in the traditional musics of several Middle Eastern cultures and of a number of European traditional musics (Irish, Scandinavian, Breton, and others)[3]
4. The association of mode and modal formulas with certain emotions, conditions, events, or topics, such as one finds on the Indian subcontinent
5. The existence of musical-poetic forms, such as the Andalusian *zajal*, that have been in continuous use since the medieval era and have marked similarities to certain medieval forms (*virelai, lauda, cantiga*).

Thomas Binkley, director of the groundbreaking Studio der frühen Musik in the 1960s and 1970s, acknowledged the difficulty that the first European and American musicians who attempted to "revive" medieval music in performance faced in finding musical models, particularly in the areas of performance that required invention. He described this firsthand experience in a 1992 radio interview:

> Improvisation is a convenient word, but it's not the word I like to use with regard to [medieval] music. Improvisation implies right off the top of the head, instant compositions. That can occur if a musician is creative and has models to follow, and has followed the models. I think a good example is recorded in [Albert] Lord's book *The Singer of Tales*, in which he listened to a Yugoslavian *jusla* player explain how he learned to play the *jusla* and sing songs. And he said that first of all he listened to the men sing, and then when he was by himself, he would practice what he heard them sing and he would play the notes on the *jusla*. And when he was able to do it very well, then he would sing for other people, and that was the way he progressed. In other words, you have a model, you imitate,

---

3. I am using the word "heterophony" here to indicate a process whereby a number of instrumentalists are playing the same melody but each is ornamenting that melody in a way that is idiomatic to their instrument.

it, and gradually you impress upon that model your own deviation, or your own musical personality. That's pretty much how we've worked. Of course, *getting the model—that's the thing.* At the time that we began doing this, there were no models to follow, and we had to search out models. We would make up models according to [a] sort of rules. We would say, well, all right: there are other places in the world where monophonic music is played, and so let's see how they work out accompaniments. And I think maybe I should say at this point, for the sake of your [radio] audience, that we're dealing with music in which the vocal line is written out, but the accompaniments are not written out, and the accompaniments often expand a piece by using a different accompaniment for every strophe of the text by having preludes, interludes, postludes—in other words, a lot of framing of the composition, so that just a few lines of the manuscript might become a twenty-minute performance.[4]

Binkley's technique of looking to Morocco and other North African or Middle Eastern musical cultures for insights into improvisational approaches to medieval music has become one of the most often-cited, and perhaps even notorious, examples of the incorporation of ethnomusicological or "world music" elements into medieval music. Binkley saw in the music of Morocco, in particular, characteristics that seemed to be especially applicable to some of the musico-poetic materials that exist from the Middle Ages, especially those of Andalusia and the regions around the Mediterranean, where a great deal of exchange happened between medieval Western and Eastern musicians. We may imagine, for example, that a performer is considering a medieval European song that is comparable in its poetic form to the Arab-Andalusian *zajal*, and it is known that these were accompanied by instruments, but no information survives to tell us which specific instruments. Binkley's process in the early days of the Studio was to find performances of living traditional musicians who still perform *zajals* and observe how they are performed. In fact, he traveled to Morocco in order to do so.

While Binkley was not the only early music performer in the 1950s and 1960s to look eastward for musical inspiration, it is largely from Binkley's influence that we find long introductory *taqsim* (preludes) at the beginning of performances of troubadour songs and the heterophonic performance of medieval instrumental music that has been adopted almost universally by medieval music performers.[5] Binkley's approach was not without controversy;

---

4. Thomas Binkley, interview with author, 1992, for the syndicated radio program *Harmonia*. Italics were used here to convey a point emphasized by tone of voice in the interview.

5. See John Haines, "The Arabic Style of Performing Medieval Music," *Early Music* 29, no. 3 (August 2001): 369–80. On p. 370, citing the New York Pro Musica's performance of *The Play of Daniel*, Haines points out that "the only instruments the New York

many hailed these ethnomusicological innovations as groundbreaking, while some later detractors infamously referred to the Studio's musical experimentations as "Radio Baghdad" (a dubious attempt at a humorous label, considering the geographical, musical, and cultural distance between Morocco and Iraq).

In Binkley's defense, it has been suggested that the Studio actually provided a historical "correction" to the perceived heterogeneity of medieval European culture, offering what Kirsten Yri referred to as a "corrective to what Hispanist Maria Rose Menocal, among others, has called 'the myth of Westernness,' the systematic attempt to censor the Arabic or Semitic elements from European and Western history."[6] Binkley himself insisted that the Studio's music was not intended to sound uniformly "Middle Eastern" or "Arabic."[7] The medieval songs they played did not use Arabic scales; neither Andrea von Ramm, Nigel Rogers, Willard Cobb, nor Richard Levitt used Middle Eastern vocal techniques; and the instruments by Binkley and Sterling Jones, while they may have had distinctly Middle Eastern analogues, were well-documented in medieval Europe, at least in the areas surrounding the Mediterranean. Any comprehensive examination of their recorded output will also reveal that they varied their arrangements, their techniques, their approach, their *instrumentarium*, and even their supporting players from one recording project to another, depending on repertoire.[8]

Ultimately, the Studio der frühen Musik's contribution to the development of medieval music performance practice was not about "Arabic influence" but rather about process. In their search for living models, they discovered that some of the processes implied by the oral versus "literate" transmission of medieval music genres might be shared by living musical traditions that employ those same processes with analogous or similar genres. At the same time, adopting a process used in a living musical tradition did not necessarily

---

Pro Musica actually imported from the Orient were percussion, but as well-known signifiers they were all that was needed to evoke things Arabic."

6. Kirsten Yri, "Thomas Binkley and the Studio der Frühen Musik: challenging 'the myth of Westernness,'" *Early Music* 38, no. 2 (May 2010): 274.

7. See Haines, "Arabic Style," and Yri, "Thomas Binkley." I do not know who first applied the "Radio Baghdad" descriptor to the work of the Studio; I have heard it used casually multiple times over the years. Binkley told me more than once in the course of informal conversation that he never intended his music to sound "Arabic" or Middle Eastern, and in one case he told me that "any Arabic person would instantly be able to tell that it was not Arabic music."

8. The styles used by the Studio for different repertoires were quite diverse. Indeed, given the process, the abundance of plucked strings, Dorian mode, and the percussive rhythms, "L'afar del comte Guió" from the Studio's recording *L'Agonie du Languedoc* would have required only heavy amplification and the addition of a full trap set of drums to fit comfortably onto a 1970s "progressive" rock and roll album. Studio der frühen Musik, *L'Agonie du Languedoc*, EMI Reflexe 7243 8 26500 2 7, 1976.

negate considerations of historical credibility. On the contrary, Binkley asserted:

> The one test that we have to make, that they did not have to make, is that we have this question of historical credibility. And that's important in improvisation, just as it's important in other musical decisions when we're playing music. They didn't have to ask "Is this the way it was done?" We do ask that question, and I'm afraid we get many conflicting answers, if you quiz people around the world who are involved with this profession.[9]

Binkley's groundbreaking contribution to medieval performance practice was the recognition that a living musical process can serve as a model for music of the past that shared those processes, and that the shared process supports the historical credibility of the end product even if it cannot provide complete historical accuracy. It is therefore because of process that we sometimes seek clues to medieval music performance practice in world music traditions.

In the decades that followed the Studio's recordings, the inventive processes used by contemporary performers of medieval music have included detailed study and exploration of European modal music and plainchant, rhetorical delivery of lyric and epic poetry, improvisatory techniques described or implied by medieval treatises, and various aspects of relevant world music traditions. Interpretations have ranged from the incorporation of extensive arrangements, multiple instruments, and various exotic elements to a pared-down approach that focuses on a cappella performance and rarely uses instruments for anything but dance tunes such as *estampies* or notated instrumental intabulations of vocal pieces. Some have attempted to hold as strictly as possible to techniques and repertoires documented in medieval sources; others make no apologies for the incorporation of improvisatory techniques already internalized from years of playing folk and rock and roll music and have no qualms about mixing medieval repertoire and later "traditional" tunes and ballads in the same performance.[10]

---

9. Binkley, interview with the author.
10. It is important to acknowledge that there is nothing to prevent a performer in any genre of music, from folk to electronica, from treating a medieval song with the same musical process one might use for a performance any genre of traditional folk music. One may render the original into modern language, use modern instruments, apply a harmonic accompaniment to it, and not be concerned as to whether the song originated in the thirteenth, seventeenth, or twentieth century. However, this represents a different set of processes and intentions than those that by consensus have informed at least three generations of historical performance practitioners. In some cases, there is overlap; many early music players and singers recognize and celebrate the fact that there are both commonalities and distinct differences in the processes and intentions of folk and "trad" musicians and "early music" performers. Indeed, a

Some of the most effective and creative performances have resulted from the skillful scholarly and artistic integration of a number of different elements. A particularly effective example of the use of ethnographic inquiry to inform medieval music performance practice can be found in the work of Sequentia Ensemble for Medieval Music, directed by Benjamin Bagby. In the notes to Sequentia's 1999 CD *Edda: Myths from Medieval Iceland*, Benjamin Bagby explains that no known medieval musical sources exist for this repertoire other than a "scrap of melodic material from the late 18th century." He chose therefore to draw on Sequentia's years of working with the modal language of plainchant and medieval song, using mode as a "collection of gestures and signs which can be interiorized, varied, combined and used as a font to create musical 'texts' which can be completely new while possessing the authentic integrity of the original material."[11]

Bagby stresses, however, that this process needed to be combined with "a strong knowledge of the practice of singing epic poetry as it still exists in various world cultures to show us how such performances must be given a form and a soul, to temper the limitless freedom of modal intoxication." So he examined Iceland's tradition of sung oral poetry (*rímur*), a tradition that dates back to the Middle Ages, listening to "hundreds of recorded performances of *rímur* and related song-types, making notes and analyses of the types and uses of modal materials." He came up with a series of "modal vocabularies," which were then taught to the other Sequentia singers by ear. "We have only worked with the Edda texts and our memories; there were never any musical scores." This is, of course, in addition to extensive study of the texts themselves, the language, the history, and many other historical considerations.[12] With the musicians having contemplated, practiced, and internalized music, text, and context, the resulting performance then appears both effortless and convincing, particularly when delivered with the musicianship, acting, and rhetorical skills of world-class performers like Bagby and his Sequentia colleagues.

In a review of Sequentia's CD *Fragments for the End of Time* written for the French music magazine *Diapason* in February of 2009, David Fiala testifies to the effectiveness of the group's integrated process:

> All of the melodies which he realizes on his harp in unleashing haunting formulas of accompaniment or marked punctuations . . . bear witness to an exceptional art of the large form, which permits us to keep our attention focused during long stretches of recitation, the performance of which has become his

---

number of musicians successfully navigate in both worlds, just as many musicians play both modern and historical versions of the same instrument.

11. Benjamin Bagby, liner notes to Sequentia, *Edda: Myths from Medieval Iceland*, DHM 05472.77381-2, 1999.

12. Bagby, liner notes to Sequentia, *Edda*.

specialty. And this, to the point where one is surprised to have put aside the translation and notes while listening to ten minutes of Old Saxon dialect from the ninth century, as if it were perfectly normal. All of this is as much from the tenth century as it is from today: beautiful, strange and intelligent.[13]

The twentieth-century groundbreakers in the field of medieval music performance have created, in a sense, a new syncretic model derived from medieval materials, imagination, extant world traditions, and their own musical heritage. The model requires a labor-intensive process; contains musical, textual, and procedural substance that is indeed medieval; and also results in the creation of "new" music. In turn, the resulting performances, both live and recorded, have become models for the next generation of players and singers.

These next generations continue to refine and add to the scholarly accumulation of historical data from which the imagined model is continually created and recreated in the mind, but now, we also have living models—models we can hear. The performer of medieval music therefore has a "layered" musical lineage, one layer consisting of scholarship based on historical artifact and primary sources (notation, iconography, instruments, texts, literature, theory, pedagogical materials) and the second layer consisting of other performers' interpretations of the materials in the previous layer. Each generation adds new discoveries about the primary sources, additional input from vernacular and world music traditions, and its own imagination. In attempting to revive a "lost" or oral tradition, we have in fact created a new one that combines some of the processes of an "oral" tradition with some of the processes of "literate" scholarship: both "fish and fowl," appropriately resembling some hybrid creature from a medieval bestiary.

FOLLOWING THE MODEL: DISCRIMINATION AND IMITATION SKILLS

The preceding section served to provide an exploration of ways in which performers have drawn upon imagined or existing models to invent a new performance practice for medieval music. This section will suggest strategies and exercises for performers who wish to examine their own relationship to performance models and musical lineage, to apply their own inventive process to medieval performance practice, and to work on skills that are crucial to the demonstration-imitation-critique paradigm of musical transmission.

When working with living models for the purpose of developing a process for medieval performance practice, two initial questions are critical. First, what criteria should be considered when choosing models? Second, what skills and

---

13. Quoted from Sequentia's website, http://sequentia.org/press/index.html#n4.

procedures should be employed in order to make use of those models? The first set of practices is analytical rather than technical; the main intention is to invite critical thought and to encourage performers of medieval music to be aware of the ways in which they take part in the process of oral transmission. Some of the suggested practices include questions that may be addressed alone or in discussion with colleagues or students, in coaching sessions or classes, or in writing. What is your own "performance lineage"? Are you making performance practice decisions yourself, or just imitating previous performers?

Practice 2.1 is aimed at musicians who would like to explore the possible connections between medieval music, various world music and vernacular

---

Practice 2.1

USING MODELS FROM VERNACULAR AND WORLD MUSIC TRADITIONS

1. When considering a particular genre of world music as a potential model for the performance of medieval music, explore the following questions:
   - What does this particular world music tradition have in common with medieval music (heterophony, monophony, primacy of text, formulaic modal content, similar instruments, similar performance circumstances, poetic structures)?
   - Which elements of this particular world music tradition are *not* likely to have been present in medieval music (different modes and scales, different kinds of modal patterns, instruments unlikely to be encountered in medieval Europe, different sorts of poetic structures, different kinds of text content)?
   - Does this world music tradition or genre have characteristics, processes, or qualities that may have been present in medieval music, even if that presence is still a matter of conjecture (vocal quality, improvisational sections, rhythms)?
2. If the answers to the questions in no. 1 above indicate that a particular world tradition may offer some useful models for the genre of medieval music in question, the next step is to consider what kinds of specific actions you might take in order to acquire the information you need:
   - consult active performers in that particular genre
   - listen to and study commercial recordings of that genre
   - listen to and study field recordings of that particular genre (these are particularly helpful)
   - consult literary resources (Are there commonalities in lyric genres, text delivery, and so on?)

music traditions, and the places where the performance practices of medieval and world musics may overlap. In terms of living models, these interconnections may manifest as illustrated by Figure 2.1:

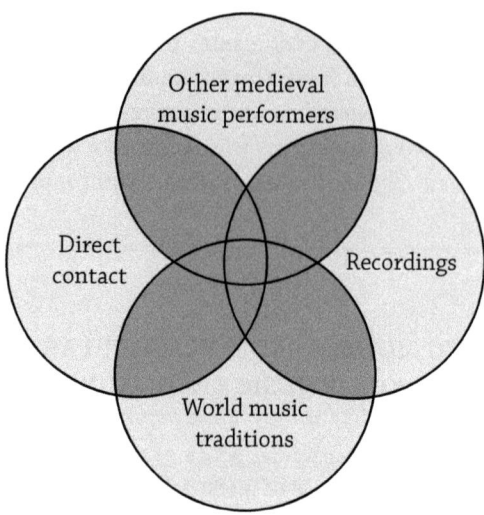

Figure 2.1: Living models and mode of transmission

The questions in Practice 2.2 require us to think about our own musical lineage and how oral transmission has been part of our own musical process. The questions can be considered in any order, although following the steps presented here may work best for creating continuity in a discussion situation.

The purpose of Practices 2.3 and 2.4 is to foster a conscious awareness of the many layers of lineage and transmission that are operating when you learn a piece of medieval music from a recording or another musician's performance. What is the medieval material you are learning? What aspects of the performer's own invention, interpretation, and style are you emulating? (No value judgment is implied; you may wish to emulate the model, or you may wish to learn some useful techniques from the model and then add your own unique aspects of interpretation and expression.)

Practice 2.4 expands directly on 2.3. In the modern world, recorded performances afford us the luxury of repeated listenings, making it much easier to replicate another performer's rendition of a piece in great detail. Is it possible to learn from a recorded model but retain our own voice?

Medieval music's lack of prescriptive notation is one of the strongest indications that the repertoire has always required a certain amount of inventive, improvisatory, and compositional skill on the part of the performer. Reflecting on our musical lineage and the inventive processes of our musical models can

Practice 2.2
WHAT IS YOUR MUSICAL LINEAGE?

It may be particularly useful to address these questions in the context of a discussion between two or more colleagues.
1. *Questions related to models*: What music do you perform most frequently? Classical? Jazz? Rock? Folk? Who was your most influential teacher in that area? Can you cite specific stylistic characteristics and techniques that you have acquired through the demonstration-imitation-critique model?
2. *Questions related to memory*: Of the different musical styles you have played, which one is held most in memory? For example, you may have played mostly Baroque music for the last five years but have an enormous memory storehouse of rock music that you could play from memory at a moment's notice. What teacher or artist was your strongest influence in the "memorized" area? How did that music become stored in your memory? Was it a conscious effort, or did it simply "happen" through playing it and hearing it repeatedly?
3. *Questions related to lineage:* How would you describe your "musical lineage?" Do you feel as though you might have several?
4. *Questions related to your experience with medieval music*: Who are your models? Who are your teachers? Do you see yourself as part of a medieval performance practice lineage? Can you cite specific stylistic characteristics and techniques of that lineage? Sometimes our own style adheres to certain aspects of our musical lineage and diverges from others; what is your experience with this?

Practice 2.3
LISTENING FOR "INVENTION"

This can be a solo or a collaborative practice. Choose a track from a specific medieval music recording and make two lists, as follows:
List 1. What part of the content of this track is "medieval"? Examples of content that might fall into the medieval category are:
- the melody/polyphony itself
- the mode, melodic patterns, etc.
- the rhythm (depending on the notation)
- the text
- use of "historical" instruments

List 2. What part of the content of this track is probably interpretation or invention? Answers can be as simple as "phrasing and expressive nuance," or they could fill a whole page:
- instrumental accompaniment
- melodic material: prelude, interludes, postlude, perhaps even the main melody
- rhythm
- tempo
- rhetorical declamation, phrasing, expressive gesture
- dynamics
- articulation
- ornamentation

More can be added to the list of invented material above; there are many possibilities.

Practice 2.4
DISCERNING LAYERS OF MODELING

Question 1. Imagine that you are going to create your own performance of the same piece that you have been listening to in Practice 2.3. How much of the content of this recorded arrangement would you actually attempt to replicate?

Question 2. Does the musical material that you would attempt to replicate from your model go beyond learning the melody of the tune or, in the case of a song, the melody and text? If so, what is the critical transition point at which the recording ceases to be a model for learning a particular piece of music and instead becomes a model for learning or absorbing that performer's particular approach to medieval music performance practice? Since both models can be beneficial, why is it important to be aware of that critical transition point?

Question 3. Having decided upon the musical content to be learned or emulated from this recorded model, explore how much you can remember without resorting to writing it down. Ask yourself if you might be able to remember the melody without writing it down or whether you could use minimal notation as a memory aid. Since most medieval music was written down with minimally prescriptive notation, what does that suggest about the extent of oral transmission from one musician to another? How much performance content may have been subject to variation and invention?

lend valuable insight to our own process of determining what we will bring to the musical content of a performance of medieval music—those aspects of the performance that will make it "our" music. Indeed, the same could be said for jazz, folk music, improvisation over a ground bass, an improvised cadenza, an aleatoric composition, or anything that requires invention or improvisation on the part of the performer. In chapter 3, we begin to discern and analyze what information is and is not on the page in the case of medieval repertoire and to consider the role of memory in creating a storehouse of idiomatic musical language from we draw to create a dynamic performance in the present moment.

CHAPTER 3

Notation and *Memoria*

What's Not on the Page

Every process has a beginning, and when we embark upon a serious study of the performance of medieval music, we usually begin by learning specific pieces. Whether we learn the pieces from transcriptions or from the actual medieval manuscripts themselves, we soon discover that only a limited amount of information about any given medieval piece exists "on the page." If we learn a medieval piece by ear from another musician or from a recording and then look at the written notation, we usually discover that we have learned quite a bit of material that is not written into the original manuscript or transcription: the other musician's phrasing, gesture, rhythmic interpretation, and any number of other unwritten factors.

If we endeavor to learn a piece from the page without the benefit of any living model or sound recording, we can gather as much information as possible from theorists, pedagogical treatises, literature, iconography, and the notated music itself, but ultimately we must synthesize that pile of books, notes, and articles into a performance. Therefore, we must bring together our artistic, interpretive, communicative, scholarly, performative, and inventive skills to create a process or set of processes that we can use as a model for negotiating the vast uncertain space of missing written data and for establishing a memorized and internalized collection of idiomatic musical materials with which to fill that space.

Every musician who embarks on the study of medieval music brings a different set of tools and experiences to the table, and this affects how we respond to the initial challenge. Even if we have experience in improvisation of one kind or another, most of us have no internalized medieval music language to draw upon. If we come to medieval music through the world of classical music, it is often the case that this new enterprise will require more of our own invention or interpretation than we have heretofore been asked to provide. Players who are well versed in jazz, rock, and various other kinds of vernacular music may be perfectly comfortable with the idea of improvisation, invention, and "fluid" composition, and they generally have accumulated a substantial vocabulary of patterns, rhythms, formal structures, scales, harmonies, timbres, techniques, and tunings. However, those elements may have little to do with medieval music. Even those of us who have played a lot of modal folk music or sung in a *schola cantorum* may have only learned selected portions of the grammar and rhetoric of medieval musical language.

We are also at a disadvantage because we cannot possibly hear or experience medieval music as medieval listeners heard and experienced it, whether they were musicians or non-musicians. We cannot "unhear" Josquin, Mozart, Beethoven, Schoenberg, or Duke Ellington. Listeners born after 1950 in any region or country where Western popular music was disseminated widely on radio and television had likely internalized the sound characteristics of rock and roll by the age of ten, at least to the point where they could identify a piece of music as "rock and roll" as opposed to classical, jazz, or folk music. In fact, many popular music devotees could, if called upon to do so, sing their favorite guitar solos from beginning to end, even if they do not read a single note of music. This constitutes a rich, internalized storehouse of musical language. For a musician, such an internalized vocabulary will greatly facilitate improvisation in that idiom, but not necessarily other idioms—not without a lot of study and exposure. Kenneth Zuckerman aptly expresses the problem that may arise in the case of medieval music performance:

> One of the most serious problems in improvising medieval or for that matter, any music, is that the basic rhythmic and melodic building blocks are not an integral part of the musical consciousness. All of these elements must be second nature—automatic, so to speak. . . . For a musician trying to improvise in the medieval style today, the problem is extreme. Not only is he cut off from the roots of the style, but often times he has already been exposed to and performed in repertoires as diverse as those of the renaissance, baroque, classic, romantic, avant-garde, pop, rock, etc. When it comes time to improvise, all of these styles and formulas tend to get mixed up and the resulting improvisation has no identity at all![1]

If musicians born in the twentieth and twenty-first centuries wish to perform medieval music, breathe life into it, and make it our own music, we

---

1. Zuckerman, "Improvisation in Medieval Music," 140–41.

must begin the process by listening to it and familiarizing ourselves with the repertoire. Learning one trecento *ballata* will not suffice; one has to listen to, read through, and live with dozens of pieces in a particular genre to begin internalizing the sounds in the memory. But that is not all. We must also (a) develop the ability to define and articulate what is "not on the page" when looking at notated medieval music and (b) set the intention to accumulate not just a storehouse of specific medieval repertoire, but our own internalized and memorized vocabulary of melodic patterns, modes, rhythms, formal musical and poetic structures, polyphonic constructions, instrumental techniques, timbres, tunings, and other elements that constitute what we know of medieval music. Item (a) is relatively simple, and this chapter will provide the reader with enough information to begin that process. Item (b) is a lifelong pursuit, but it is necessary if we are to create engaging, "living" performances that still have some relation to the musical world from which medieval repertoire originated.

In the introduction to her important work *Medieval Music and the Art of Memory*, Anna Maria Busse Berger refers to the memory storehouse as a memorial archive, drawing on the connection between composition and memory articulated by rhetoric scholar Mary Carruthers:

> A scholar built up a memorial archive throughout his life from which he would draw in the process of composition. Thus, composition was not about creating a new, innovative work, as it has become in modern times: "Composition is not an act of writing," Carruthers says, "it is rumination, cogitation, dictation, a listening and a dialogue, a 'gathering' (*collectio*) of voices from several places in memory." But perhaps most importantly, [Carruthers] demonstrates that the same techniques that were used to memorize existing texts were also used to create new works. An author who composed a work in his mind visualized it, usually with the aid of an imaginary architectural structure, or on a written page. These ideas are of central important for our own understanding of the medieval compositional process in any field, music included.[2]

In this chapter, we will begin the process of identifying what is and is not on the page, and what must be "invented," and we will explore practical mnemonic strategies for building a memorial archive on which we can draw in order to "invent," using techniques that were well known to the creators of the music we seek to perform.

---

2. Mary Carruthers, *The Book of Memory: A Study of Memory in Medieval Culture* (Cambridge, UK: Cambridge University Press, 1990), 197–98, quoted in Berger, *Medieval Music and the Art of Memory*, 4.

NOTATION: MISSING DATA VERSUS DIFFERENT DATA

As modern performers educated in a primarily literate culture, we may be challenged by texts and notations that originated in a culture that depended heavily on memory and oral transmission.[3] Musical notation, like an alphabet, provides a graphic representation of aural phenomena: a written symbol represents a particular aspect of sound. Notational symbols can thus denote pitch, duration, dynamics, phrasing, meter, and many other characteristics. Often, when modern performers first encounter medieval neumes, our first impression is that the notation is missing a considerable amount of data that we are accustomed to receiving from modern musical notation, especially in the area of rhythm and meter. However, rather than perceiving this absence of notational directive as a deficiency on the part of medieval notation, I would argue that we are better served to think of medieval notation as containing a different set of data than modern notation, and that this different set of data affirms the importance of Berger's memorial archive to the performance of medieval music both then and now.

A large amount of performance data in medieval notation is indicated graphically in a way that allows for multiple possibilities, thus placing responsibility for the sonic manifestation of those graphic images squarely in the hands and voice of the performer rather than the composer. Thus a convincing performance may include some degree of performer-generated data in the form of invention, arrangement, "oral" or "fluid" composition, or improvisatory processes. This is true even in the case of unaccompanied monophonic song, in which the performer still must make choices about rhetorical declamation, phrasing, expression, dynamics, articulation, ornamentation, and tempo (at the very least). The lack of prescriptive notation is an important clue to the process of medieval music performance and is characteristic of musics that are transmitted from one person to another by demonstration and imitation (i.e., by ear), held or even composed primarily in the memory, and dependent to some extent upon the inventive skill of the individual performer.

An extensive discussion of medieval notation is far beyond the scope of this book.[4] Nevertheless, it is important to consider performance implications that arise from the nature of medieval notation, particularly in relation to improvisatory processes such as inflection and ornamentation.

---

3. Leo Treitler and others have pointed out that written music can be produced by a culture that is still primarily oriented toward oral transmission; see "Oral, Written and Literate Process" in Treitler, *With Voice and Pen*, 230–51.

4. For a beautifully illustrated and engaging history of notation, see Thomas Forrest Kelly's *Capturing Music: The Story of Notation* (New York: W. W. Norton, 2014). Other works on medieval notation include Constantin Floros, *Introduction to Early Medieval Notation*, trans. Neil K. Moran (Warren, MI: Harmonie Park, 2005), and Richard Rastall, *The Notation of Western Music: An Introduction*, 2nd ed. (London: Travis & Emery, 2008). A very interesting introduction to the concept of neumes that also connects the notation to the practice of improvisation or "musical composition in an oral

One of the most obvious examples indicating that medieval notation contains a different set of data from modern notation lies in the number of different graphic neumes that can represent the same two pitches. For example, in modern Western notation, the representation of two precise ascending pitches is indicated by their relative position on a staff, as shown in Example 3.1. Variations in that representation will only occur in terms of duration or clef.[5]

Example 3.1: D to F

In the case of medieval neumes, on the other hand, a diversity of graphic characters such as those illustrated in Figure 3.1 can be used to represent the exact same pitches and can be irrelevant of duration.

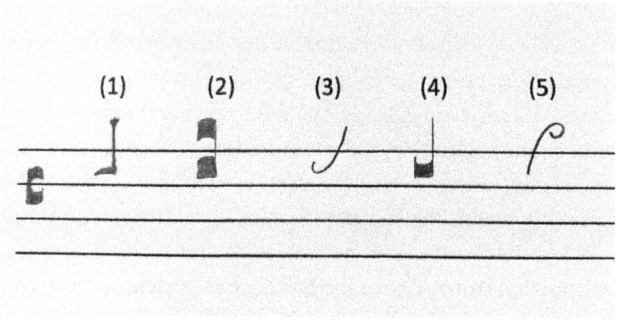

Figure 3.1: D to F, various neume shapes

While specifically quantitative durational data may be missing, the different neume shapes carry meaning that is not contained in modern notation. For example, in Figure 3.1, (5) is a *liquescent* neume. "Liquescence" refers to a quality

context" can be found in Richard Taruskin, *The Oxford History of Western Music*, vol. 1, *The Earliest Notations to the Sixteenth Century* (Oxford: Oxford University Press, 2005), 13.20. A short and very concise introduction to the basic concept of early notation is also included in J. Peter Burkholder, Donald Jay Grout, and Claude Palisca, *A History of Western Music*, 9th ed. (New York: W. W. Norton, 2014), 32–38.

5. To clarify, I am referring here to standard modern five-line-staff notation and not to the many innovative graphic representations that have developed in the twentieth and twenty-first centuries to indicate indeterminate pitch, clusters, extended techniques, or other sounds.

described by Guido d'Arezzo as "passing from one note to the other in a smooth manner" and is often interpreted as a slur or small glissando between the two pitches. In some cases, as in (5) in Figure 3.1, one pitch in the liquescent neume is drawn in a way meant to indicate that the smaller note is the endpoint of the glissando and not sung as "fully," or in some cases is sung on an "m" or "n" consonant, and therefore the very end of the note carries a more closed sound, almost like a hum.[6] Therefore the neume carries data about articulation that in modern notation would have to be provided by additional graphics such as slurs or glissandi, or perhaps is not accurately translatable by modern notation at all.

In some ways, the fact that neumatic notation contains "different" data opens Pandora's box for practitioners of historical performance. It is possible, and in my opinion quite likely, that neumes represent vocal nuance, pitch-bending, and articulations that were an inherent part of medieval vocal production—subtleties that are essentially lost to us forever. We often describe liquescent neumes such as the *quilisma, oriscus,* and *pressus* as "ornamental neumes," but "ornament" implies something that is added—in other words, ornaments are part of the improvisational process and not a byproduct of a received process of vocalization transmitted by ear and in the memory. In his book *The Sound of Medieval Song*, Timothy McGee makes a critical point about this distinction:

> It is possible to view the many different neume forms in the early manuscripts as records of an integrated vocal style that included a large number of sounds that are foreign to the later Western practice. If we observe the quantity of ornamental neume shapes in any one chant in the early manuscripts, the extent to which these "ornamental" sounds were in use removes them from the category of "ornamental." ... We are left with an impression of a medieval vocal technique that had within its basic vocabulary such sounds as inflected tone, sliding and pulsing sounds, throat vibrato, and indefinite pitch as well as what we might think of as the more normal ingredients of full tone and stable pitch.[7]

McGee also provides a strong argument that regional differences in neume shapes reflected differences in regional vocal styles, stating:

> The fact that neume shapes were closely connected with the desired performance practices also suggests that the differences in their forms from one region to another can assist us in identifying some elements of local performance styles.[8]

---

6. Timothy J. McGee, *The Sound of Medieval Song: Ornamentation and Vocal Style According to the Treatises* (Oxford: Clarendon, 1998), 46.
7. McGee, *Sound of Medieval Song*, 60.
8. McGee, *Sound of Medieval Song*. In his concluding chapter, McGee provides a list of "descriptions of regional style characteristics" that, even when considered in conjunction with local monastic affiliations and vernacular language and practices, may serve as a "distillation of the evidence of notational practices as they relate to an analysis of performance style." See 144–51 (the list is on pages 146–47).

For practitioners of medieval music, I suggest that these issues lead to three considerations that must be part of our process. First, we must make friends with uncertainty. This may seem abundantly obvious, but in a discipline in which the quest for historical verisimilitude is understood to be a *sine qua non*, uncertainty is uncomfortable. Yet we must accept it—even the most assiduous study of regional neume shapes will never tell us what a recording or video would have been able to convey about the precise sound of Aquitanian singers as opposed to young nuns from the Rhineland. Not only would their vocal technique have likely been different from one another, but even their Latin would have been pronounced differently.[9]

Second, where uncertainty exists and no historical data is available, we must make educated decisions regarding the improvisation, composition, or invention of musical material that is critical to the creation of a viable performance. Third, as stated earlier, we must cultivate clarity in discriminating between musical and textual information that is actually being transmitted to us by medieval sources; musical styles, approaches, and content that we have absorbed from our teachers and colleagues; and musical content that we bring to a performance as a result of our own musical experience and memorial storehouse. Chances are that we will employ all three, and all three contribute to our individual storehouses of musical memory. I offer here a systematic approach to sorting and analyzing what is and is not on the page, and provide a basic introduction to the role of memory in retrieving the contents of our musical storehouses for the purpose of invention.

WORKING WITH THE DIFFERENT DATA: TWO EXAMPLES

We have established thus far that both the data contained in medieval neumes and the data that is missing from neumatic notation carry implications about performance practice, memory, transmission, and elements of improvisation. The missing data in a particular notation signals that improvisation, oral transmission, memory, or some combination of the three will play a large role in the way the music is transmitted and presented by the performers, either in a premeditated way or somewhat spontaneously in the course of performance.

To illustrate this, here is an example from the works of twelfth-century abbess and composer Hildegard von Bingen: an antiphon shown in facsimile

---

9. The definitive guide to historical pronunciation for early music singers is Timothy J. McGee, A. G. Rigg, and David Klausner, eds., *Singing Early Music: The Pronunciation of European Languages in the Late Middle Ages and Renaissance* (Bloomington: Indiana University Press, 1996).

in Figure 3.2.[10] The two primary manuscript collections of Hildegard's music contain early German neumes of a style somewhat later than those found in the Saint Gall manuscripts, but earlier than Gothic neumes. In this type of notation, groups of ascending or descending pitches can be represented graphically in multiple ways.[11]

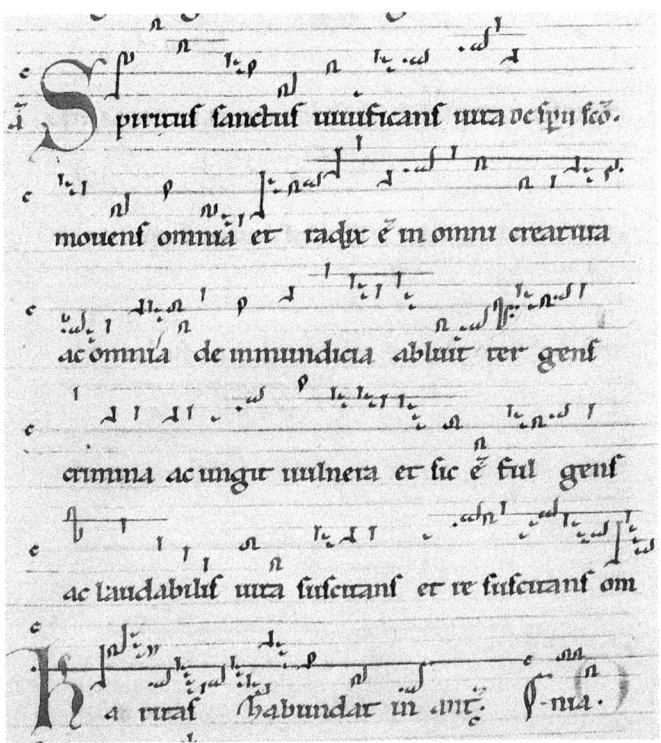

Figure 3.2: Hildegard von Bingen, "Spiritus sanctus vivificans vita" (reproduced with permission, Hochschul- und Landesbibliothek RheinMain, Riesencodex, Hs 2, 466v)

10. Fortunately, there are two excellent facsimile editions of Hildegard's music: Hildegard von Bingen, *Symphonia harmoniae caelestium revelationum: Dendermonde, St.-Pieters & Paulusabdij, Ms. Cod. 9*, ed. Peter van Poucke (Peer, Belgium: Alamire, 1998), and Hildegard von Bingen, *Lieder; Faksimile; Riesencodex (Hs. 2) der Hessichen Landesbibliothek Wiesbaden, fol. 466–481v*, ed. Lorenz Welker (Wiesbaden, Germany: Dr. Ludwig Reichert, 1998). A public domain version of the Riesencodex facsimile is also available online through the IMSLP/Petrucci Music Library: "Symphonia et Ordo Virtutum," http://imslp.org/wiki/Symphonia_et_Ordo_virtutum_%28Hildegard%29, accessed January 9, 2011.

11. In the notes to the facsimile edition of the Dendermonde manuscript, van Poucke describes the neumes as "early German, in notational chronology between Sankt Gallen neumes and the so-called Gothic neumes (*Hufnagelschrift*)." Hildegard von Bingen, *Symphonia harmoniae caelestium revelationum*, 11.

Both of the neumes in Figures 3.3 and 3.4 represent one syllable of text sung on a descending major second:

Figure 3.3: Non-liquescent descending major second

However, the neume in Figure 3.4 is liquescent, suggesting a different kind of vocal articulation than the first:

Figure 3.4: Liquescent descending major second

In modern notation, we might represent these two figures using the exact same notes, but with some sort of articulation mark over the second, such as a slur.

The notation does not tell us whether the two notes of either neume should be sung with exactly equal duration, whether one note should be articulated more strongly than the other, or whether one should differ in dynamic level from the other. This is a judgment call by the performer, who may choose to use the text as a guide (is it an accented syllable? beginning of a phrase? What is the meaning?). In other words, the very notation requires the performer to make some decisions that later composers would make for us with the use of slurs, staccato marks, dynamic marks, or other markings. There is room, therefore, for subtle variations from one performer to the next (and even, perhaps, from one performance to the next by the same singer).

To complicate matters further, the exact meaning of some of these neumes is still uncertain, and there are multiple scholarly opinions about their execution. In other words, as stated, there is some missing data that must be supplied by the performer. Even a brief sample of different information about just one liquescent neume shape will demonstrate the complexity of taking the process from notation to performance. The *quilisma*, shown in Figure 3.5, is an ornamental neume that appears frequently in Hildegard's work.

Figure 3.5: Quilisma

If a performer wishes to sing Hildegard's music, she or he must make some performance decisions about this neume, and it is not a simple puzzle. Richard Rastall says that the *quilisma* has been interpreted variously as a short trill or mordent, and he also cites Dom Eugène Cardine's description of it as a note that is "sung lightly, the accent being thrown on a later note."[12] Constantin Floros suggests that the *quilisma* is analogous to the "Paleobyzantine Chartres-anatrichisma," which he describes as a "shudder."[13] In *The Sound of Medieval Song*, Timothy McGee devotes nearly two pages to the *quilisma*, quoting descriptions from a number of primary sources, including Aurelian of Réôme's "tremulous and ascending note" (ninth century), the *Summa musice*'s "three or more small notes" (ca. 1200), and even Walter Odington's somewhat mysterious "moist earth," which McGee speculates might refer to the "wavy marks left on the seashore at low tide."

McGee also points out that Aribo (1078) and another anonymous eleventh-century theorist may have indirectly supplied us with the performance practice of the *quilisma* by comparing it to an unwritten ornament called a *tremula*, stating that both involve a "change in pulse but not pitch," implying that the *quilisma* was a "volume pulsation without pitch change," resulting in "a smooth motion between the two written pitches in which the voice pulses alternately strong and weak as it moves."[14] Does this "smooth motion" include the intervening pitches as well? The directions given in the *Liber Usualis*, a compilation of plainchant used in the liturgy of the Roman Catholic Church, tells us to include them and indicates that the *quilisma* slightly lengthens the note immediately preceding it. The performer has to ultimately decide which authority he or she will follow.

The interpretation of the *quilisma* is but one example of information that the musician must seek out and then put into practice in order to execute a complete and convincing performance of our Hildegard example. Further decisions will have to be made regarding ornamentation, dynamics, durations, phrasing, flow, tempo, vocal timbre, and word accent. While this does not involve the same amount of "fluid composition" as, for example, creating a modal prelude for a piece, there is still a lot that is left up to the performer, particularly in the area of rhythm or meter. In the case of rhythm, data that is missing from the neumatic notation can sometimes be found in the relationship of the text to the music, a fact that practically mandates that

---

12. Rastall, *Notation of Western Music*, 21.
13. Floros, *Introduction to Early Medieval Notation*, 105.
14. McGee, *Sound of Medieval Song*, 53.55.

both singers and instrumentalists engage with texts at a deeper and more detailed level than they may have done in their work within later musics.[15]

The second manuscript example (Figure 3.6) is "Ondas do mar de Vigo," one of the Gallego-Portuguese *cantigas de amigo* by the thirteenth-century Galician troubadour Martin Codax. The *cantigas de amigo* were strophic love songs written from a woman's point of view, although all of the named authors of extant *cantigas de amigo* are male. This cycle of songs by Martin Codax contains the only *cantiga de amigo* to survive with music intact.

The strophic form of the poetry can be determined by looking at the text. The poetry uses a technique called parallelism, in which a line recurs in a subsequent verse, but is modified with a new ending rhyme (*ondas do mar de Vigo* in strophe 1, *ondas do mar levado* in strophe 2; *se vistes meu amigo* in strophe 1, *se vistes meu amado* in strophe 2). In this example, the parallelism does not apply to the refrain, which remains constant.[16]

Ondas do mar de Vigo,	Waves of the sea at Vigo,
se vistes meu amigo;	Have you seen my friend?
E ai, Deus! Se verrá cedo!	*O God, when will he return?*
Ondas do mar levado,	Rising waves of the sea,
se vistes meu amado;	Have you seen my lover?
E ai, Deus! Se verrá cedo!	*O God, when will he return?*
Se vistes meu amigo,	Have you seen my friend,
O por que eu sospiro;	The one for whom I sigh?
E ai, Deus! Se verrá cedo!	*O God, when will he return?*
Se vistes meu amado,	Have you seen my lover,
por que hei gran cuidado;	The one for whom I have so many cares?
E ai, Deus! Se verrá cedo!	*O God, when will he return?*

Here is some other information, musical and otherwise, that is contained "on the page":

1. Relative pitch: notes placed on a staff, with a clef at the beginning
2. Text: lyrics written under the notes with subsequent verses below
3. The composer's name: written above the piece (not all instances of composer identification are 100 percent reliable, but it is one type of information that is sometimes available on the page)

---

15. In my personal observation, this critical engagement with text in medieval repertoire often has a profound effect on young musicians' approach to text-music relationships in their subsequent explorations of later music.
16. All translations are mine unless otherwise noted.

Figure 3.6: Martin Codax, "Ondas do mar de Vigo" (reproduced with permission, Morgan Library and Museum)

Does the score tell us rhythm? Even newcomers to medieval music would be able to detect notes of different shapes (longas, breves, and semibreves), so one would assume that some kind of relative duration or at least rhythmic gesture is certainly present. However, because the notation is somewhat ambiguous, it is a very complicated question; no fewer than thirty pages of the Ferreira edition of the Martin Codax *cantigas* are devoted to different theories regarding the rhythm of these pieces.[17] For our purposes,

17. Manuel Pedro Ferreira, *O Som de Martin Codax* (Lisbon: Impresa Nacional—Casa de Moeda, 1986), 90–120. The original manuscript belongs to the Pierpont

then, the safest answer to the question "Does the score tell us the rhythm?" is yes and no. The performer therefore must choose an approach:

1. Simply apply a meter to it, using the relative durations shown in the manuscript.
2. Choose text rhythm instead of a strict meter.
3. Use a combination of note duration and text rhythm.
4. Find a good modern edition, and let the editor decide the question.
5. Work through the information in the critical editions of the pieces, and draw a conclusion on the basis of that data.
6. Explore all of the above, plus one's own training in medieval notation, and make a decision.
7. Use the thirteenth-century method and learn it by ear from another musician (or a twentieth- or twenty-first-century recording), remaining aware that this process also results in the oral transmission of someone else's performance decisions.

Having addressed the content that is on the page, here are a few other things that are not indicated by anything on the written score:

1. Instrumentation (if any)
2. Tempo
3. Ornamentation (if any)
4. Phrasing
5. Context of performance (solo, private, public, and so forth)
6. Style of accompaniment (if any)
7. Historical pronunciation of the language

In the case of both the Hildegard antiphon and the *cantiga de amigo*, anything we add other than pitch and text is a matter of conjecture, subject to differences in scholarly interpretation, and completely up to the modern performer. In its original performance context, these considerations most likely would not have been present; each song in question would either have been sung by the composer or learned by ear from another musician, and the aspects of performance missing from the manuscript would have been learned by demonstration and imitation. The notation served as a quick memory refresher, a presentation volume for a patron, or documentation of the

Morgan Library in New York City (Vindel MS M979). It is used here by permission, but the entire two leaves can also be viewed on the library's website. Another website devoted to Codax and this manuscript can also be found online at La Biblioteca Virtual Miguel Cervantes; see http://bib.cervantesvirtual.com/servlet/SirveObras/89558518292445473413068/ima001.htm.

composer's work unintended for sight-reading, while the actual musical practice was characterized by unwritten content that was most likely transmitted orally/aurally. Even the complex notation of the fourteenth century, while it definitely indicates rhythm and meter, leaves out quite a bit of interpretive information.

In short, for modern players and singers, the first step toward performing music that was written in neumes, unmeasured notation, ambiguous early mensural notation, or even fourteenth-century notation involves recognizing and listing the areas in which you, the performer, must make decisions and, in some cases, invent musical content: articulation, gesture, tempo, dynamics, text declamation, accompaniment, instrumentation, perhaps even rhythm. The added material is a product of the performer's invention—just as it was for them. In our case, the added material is also a product of our historical imagination—a fact that immediately creates an unavoidable distinction between ourselves and the medieval performer. This is part of the contradiction that is "performing medieval music," and if we wish to be modern performers playing medieval repertoire, we must learn to navigate comfortably within that liminal space.

PRACTICE: CHARTING DIFFERENT DATA AND ABSENT DATA

Practice 3.1 provides a template for a simple assessment and comparison of a specific piece of medieval music: what is on the page, what musical content is not on the page and must be provided by the performer, and what, if anything, may require the performer to undertake a bit of performance practice research in order to create a performance. It provides a starting point for the process of learning the piece and making performance decisions and helps to clarify which aspects of the performance are going to require *invention*: improvisation, arrangement, or "fluid" composition.

One may be tempted simply to write something specific in categories A and B and "everything else" in category C, but it is more effective to be specific. Even in the case of an a cappella performance of a song, one must still decide tempo, dynamics, number of singers, rhythm, and whether to address issues of historical pronunciation; and therefore one must introduce unwritten elements into the performance. The nature of this music's transmission requires the singers and players to put more of an individual "stamp" on the piece than that allowed by the dynamics, slurs, and metronome markings of later music scores. The degree to which one considers this process "arrangement," "fluid composition," or "improvisation" depends on the amount of variability one chooses to allow from one performance to the next. For our Hildegard antiphon, a chart based on the Practice 3.1 categories might look something like this:

Practice 3.1
WHAT IS AND IS NOT ON THE PAGE

The following template can be used as a chart to categorize musical or textual content in a medieval piece: content included in the score, content included in the score but requiring specialized knowledge, and missing content that must be provided by the performer. (Examples of practical applications of the template are detailed in this chapter.)

Category A. Information included in the score.
   1.
   2.
   Etc.

Category B. Information included in the score but requiring specialized knowledge.
   1.
   2.
   Etc.

Category C. Information NOT included in the score, which may require research.
   1.
   2.
   Etc.

For the Martin Codax piece, the chart would be slightly different:

Table 3.1. APPLYING PRACTICE 3.1 TO HILDEGARD'S "SPIRITUS SANCTUS"

Category A. Information included in the score
   1. Pitch
   2. Text

Category B. Information included in the score but requiring specialized knowledge:
   1. Articulations, relative durations, gestures, etc. implied by neume shape
   2. Mode
   3. Liturgical context ("De spiritu sancto" = antiphon for the Holy Spirit)

Table 3.1. *(continued)*

Category C. Information NOT included in the score, which may require research:
1. Rhythm
2. Tempo
3. Dynamics
4. Phrasing
5. Number of singers
6. Use of instruments (or not)
7. Vocal tone or quality
8. Text-related info: translation, poetics, historical pronunciation, etc.

Employing the process outlined in Practice 3.1 will facilitate the identification of elements of performance that will require invention. Invention in this case can be anything from individualized phrasing and expression to improvisation, "fluid" composition, or arrangement. This is where the memorial archive comes in, with its storehouse of modal language, poetic and rhetorical content, and building blocks for the creation of polyphony, all of which will be discussed in subsequent chapters.

Next, while it helps to envision these areas of knowledge and skill as part of an archive or storehouse, it is crucial to remember that invention is a process, and that process is dependent upon memory; one cannot interrupt a performance to search the Internet for the notes in a particular mode. Just as the process of weaving requires the framework of a loom, the process of invention in performance requires a framework that includes strategies for memory. Therefore, let us take our discussion of notation one step further. Can we build working performance scores for ourselves, our colleagues, and our students that preserve the mnemonic attributes of medieval notation and remind us where invention is needed? As we create performances of specific pieces, can we draw upon any medieval techniques in order to further incorporate memory into our inventive process? The rest of this chapter will offer two ways of addressing those questions, one that draws from the mnemonic nature of the medieval notation itself and one that is related to the memory techniques put forth in sources widely used in the Middle Ages.

(44)   Improvisation and Inventio *in the Performance of Medieval Music*

Table 3.2. APPLYING PRACTICE 3.1 TO MARTIN CODAX'S "ONDAS DO MAR"

Category A. Information included in the score:
1. Pitch
2. Text

Category B. Information included in the score but requiring specialized knowledge:
1. The shapes and ligatures of thirteenth-century notation, their relative durations, implied articulations and gestures, etc.
2. Mode

Category C. Information NOT included in the score, which may require research:
1. The interpretation of the rhythm indicated in the notation
2. Tempo
3. Dynamics
4. Phrasing
5. Number of singers
6. Use of instruments (or not)
7. Vocal tone or quality
8. Text-related info: translation, poetics, historical pronunciation (*cantigas de amigo* as "women's songs" written by men; parallel poetic construction; pronunciation of Gallego-Portuguese, etc.)

MEMORIA AS LEARNING PROCESS: BUILDING MNEMONIC SCORES

Those of us born into modern industrialized societies are, for better or for worse, the product of a "literate" culture, meaning that our primary mode of information transmission involves the written word. While the architectural memory techniques were widely used in the Middle Ages, the idea of memorizing directly from a written source was not completely rejected. In *The Art of Memory*, Frances Yates states:

> In none of the evidence I have discovered is the act of writing itself regarded as a supplanter of memory. . . . Rather books are themselves memorial cues and aids, and memory is most like a book, a written page or a wax tablet upon which something is written.[18]

Yates goes on to say that the metaphor of "memory as a written surface" is "ancient and persistent in all Western cultures." As we have seen, it is possible to

---

18. Frances A. Yates, *The Art of Memory* (Harmondsworth, UK: Penguin, 1966), 16.

learn some aspects of medieval music from a written score, and, depending on the musician, it may be much faster than learning it by some method of oral transmission. Even the thirteenth-century treatise by the author known as Anonymous IV comments that the newer and more specific notation of the writer's own time allowed students to "achieve more in one hour than formerly in seven."[19]

However, learning music from notation may not facilitate the memorization process. The standard practice in creating modern editions of medieval music is to transcribe neumes into stemless noteheads; indeed, the technique is used at various points in this document. There are good reasons for using stemless noteheads. They allow an editor to transmit the pitch data that is actually on the original page without incorporating rhythmic or interpretive data that is not in the original; they are quickly understood by modern readers; they do not require an extensive study of medieval notation in order to begin working with repertoire; and they allow for quick pitch learning. However, for inexperienced performers not yet sensitive to text rhythm, stemless notehead scores also tend to result in the production of a monotonous string of pitches of equal duration, even when editorial slurs and articulation marks are used in the modern scores in conjunction with the noteheads.

It is completely possible, on the other hand, to create working performance scores for one's own personal use that incorporate some of the mnemonic characteristics of medieval notation while remaining easy to follow for the modern reader. This is to some degree what was done by the monks of Solesmes in the creation of the *Liber Usualis* in the nineteenth and early twentieth centuries, when certain common characteristics of different paleographic styles were homogenized into the notation used in modern collections of Gregorian chant. Eventually, editions of chants from the *Graduale Romanum* and the *Liber Usualis* were published with hand-drawn versions of the original neumes added above each staff; these can be found in books such as the *Graduel Neumé* and the *Graduale Triplex*.[20] However, considering the number of medieval manuscripts now available for viewing on the Internet, it is a straightforward exercise to do this oneself. This is demonstrated in Figure 3.7 by my own handwritten neumes, copied from a tenth-century manuscript originating from the monastery of Saint Gall and placed above the *Liber Usualis* notation for the chant "Viderunt omnes."[21]

---

19. Fritz Reckow, *Der Musiktraktat des Anonymous 4* (Wiesbaden, Germany: Steiner, 1967), 49–50, quoted in Treitler, *With Voice and Pen*, 249.

20. See Eugene Cardine, ed., *Graduel Neumé* (Solesmes, France: Abbaye Saint-Pierre de Solesmes, 1966), and *Graduale Triplex: Seu Graduale Romanum Pauli Pp. VI Cura Recognitum & Rhythmicis Signis a Solesmensibus Monachis Ornatum* (Solesmes, France: Abbaye Saint-Pierre de Solesmes, 1985).

21. The chant example is from the *Liber Usualis*; the neumes were copied by hand by me from St. Gallen, Stiftsbibliothek, Cod. Sang. 359, p. 40—Cantatorium, online at http://www.e-codices.unifr.ch/en/list/one/csg/0359.

Figure 3.7: "Viderunt" from the *Liber Usualis* with St. Gallen neumes

It is also possible to write neume shapes above a modern notehead-style transcription. Figure 3.8 shows an example, using a phrase from Hildegard's "Spiritus sanctus":

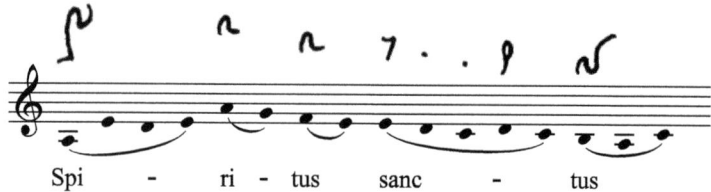

Figure 3.8: "Spiritus Sanctus" with noteheads and neumes

The method of writing neume shapes above the noteheads can provide additional information about articulation. For example, in the group E–D–C–D–C above the syllable "sanc-," the presence of the neume shape over the second D–C indicates liquescence, and thus that the second D–C is to be articulated differently from the first (see the discussion of liquescent neumes above). The presence of the two different neume shapes over that syllable also provides a very specific and more vivid visual image that will aid in the memorization of that word and its music.

Once the notes are learned, the next step toward memorization is to remove the pitches entirely, creating a handwritten or partially handwritten score that looks something like Figure 3.9:

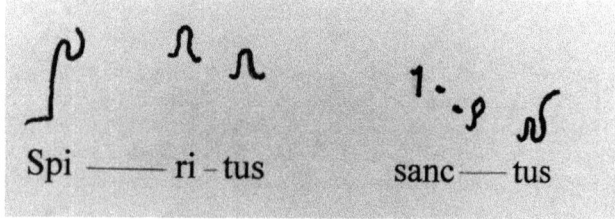

Figure 3.9: "Spiritus Sanctus" with text and neumes

The graphic style also works very well if the melody is taught orally/aurally from the very beginning of the process, omitting the use of notes altogether. When Barbara Thornton, cofounder of Sequentia Ensemble for Medieval Music, used the neume-plus-text technique in her medieval music workshops, groups of singers were able to memorize a surprising amount of music in the space of a couple of weeks. Thornton also used a system whereby the original neumes were modified slightly so that they could be placed on a staff over text that is written in modern script. This is particularly useful for those who teach medieval music students who may understand certain aspects of the manuscript's notation but have not yet had paleographic training and cannot read the text. Figure 3.10 shows another example of the same line from Hildegard's "Spiritus Sanctus," transcribed by Thornton for a group of music students:[22]

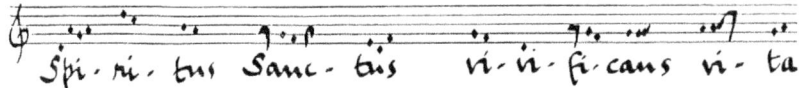

Figure 3.10: "Spiritus Sanctus," Thornton transcription

Thornton has separated some of the neumes into individual pitches, but in the case of liquescent neumes (the last two pitches above "sanc-" and the *quilismae* above "-cans" and "vi-") she has drawn the original shapes directly onto the staff as they would have been in the original Riesencodex manuscript. She has also represented literally the virga-punctum-punctum pattern (/ . .) that occurs frequently in Hildegard's work. This transcription of Thornton's is, once again, a pedagogical and mnemonic tool only, used for practical purposes.

These are just a few examples of ways in which one can combine medieval neumes with modern notation to create working performance scores with mnemonic elements. It can be tailored to the individual performer, who can then take advantage of the visual mnemonic aspects of medieval notation, either dispensing with noteheads all together as in Figure 3.9 or working with some combination of neumes and modern notation. I would strongly encourage all medieval music practitioners who are using stemless notehead transcriptions to supplement them with facsimiles of the original notation whenever possible and to either develop a basic working knowledge of the notation or gain access to notation manuals and reference books.

22. Abundant thanks to Benjamin Bagby for his gracious permission to use this fragment of Barbara Thornton's transcription, part of an unpublished working score given to students attending Vancouver Early Music's 1993 Mediaeval Programme.

MEMORIA AS DISCIPLINE: EMPLOYING LOCATION AND IMAGE

Since the purpose of constructing a mnemonic score is to facilitate memorization, at some point the process of preparing a performance must include the transition from paper to memory. The parts of a particular performance that will ultimately live in the memory include not only the melody and the text but all of the aspects of invention, including those that are fixed (arrangement) and those that involve fluid composition or improvisation. All must be held in the mind. In the Middle Ages, memory was viewed not just as a phenomenon arising spontaneously from simple familiarity or repetition but also as a skill developed by mental discipline. The imagination and visualization of images and location were important tools in this process.

The cultivation of memory was also considered to be part of the realm of rhetorical skill. Medieval scholars, orators, poets, and musicians therefore turned to the ancient rhetorical treatises to find techniques that, while originally intended to help orators, were also considered to be useful for the construction and delivery of poetry. Poetic skill, in turn, was directly related to music; Quintilian, in his *Institutio Oratoria*, reminds us that "music was the most ancient of sciences connected with literature" and that "the most celebrated poets" agree.[23] In an article concerning rhetoric and late medieval polyphony, Margaret Bent points out that music and rhetoric had "a large shared vocabulary of technical terminology" and that medieval theorists often modeled "musical definitions on those of grammar and rhetoric" and "music treatises on their verbal counterparts."[24]

The *Rhetorica ad Herennium* is a Latin text on rhetoric written in the first century BCE. It was formerly thought to have been written by Cicero, and in the Middle Ages it was widely used as one of the major pedagogical texts for the study of the rhetorical arts. *Rhetorica ad Herennium* was also important because it was one of the first rhetorical texts to systematically discuss memory.

---

23. Quintilian, *The Orator's Education, Books 1–2*, trans. Donald A. Russell (Cambridge, MA: Harvard University Press, 2001). See chapter 7 for a more complete discussion of Quintilian's association of poetry to music.
24. Margaret Bent, "Grammar and Rhetoric in Late Medieval Polyphony," in *Rhetoric Beyond Words*, ed. Mary Carruthers (Cambridge, UK: Cambridge University Press, 2010), 52–53.

In her book *The Art of Memory*, Frances Yates gives an extensive discussion of the *Rhetorica*, explaining that the treatise names two kinds of memory, natural and artificial.[25] The natural memory is "that which is engrafted upon our minds, born simultaneously with thought," and the artificial memory is "memory strengthened or confirmed by training." Artificial memory is extremely important, because "a good natural memory can be improved by this discipline and persons less well-endowed can have their weak memories improved by the art." This artificial memory can be developed by way of specific techniques, including the skill of establishing mental "places," or loci, and mental "images." A mental place can be defined as "a place easily grasped by the memory, such as a house, an intercolumnar space, a corner, an arch, or the like." Images, on the other hand, are "forms, marks or simulacra (simulations)" of what we wish to remember." This is not entirely separate from the act of learning something through the action of reading: "The places are very much like wax tablets or papyrus, the images like the letters, the arrangement and disposition of the images like the script, and the delivery is like the reading."

The *Rhetorica* author says an orator should have a store of a large number of these "places" and advises those aspiring to improve their memory capacity to remember them in a series that goes in a particular order, so that you can start from any one of them and move forward or backward. This same set of loci can be used "again and again for remembering different material." Every fifth locus should have an image; the author suggests something like "a golden hand" on number five.[26] The reader is advised to create these loci in a quiet and solitary place without distractions. The author gives extremely detailed instructions about the nature of these locations, how much space should be between them, how they should be lit, and so on, the main point being that the more vivid the images, the stronger the memory imprint.

As for the images that are placed upon these locations, the *Rhetorica* tells us that there are two kinds of images: one for things (*res*), the other for words (*verba*).[27] "Things are thus the subject matter of speech; words are the language in which that subject matter is clothed." Material can be memorized word for word (*memoria verborum*) or according to events or ideas (*memoria rerum*). Ultimately, both are needed; in his *De inventione*, Cicero says that

---

25. Yates, *Art of Memory*, 21–32. The quotations are taken from Yates.
26. Presumably because of the presence of five fingers on the hand. One cannot help but be reminded of the "five golden rings" verse in the carol "The Twelve Days of Christmas."
27. Yates, *Art of Memory*, 24.

memory is the "firm perception in the soul of things and words." Both the author of *Rhetorica* and Cicero agree that word-for-word memorization is more difficult, but the memory of the events or ideas is even more effective.[28] Mary Carruthers describes the distinction thus:

> Human memory operates in signs, images that call up material which is not immediately present to one. So all memories are images. Then there is the distinction in remembering something between its exact reproduction and its reconstruction or "translation" in memory. The former, what we now call rote memorization, was called in Latin *memoria verborum* or *verbatim* and was always thought to be *by itself* an ability of minor cognitive value. The latter, reconstructive memory, was called *memoria rerum* or *sententialiter* and is fundamental to understanding human learning. The phrase is best translated into English as "remembering the substance"—it should be left as open-ended as that.[29]

Both the *Rhetorica* and Cicero are speaking quite literally of creating architectural images in the mind. Using the framework of this image, content that needs to be memorized is placed in very specific locations. A very famous musical example of a locational mnemonic image is the "Guidonian hand," found in Guido D'Arezzo's eleventh-century pedagogical and theoretical treatise *Micrologus*, in which the notes of the medieval hexachord system (*ut, re, mi, fa, sol,* and *la*) are visualized on the joints of the hand rather than in a graph or chart.[30] Figure 3.11 illustrates the hexachord system as it might appear in a chart:

---

28. Yates, *Art of Memory*, 24–25.

29. Mary Carruthers, "The Poet as Master Builder," *New Literary History* 24 (1993): 881.

30. For those unfamiliar with the medieval hexachord system, the "scale" consisted of six consecutive notes that ascended in the following interval pattern: tone, tone, semitone, tone, tone. These notes were designated by the syllables *ut, re, mi, fa, sol,* and *la*, and were used for sight-singing, much like our "do-re-mi" solfege system today. There were three hexachords, one beginning on G, one on C, and one on F. In order to conform to the T-T-S-T-T formula, the F hexachord included a B♭. If the range of a piece went beyond the top note of the hexachord, the singer would have to "mutate" to the next hexachord. For example, referring to Figure 3.13, if you were singing in the lowest G hexachord (lower left-hand corner), and you ascended beyond E "la" to F, that F would be sung as "fa" in the C hexachord. With the use of the Guidonian Hand, young singers were taught to visualize on their hand the entire range of hexachords, or "gamut" (named after the first note, gamma ut), pointing to specific joints as they sang the syllables.

e'							la
d'						la	sol
c'						sol	fa
b'							mi
b'(flat)						fa (b)	
a'					la	mi	re
g					sol	re	ut
f					fa	ut	
e				la	mi		
d			la	sol	re		
c			sol	fa	ut		
b				mi			
b(flat)			fa (b)				
a		la	mi	re			
G		sol	re	ut			
F		fa	ut				
E	la	mi					
D	sol	re					
C	fa	ut					
B	mi						
A	re						
Γ	ut						

Figure 3.11: The medieval hexachord system

Figure 3.12 shows how this same data was illustrated through a mnemonic placement technique that located each note of the hexachord on a joint of the hand. A number of variations on this image exist in medieval and later treatises.[31]

These mentally constructed loci can be created in any number of different ways and can be as diverse as the individuals creating them. The more personal

---

31. As David E. Cohen points, while the hand is "universally attributed to Guido," it is also the case that "no extant text by him mentions it." Cohen, "Notes, Scales, and Modes in the Earlier Middle Ages," in *The Cambridge History of Western Music Theory*, ed. Thomas Christensen (Cambridge, UK: Cambridge University Press, 2006), 344. Regardless of origin, the "solmisation hand" remains a useful tool and an excellent example of the use of placement as a mnemonic device.

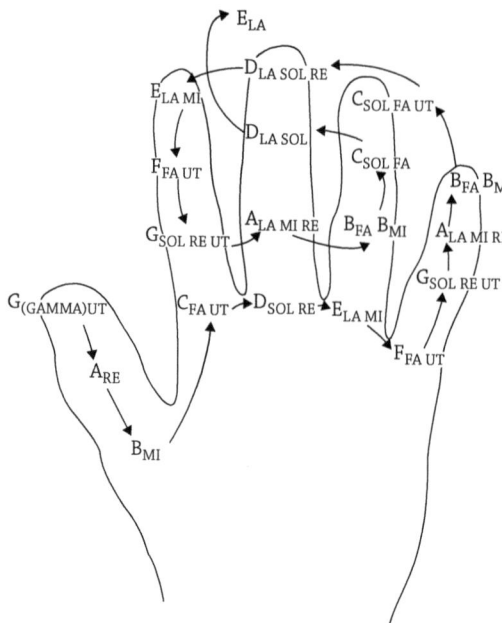

Figure 3.12: Hexachord placement, modeled after the Guidonian hand

they are, the more effective they will be for the individual using them. Mary Carruthers compares them to computer icons that "set in motion" a task:

> A locational memory system is any scheme that establishes a set of ordered, clearly articulated, and readily recoverable background locations into which memory "images" are consciously placed. These images, often called *agent images* for they are active, function like the icons in a computer program in that they set in motion a task, the associative procedures of recollection. Within each background, discrete images can be grouped together in scenes, their number limited only by short-term memory. The images provide the associative cues to particular material; their "places" provide the relationship of their matters to one another. The power of this elementary technique is that it provides immediate access to whatever piece of stored material one may want, and it also provides the means to construct any number of cross-referencing, associational links among the elements in such schemes. It provides one with a random access memory as well as schematics or templates upon which to construct any number of additional collations and concordances of material.[32]

32. Mary Carruthers, "The Poet as Master Builder," *New Literary History* 24 (1993): 881–82.

Carruthers points out that this construction of associational links and template-based collations and concordances of material comprise "what we might recognize as 'composition.'" She lists the various architectural constructs that were used as templates: amphitheaters, labyrinths, churches, monasteries, castles, towers, ladders, rose windows, and wheels, as well as things from nature such as trees, gardens, and so forth. One learns things twice: once by rote, and then a second time to "attach those sounds to their meaning and commentary."[33]

Figure 3.13 shows an example of this architectural technique as one might apply it to the Martin Codax "Ondas do mar" *cantiga*.

This little building provides a template for a four-strophe song with a refrain. Note the symmetrical placement of the verses, the alternation of the *i-o* and *a-o* vowel endings, the graphic representation of the parallelism, the curvature of the superimposed image where there is a prominent "o" vowel at the beginning of the line. The staircases lead down to the refrain, which is identical for each stanza.

The medieval treatises suggest that we visualize a building, architectural construction, or shape that actually exists, preferably one that we can call up in the memory easily. Today, we have the added advantage of all kinds of shapes, charts, and templates that we can access via computer; one can easily create a mnemonic image by experimenting with various software programs. It is most effective if performers create their own templates and mnemonic images, as learning and memorization styles vary greatly among individuals. By personalizing these "icons," to use Carruthers's apt analogy, the images set in motion an even stronger "associative procedure of recollection." My own

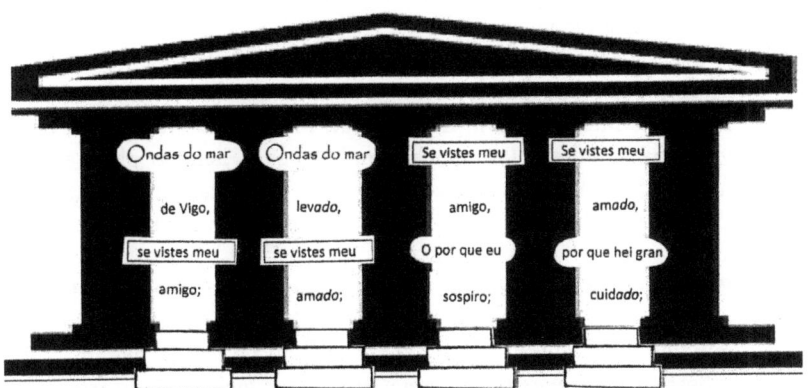

Figure 3.13: The "Ondas do mar" building

33. Carruthers, "Poet as Master Builder," 888.

experience suggests that after a mnemonic image is recalled in the mind a certain number of times, the content is internalized and the image no longer needed; however, if an external stimulus such as performance anxiety causes a memory slip, the instant engagement of the mnemonic image can save the day. Practice 3.2 provides a step-by-step process for using placement as a memory technique.

> *Practice 3.2*
> **USING "PLACEMENT" AS A MEMORY TECHNIQUE**
>
> 1. Having chosen a specific piece that will be committed to memory, choose an architectural form or graphic image that can be held easily in the mind. It could be the façade of your childhood home, the building where you work, a famous location that you can visualize easily, or a simple shape such as a wheel, star, concentric circle, and so on.
> 2. Make sure that the structure of your mental image will fit the structure of the piece you wish to memorize. For example, if the piece has five verses, it will be most effective to mentally place each verse in the window of a building façade that has five windows. Adjust the template on which you are placing your memorized data, or use a different one.
> 3. Keep in mind that you can include multiple types of data on a template such as this. Lyrics are the obvious choice, but an instrumentalist might write in the first few notes of a particular section or words such as "prelude," "stanza 1," or "interlude." One might also include things like stage blocking—spokes in a wheel, for example, could be a template for stage movements.
> 4. It may be beneficial to draw a representation of the mental image, including the data (words, directions, and so forth).
> 5. Begin the memorization process. How much of the image can you visualize at once? How much detail? Does it help to place extra images that "trigger" the recollection of a particular line or section? Can you visualize your way through the image forward, backward, up and down?
> 6. Personalize the process. Since people have different learning styles, memorization can be a highly individualized process. Some people remember actual written words better than representative images; others are the opposite. For some, simply remembering the arrangement of verses in a written poem is enough to create a mental image that stays in the mind; others find that the more elaborate and colorful the image, the more they retain.
>
> It can also be useful to apply this process to non-musical material such as phone numbers, lists, or names.

THE NEXT STEP: BUILDING THE STOREHOUSE OF INVENTION

In this discussion of medieval notation and memory, we have outlined the "big picture" of the process that we call medieval performance practice: *Medieval notation points to what must be invented, and memory is our storehouse of invention.* In the following chapters on mode, rhetoric, and polyphony, we will discover that some of the processes of musical training in the Middle Ages were geared toward filling the storehouse of invention. Mnemonic-friendly notation, the visualization of images, and memorized intonations and melodic patterns were built into the pedagogical methods and even compositional techniques used in the medieval period. It is important to note, however, that as modern musicians, we do not attempt to learn these skills and use these tools because we wish to exactly replicate, for example, a specific twelfth-century performance. Not only is that impossible, but if we are trying to be true to some notion of "authenticity," we would have to consider that a medieval audience that placed such value on musical invention would probably have been bored with the replication of a performance from the previous week. Rather, we endeavor to learn and use the medieval musician's tools because a musical repertoire does not exist in a vacuum separate from the process used to create it, and the tools that the medieval performers used were integral to the repertoire that they performed. If we are going to engage with medieval repertoire and make it our own, we must explore the contents of the medieval musical storehouse and add it to ours.

CHAPTER 4

✧

Mode

The Vocabulary of Melody

When discussing style in music history classes, a student will often make a comment such as "When I hear *Eine kleine Nachtmusik*, I know it's Mozart, but I don't know why." The student has heard Mozart's works so many times that she has internalized the sound of Mozart's compositional thumbprints—the melodic patterns, rhythmic gestures, orchestral color combinations, phrase structures, and Alberti bass patterns, among other things, that are characteristic of Mozart's work. Up to that point in her studies, this process of internalization has been unconscious; that is, the student did not purposely make an effort to memorize and categorize these Mozart thumbprints. Through repeated encounters with the music, however, a categorization process was taking place, as the mind recorded and catalogued musical characteristics in a folder labeled "Mozart."

To extend this metaphor, the data previously stored in the student's mental folder contains audio files (e.g., the sound of the opening phrase of *Nachtmusik*) but not text files ("Mannheim-influenced rocket theme"). Therefore, the student is having difficulty in a style analysis class that is requiring her to retrieve words to describe what she is hearing—it just "*sounds* like Mozart." This *nonverbal process of cataloguing and categorizing internalized musical data* may pose a problem in a music history class, but it is critical to the process of improvisation, just as we reach fluency in a language when we stop thinking about the meaning of every word. It is this nonverbal process that allows a blues guitarist to improvise in the blues idiom or an Irish fiddler to improvise on a slow air or, for that matter, to compose his own air in the traditional style.

In order to be able to improvise or invent a musical performance in the context of medieval performance practice, it is necessary to internalize the thumbprints of medieval modes, just as earlier musicians did either through training or by absorbing the sound of the music they heard every day. However, in addition to memorizing the melodic patterns and cadences that characterize each mode, one must also learn how to hear modal melody outside the context of functional harmony, as a musician trained in pre-Baroque-era or certain vernacular musics would have been more likely to do, but which can be challenging for modern musicians. This chapter is intended to be a practical pedagogical or autodidactic tool offering suggested practices and techniques for internalizing the modal language of medieval Western music. While inclusive of some rudimentary theoretical content, the chapter is not intended to provide a thorough theoretical discussion of medieval mode; that has been covered extensively elsewhere in the literature of musicology and music theory. The chapter will, however, include techniques for recognizing modes and learning modal patterns and formulas and attempt to distill out of a vast pool of information a modal primer that will be useful even to players who have had little or no previous training in modal music.

WHAT IS A "MODE"?

The concept of "mode" is covered in most introductory or undergraduate music theory classes. Beyond that, unless a musician engages with jazz, traditional folk, non-Western, or early music, its practical application is seldom emphasized. The following review of the basic concept of mode therefore assumes a certain familiarity on the part of the reader and is not intended be didactic. Its purpose is rather to demonstrate the difference between modern uses of modes that place them in harmonized contexts and the medieval modal system associated with plainchant beginning around the time of Charlemagne (768–814), which also works for a large percentage of medieval secular songs.

Modes in modern Western music are often introduced to the student by way of a system based on a series of diatonic "scales" corresponding to the white keys of the piano. These scales and their mode names are shown in Table 4.1:

Table 4.1. MODE NAMES (MODERN USAGE)

Ionian	C D E F G A B C
Dorian	D E F G A B C D
Phrygian	E F G A B C D E
Lydian	F G A B C D E F
Mixolydian	G A B C D E F G
Aeolian	A B C D E F G A
Locrian	B C D E F G A B

In order to facilitate quick aural recognition of the modes, music theory students are often encouraged to think of these modes as "altered" versions of the major and natural minor scales, as shown in Table 4.2:

Table 4.2. MODES AS "ALTERED SCALES"

Mode	Alteration	Position of altered note
Ionian	(same as major scale)	—
Dorian	natural minor with raised sixth	D E F G A B C D
Phrygian	natural minor with lowered second	E F G A B C D E
Lydian	major with raised fourth	F G A B C D E F
Mixolydian	major with lowered seventh	G A B C D E F G
Aeolian	(same as natural minor scale)	—
Locrian	natural minor with lowered second and fifth	B C D E F G A B

For a person trained in either classical or popular Western music, hearing modes in terms of these alterations helps identify modes when we hear them in folk, rock, or other vernacular musics, or in classical and church music that borrows from folk, medieval, or Renaissance musical material.

It can also be the case that past experience with modal folk and rock music can facilitate the speed at which a musician becomes fluent in medieval modal language. Those who have had extensive experience with Anglo-Celtic folk music and/or rock and roll often need almost no prompting in order to improvise or create new melodies in Dorian and Mixolydian modes, since they are part of the internalized language of those vernacular idioms as well. However, our twentieth- and twenty-first-century ears are trained to hear music in terms of functional harmony, and modern musicians naturally gravitate toward hearing these modal musics in the context of chordal accompaniment. Indeed, one can build a set of "diatonic" triads for each mode, as illustrated for Dorian mode in Table 4.3:

Table 4.3. DORIAN "DIATONIC" TRIADS

i	minor	D F A
ii	minor	E G B
III	major	F A C
IV	major	G B D
v	minor	A C E
vi°	diminished	B D F
VII	major	C E G

These triads can also be expanded to diatonic seventh and ninth chords, as was the case with the modal jazz that became prominent in the late 1950s and 1960s. Two Dorian mode examples from jazz would be the Dm7–Em7 progression that characterizes the harmonization of John Coltrane's famous solo on "My Favorite Things" (although the original tune itself is not strictly Dorian), and the famous Dorian bass motive and responding chord changes that begin the main theme of Miles Davis's "So What."

Simpler modal harmonizations can be found in hundreds of folk and popular songs. Just as "So What" is often cited as an example of the use of Dorian mode in jazz, "Scarborough Fair" is a frequently used example from folk music. The use of the Dorian and Mixolydian modes is found often in the music of rock and roll bands that were influenced by Anglo-Celtic folk and country music, and as a result we also frequently hear those modes in the music of bands associated with the 1960s British Invasion. A considerable number of the Beatles' songs employ either Dorian or Mixolydian mode, although few of the songs stay in the mode throughout, often deviating at the bridge ("Norwegian Wood" and "If I Needed Someone" are two notable examples). Another frequently cited British Invasion example is the Mixolydian verse of Gerry and the Pacemakers' "Ferry Cross the Mersey" (now played in a continuous loop on the actual ferry that crosses the Mersey in Liverpool, providing passengers with a Mixolydian aural immersion experience). The British Invasion rockers, in turn, brought the Anglo-Celtic modal influence into the next wave of rock and roll music as well. The phrase shown in Example 4.1, with the harmonic context removed, could easily be a piece of plainchant in transposed *a* Dorian mode, complete with a characteristic whole-step cadence:

Example 4.1: Dorian melody (final transposed to A)

The sequence of pitches in Example 4.1, however, is the same as part of a phrase found in a passage from Led Zeppelin's "Stairway to Heaven." The Phrygian and Lydian modes are rarer in Western popular music, although examples do surface occasionally.[1]

In short, between vernacular music and some of the older church music that is still in use, both American and European music listeners have been surrounded

---

1. Perhaps one of the best examples of a globally known Lydian popular tune is composer Danny Elfman's theme for the American cartoon series *The Simpsons*, which has been broadcast all over the world in at least a dozen languages, including Mandarin. The Simpson's Lydian theme itself is very reminiscent of another, less globally known TV theme, which is the 1960s sci-fi cartoon series *The Jetsons*.

by modal music. However, because modern musicians are trained to hear melodies in the context of functional harmony, we have learned to hear modal melodies in a harmonized context as well. Thus, it is difficult to change one's aural perspective; if one is accustomed to hearing a melody in relationship to chords, it can be more challenging to hear a melody in relationship to the "final" of a mode without mentally harmonizing that melody. Even those of us who have played medieval music for years often find that the retrieval system in our own storehouses of memory automatically engages the "chordal accompaniment" function when we hear a melody, whether that melody was composed by Mozart, John Lennon, or Hildegard von Bingen. This is particularly true for those of us who spent years playing keyboard, rhythm guitar, or any other musical role in which the primary function is to provide harmonic support for a melody.

To learn the language of modes for the purpose of medieval music, musicians must learn to think of mode in a different way, immersing themselves in a musical language that is not simply a matter of "altered" major or minor scales and is not based on the concept of tonal harmony (even if it sounds "tonal" to modern ears).

MEDIEVAL MODE: A BRIEF HISTORICAL BACKGROUND

Far from being just a series of intervals or an "altered" octave species scale, a medieval mode consists of a collection of melodic phrases, patterns, incipits, gestures, and cadences that appear in a particular mode, in both sacred chant and secular melodies. This way of identifying the character of a mode involves far more than simply looking at the last note of a piece to determine what the final of the mode must be. In this section, I will attempt to distill from the multitude of medieval treatises a very basic and practical amount of historical and theoretical information that will illustrate some of the ways in which medieval mode differs from our modern major and minor scales.

Many of the theory treatises of the ninth and tenth centuries were intended to be of practical use, written to educate plainchant singers. Even before Charlemagne was crowned first emperor of the Holy Roman Empire in 800 CE, one of his goals had been the establishment of a unified Roman liturgy throughout his empire (an initiative that had actually begun during the rule of his father, Pepin III).[2] Since hundreds of Frankish singers had to learn a lot of Roman chant in a hurry, some of the theoretical treatises of the time were written from a distinctively pedagogical and practical point of view,

---

2. See Charles Atkinson, *The Critical Nexus* (Oxford: Oxford University Press, 2009), 85, and J. Peter Burkholder, Donald Jay Grout, and Claude V. Palisca, *A History of Western Music*, 9th ed. (New York: W. W. Norton, 2014), 30–31.

a trend that continued well into the century after Charlemagne's death. The need for practical manuals led to the creation of books called *tonaries*, which will be discussed later in this chapter; but in order to understand the tonaries, it is necessary to first be familiar with the structure and content of the eight modes that are now sometimes referred to as the "medieval church modes."

The eight medieval modes are thought to have come from a system called the *oktoechos* used in the Byzantine chant tradition. The Byzantine system divided its chant repertoire into tonal categories called *echoi*, of which there were eight—hence the Greek term *oktoechos*, or "eight *echoi*."[3] Both the Byzantine and the Western systems contained four pairs of modes. Taking their cue from the Byzantine tradition, Carolingian-era writers such as Aurelian of Réôme (*Musica Disciplina*, ninth-century) and the compilers of the earliest tonaries grouped the modes into pairs. These pairs were labeled according to the first four Greek ordinal numbers. Thus, modes 1 and 2 were the *protus* (first) pair; modes 3 and 4 were the *deuterus* (second) pair; modes 5 and 6 were the *tritus* (third) pair; and modes 7 and 8 were the *tetrardus* (fourth) pair. The modes, or *toni*, are defined in terms of characteristic melodic patterns, or *intonation formulas*, often set to a sequence of syllables such as "no-e-a-ne" or "no-e-a-gis." Each mode also is assigned a certain number of formulaic melodic patterns that can be used to end one chant and move smoothly to another (this will be discussed more fully later, in the discussion of tonaries).

Each of the four pairs of medieval modes also shared a *final*. This was the most important note, the "home" note on which the chant usually ended. To our modern ears, the modal melody will seem to come to rest on this note. It is important to note here that the earliest medieval treatises on mode do not describe the modes in terms of finals; however, finals are introduced by the time we get to the writings of Hucbald of Saint-Amand (*De harmonica institutione*, ca. 870–900) and the treatises known as *Musica Enchiriadis* and *Schola Enchiriadis* (ca. 850–ca. 900). In *The Cambridge History of Western Music Theory*, David E. Cohen points out that "Hucbald and the *Enchiriadis* treatises are the first known sources to define and use the concept of modal finals, and to locate them as specific notes in the scale."[4] The *protus* modes shared the final we would call D; the *deuterus*, E; the *tritus*, F; and the *tetrardus*, G. In each pair of modes, the first of the pair was called *authentic* and was characterized by a range that extended in theory from the final to one octave above the final, but in practice often included the step below the final and sometimes extended past the top octave. The second mode of the pair sharing the same final was called *plagal*, characterized by a range that extended in theory a fifth above the final and a fourth below, but in practice could descend to at least a fifth below and occasionally rise higher than the fifth above.

3. Cohen, "Notes, Scales, and Modes," 310.
4. Cohen, "Notes, Scales, and Modes," 322.

In addition to the final, each individual mode had a *reciting tone*, a note that was secondary only to the final in importance. In the context of plainchant, the reciting tone featured prominently in psalm recitation formulas, and often long phrases of text were chanted on this note before a formulaic cadence led back to the final. Each mode, both authentic and plagal, has its own individual reciting tone. In most cases, the reciting tone in the authentic mode is the fifth above the final, and the reciting tone in the plagal mode is a third above the final; however, there are three important exceptions to that rule: in mode 3, the reciting tone is C; in mode 4, A; and in mode 8, C.

It is worth noting here that Hucbald was trying to reconcile the mathematical approach of previous authorities such as Boethius (ca. 480–525) with the practical task of educating plainchant singers. Instead of using math to explain intervals, for example, Hucbald uses examples from plainchant that his singers would have already had stored in their memories, or from common instrumental use (for example, he tells us that a semitone can be heard "between the third and fourth strings of a six-stringed cithara").[5] The practical intention of these treatises is worth noting for our purposes, because the writers are attempting to help the singers fill their storehouse of memory with the tools that they will need in order to recognize modal formulas by ear.

There remains one more thing to discuss in our short historical background of medieval mode, and that is how the modes got the names that we now associate with them: Dorian, Phrygian, Lydian, and Mixolydian. Up to this point, we have established the following:

1. There were eight medieval modes.
2. The eight medieval modes were grouped into four pairs, labeled *protus, deuterus, tritus,* and *tetrardus.*
3. Each pair of medieval modes shared a final.
4. The finals of the medieval modes were D (*protus*), E (*deuterus*), F (*tritus*), and G (*tetrardus*).
5. Each mode had a note of secondary importance that was called a reciting tone.

To this list, we will now add another layer of nomenclature. In the late ninth or early tenth century, one of the authors of a group of theoretical texts now known as *Alia Musica* applied the Greek ethnic appellations Dorian, Phrygian, Lydian, and Mixolydian to the *protus, deuterus, tritus,* and *tetrardus* modal pairs.[6] Unfortunately, the *Alia Musica* author's use of these names is based on a misunderstanding of earlier Greek theory and Boethius's octave species modes; nevertheless, the names stuck. Since then, the term Dorian has been applied to the

---

5. Atkinson, *The Critical Nexus*, 150–51.
6. Cohen, "Notes, Scales, and Modes," 333–34.

protus authentic mode, and Hypodorian to *protus* plagal; Phrygian to the *deuterus* authentic mode, and Hypophrygian to the *deuterus* plagal; Lydian to the *tritus* authentic mode, and Hypolydian to the *tritus* plagal; and Mixolydian to the *tetrardus* authentic mode, and Hypomixolydian to the *tetrardus* plagal.

THE EIGHT MEDIEVAL MODES

With this historical background in mind, let us now consider each of the eight modes in terms of their specific intervals and range. While mode is often taught in modern music theory classes as a series of diatonic "scales" corresponding to the white keys of the piano and spanning an octave, as shown in Table 4.1, in medieval theory they were conceptualized as overlapping species of fourths and fifths.

This difference can be illustrated by using a rudimentary explanation of the construction of a major or minor scale as a point of reference. Both the major and minor scales of Western tonal music are comprised of a specific succession of smaller intervals that ends on a note one octave higher than the note on which it began. If you wish to construct a major scale, you would begin on any note and proceed according to the following pattern of tones (whole steps) and semitones (half steps):

tone → tone → semitone → tone → tone → tone → semitone

If one begins with the note C, the result will be C–D–E–F–G–A–B–C. If one begins on a G and follows the same pattern of intervals, the result will be G–A–B–C–D–E–F♯–G.

If you wish to build a minor scale, the succession of intervals will be different. The natural minor scale gives us the following pattern:

tone → semitone → tone → tone → semitone → tone → tone

If one begins with the note C, the result will be C–D–E♭–F–G–A♭–B♭–C. If one begins on a G and follows the same pattern of intervals, the result will be G–A–B♭–C–D–E♭–F–G.

Both the C minor and the C major scale span an octave, but the pattern of intervals included in that octave is different. The pattern of intervals, or *species*, of both scales spans an octave; therefore, the two scales comprise two different octave species. (For those who may not have encountered the term *species* in music theory, I offer an analogy from nature: the octave is like the genus *Panthera*, and the major, natural minor, melodic minor, and harmonic minor scales would be the species of lions, tigers, leopards, and jaguars.)

In the Western tonal system, any interval larger than a whole step can technically have different species. For example, a minor third could be comprised of a tone followed by a semitone, or a semitone followed by a tone. In the system of medieval church modes, species of fifths and fourths are particularly important, as we will see.

A number of different patterns of tones and semitones can be placed in order in such a way that the first and last of the resulting succession of notes spans a perfect fifth. Here are three different examples of combinations of intervals that comprise a species of fifth, starting on the note D:

> tone → tone → semitone → tone (D–E–F♯–G–A)
> tone → semitone → tone → tone (D–E–F–G–A)
> semitone → tone → tone → tone (D–E♭–F–G–A)
> tone → tone → tone → semitone (D–E–F♯–G♯–A)

Here are three different examples of combinations of intervals that comprise a species of fourth, starting on the note A:

> tone → tone → semitone (A–B–C♯–D)
> tone → semitone → tone (A–B–C–D)
> semitone → tone → tone (A–B♭–C–D)

Rather than think of a medieval mode as an octave species scale, it is more accurate to think of a medieval mode as overlapping species of fifths and fourths. This way of conceptualizing the modes differs considerably from defining Dorian mode, for example, as a scale that "starts on the second scale degree of a major scale and extends up an octave." Unlike our modern octave species scales, the final of a medieval mode is not always located at the beginning and end of the octave species like goalposts. In the plagal modes, the final appears in the middle (see Table 4.4). Therefore, it is easier to understand the distinction between the authentic and plagal modes by thinking of the eight modes in terms of overlapping species of fourths and fifths, with some additional modifications dictated by common use, such as the occasional use of B♭s and of notes that extend outside the fourth and fifth species, particularly at cadence points.

Mode 1, Dorian, is characterized by the interval pattern shown in the first part of Table 4.4, with D as the final.[7] Mode 2, Hypodorian, shown in the second part of Table 4.4, also has D as the final, but notice that the species of fourth is placed below the final, rather than above it, affecting the range, or ambitus, of the mode. (In Tables 4.4–4.7, "T" refers to a whole tone and "S" to a semitone; "RT" stands for "reciting tone.")

---

7. It is important to note that musicians of the Middle Ages did not have absolute pitch standards as we do today, so what they were calling D may not be the same as the approximately 147 Hz that we would now associate with the D below middle C.

Table 4.4. THE *PROTUS*/DORIAN MODES

Mode 1: Protus Authentic (Dorian)							
T →	S →	T →	T →	T →	S →	T →	
D (Final)	E	F	G	A (RT)	B	C	D

fifth (D–A); fourth (A–D)

Mode 2: Protus Plagal (Hypodorian)							
T →	T →	S →	T →	T →	S →	T →	
A	B	C	D (Final)	E	F (RT)	G	A

fourth (A–D); fifth (D–A)

The two formulaic melodies shown in Example 4.2 and Example 4.3 were used in the Middle Ages to illustrate the difference between the authentic and plagal *protus*/Dorian modes. (We will encounter these melodies again in more detail later in the chapter, where we will see them along with the mnemonic texts that accompanied them in various medieval treatises.)[8] Example 4.2 illustrates the *protus* authentic or Dorian mode.

Example 4.2: *Protus* authentic/Dorian formulaic melody (mode 1)

Example 4.3: *Protus* plagal/Hypodorian formulaic melody (mode 2)

In actual practice, in many Dorian and Hypodorian melodies the B♮ is modified to a B♭, particularly when used as an upper neighboring tone between two iterations of the note A, as is the case with Example 4.2. It is also quite

---

8. These formulaic melodies are found in a number of medieval treatises, accompanied by mnemonic Latin texts. An extensive discussion of the melodies, their provenance, and their Latin texts can be found in Terence Bailey, *The Intonation Formulas of Western Chant* (Toronto: Pontifical Institute of Mediaeval Studies, 1974), a treasure trove of medieval mnemonic and pedagogical formulas compiled from no fewer than thirty-eight manuscripts. The melodies in Examples 4.4 through 4.11 are from a manuscript from Reichenau (Bamberg, Staatsbibliothek, Ms. Lit. 5), cited by both Bailey and by Berger in *Medieval Music and the Art of Memory*, 69. The formulas will be discussed in conjunction with their texts later in this chapter.

common to find the B♭ on the fourth degree of modes 5 and 6 and as a lowered fifth scale degree in mode 4.[9] Since the overall purpose of this chapter is to provide techniques for internalizing and becoming familiar with the actual sound of the different modes, a complete discussion of the theory behind the use of B♭ in the eight church modes is beyond our scope, but suffice it to say that B♭ can appear because of several factors, including the desire to avoid a tritone or to follow the medieval rules of solmization.[10]

The tables that follow contain modes 3 and 4 (Table 4.5, *deuterus*/Phrygian, with formulaic melodies shown in Examples 4.4 and 4.5); modes 5 and 6 (Table 4.6, *tritus*/Lydian, with formulaic melodies shown in Examples 4.6 and 4.7); and modes 7 and 8 (Table 4.7, *tetrardus*/Mixolydian, with formulaic melodies shown in Examples 4.8 and 4.9). The formulaic melodies from the same source as the previous Examples 4.2 and 4.3. The figure shaped like a "w" indicates the presence of a *quilisma* in the original source.

Table 4.5. THE *DEUTERUS*/PHRYGIAN MODES

Mode 3: Deuterus Authentic (Phrygian)							
S→	T→	T→	T→	S→	T→	T→	
E (Final)	F	G	A	B	C (RT)	D	E
					fourth		
fifth							

Mode 4: Deuterus Plagal (Hypophrygian)							
S→	T→	T→	S→	T→	T→	T→	
B	C	D	E (Final)	F	G	A (RT)	B
fourth							
			fifth				

Example 4.4: *Deuterus* authentic/Phrygian formulaic melody (mode 3)

Example 4.5: *Deuterus* plagal/Hypophrygian formulaic melody (mode 4)

9. Later theorists such as Glareanus expanded the system to twelve modes, each having an octave species. From the modern standpoint, modes 5 and 6 (Lydian) with a B♭ are actually Ionian, and Dorian with a B♭ is Aeolian (see Table 4.2).

10. For an excellent basic summary, see William P. Mahrt, "Gamut, Solmization, and Modes," in Duffin, *Performer's Guide to Medieval Music*, 482–95.

Table 4.6. THE *TRITUS*/LYDIAN MODES

	Mode 5: Tritus Authentic (Lydian)
T →	T →	T →	S →	T →	T →	S →	
F (Final)	G	A	B	C (RT)	D	E	F

fifth (F–C); fourth (C–F)

	Mode 6: Tritus Plagal (Hypolydian)
T →	T →	S →	T →	T →	T →	S →	
C	D	E	F (Final)	G	A (RT)	B	C

fourth (C–F); fifth (F–C)

Example 4.6: *Tritus* authentic/Lydian formulaic melody (mode 5)

Example 4.7: *Tritus* plagal/Hypolydian formulaic melody (mode 6)

Table 4.7. THE *TETRARDUS*/MIXOLYDIAN MODES

	Mode 7: Tetrardus Authentic (Mixolydian)
T →	T →	S →	T →	T →	S →	T →	
G (Final)	A	B	C	D (RT)	E	F	G

fifth (G–D); fourth (D–G)

	Mode 8: Tetrardus Plagal (Hypomixolydian)
T →	S →	T →	T →	T →	S →	T →	
D	E	F	G (Final)	A	B	C (RT)	D

fourth (D–G); fifth (G–D)

Example 4.8: *Tetrardus* authentic/Mixolydian formulaic melody (mode 7)

Example 4.9: *Tetrardus* plagal/Hypomixolydian formulaic melody (mode 8)

Mode in Western medieval practice, therefore, was not simply a matter of range alone but also was understood in terms of melodic formulas around a particular final within a particular range, or ambitus. This is important, because it differs profoundly from our modern idea of "key." For us, a key involves an understanding of melody as it relates to a particular octave species scale and its tonic, and a set of diatonic chords that tend to function in certain expected ways. For the modern musician, therefore, there would be no discernible difference between modes 1 and 2; they would both sound like "D minor with a B natural." J. Peter Burkholder, in the textbook *A History of Western Music*, makes the excellent point that this difference in the location of the final note within the ambitus of the mode would have been perceived by the medieval listener as a very great difference in the sound and character of the melody:

> The effect of cadencing around the middle of that octave in the plagal modes was heard in the Middle Ages as quite distinct from closing at or near the bottom of the range in the authentic modes. Modern listeners may find this difference hard to understand, since we consider both *Row, Row, Row Your Boat* and *Happy Birthday* to be in the major mode, despite the different ranges of their melodies in respect to the tonic. But to medieval church musicians, the combination of different intervals around each final with different ranges relative to the final for authentic and plagal modes gave each of the eight modes an individual sound.[11]

The next step involves learning techniques to help us become fluent in formulaic modal language and to become more familiar with this modal "repertoire of melodic gestures."[12]

TONARIES, MODAL FORMULAS, PSALM TONES, AND THE *LIBER USUALIS*

Modal patterns and formulas can be found in both original and modern collections of liturgical chant. Two examples are tonaries and the more modern *Liber Usualis*, both of which we will consider in the next section. Each of these sources can, in different ways, demonstrate methods that were used in the

---

11. Burkholder, Grout, and Palisca, *History of Western Music*, 40–41.
12. I am indebted to Benjamin Bagby for the use of the term "repertoire of melodic gestures" in this context.

Middle Ages to categorize and memorize modal patterns and formulas and provide us with specific examples.

Tonaries

Certain mnemonic modal patterns and formulas used by musicians in the Middle Ages have been passed down to us in the liturgical books known as tonaries. Tonaries can be thought of as the equivalent of a database in which a large number of chants are sorted according to various parameters. In addition to sorting them according to their *protus, deuterus, tritus,* or *tetrardus* designation, they are also sorted into subcategories, such as liturgical use, the proximity of the first note to the final, the similarities of their opening melodic phrases, their level of complexity, or simply alphabetical order.[13]

The critical difference between a tonary and a database, however, is that the material in the tonary was meant to be eventually memorized. As we noted in our brief historical overview, the theorists writing for singers in the Carolingian era and the generation that followed did not necessarily expect their singers to retain the mathematical aspects of their treatises, but they absolutely expected them to know that a chant was in mode 1 just by hearing it. This is why the material that is presented in tonaries is especially useful for our purpose, which is to become familiar with the repertoire of melodic gestures that characterizes specific modes. The tonaries, therefore, are most useful in the context of this document because of their intonation formulas, Latin mnemonic verses, and textless melismas called *neumae* (not to be confused with neumes), as well as the psalm tones and their various termination formulas.

In addition to looking at early tonaries, another compendium of plainchant that may be helpful is the more recent *Liber Usualis*, a book containing large collection of chants used in the Roman Catholic liturgy. Compiled and edited in the late nineteenth century by the monks of the Abbey of Solesmes and now available on several websites, the *Liber* uses a type of square notation that is not actually medieval but shares some properties with earlier notation. The introductory chapters of every copy of the *Liber* provide a comprehensive explanation of the notation.[14]

Let us begin our discussion of modal formulas with a consideration of psalm tones as they are explained and catalogued in the *Liber Usualis*. It should be noted that since our goal is to become familiar with sources for modal formulas, our examination will cover the mechanics of the psalm tone formulas and will not include a detailed discussion of the liturgical role of the psalm tone.

---

13. Berger, *Medieval Music and the Art of Memory*, 58.
14. Musica Sacra's website contains a downloadable version of the *Liber Usualis* at http://musicasacra.com/2007/07/17/liber-usualis-online/. A searchable database of plainchant can be found at the Global Chant Database, http://www.globalchant.org; this indexes the *Liber Usualis* as well as other sources.

In plainchant, the chanting of a psalm is usually preceded and followed by a chant called an *antiphon*. In other words, the antiphon "frames" the psalm, so that the whole thing is heard in this order: antiphon-psalm-antiphon. The antiphons have pre-composed melodies, but the psalms are chanted according to formulas. There is a formula for each mode, chosen with the intention of matching the mode of the chanted psalm to the mode of the antiphon. These formulas are called *psalm tones*.

Psalms tend to be sung antiphonally, meaning with two alternating choirs. This may be done in either of two ways: choir 1 sings the first half of a psalm verse, and choir 2 sings the second half of the psalm verse, or the two choirs simply alternate entire verses. These formulas are best understood by going through the step-by-step process of applying one to a specific psalm, so here is an example. Let us begin with psalm tone formula for mode 5 (Example 4.10), using the same kind of notation as is found in the *Liber Usualis*.[15] Note that the staff has only four lines, and the "C" clef that identifies "middle C" is on the second line down from the top:

Example 4.10: Psalm tone for mode 5

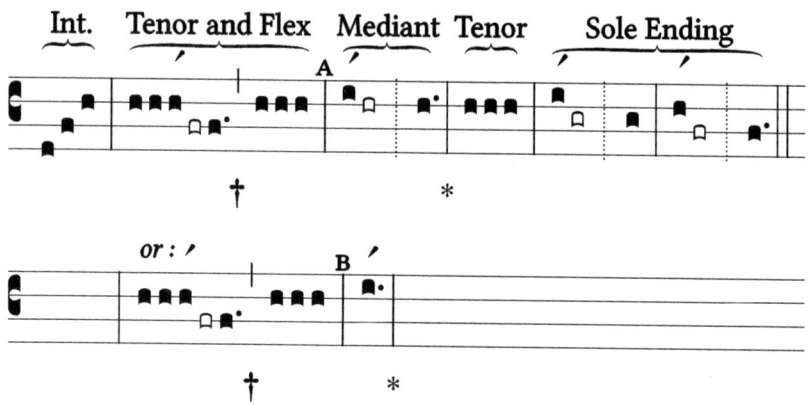

Applying the formula to a specific psalm will demonstrate the way in which the different parts of the psalm tone formula work. This is Psalm 23, "The Lord Is My Shepherd," or, in Latin, *Dominus regit me*.[16]

> *Dominus regit me, et nihil mihi deerit;*
> The Lord is my shepherd, I shall not want.
>
> *In loco pascuae ibi me collocavit.*
> He makes me lie down in green pastures.

---

15. Note that *Liber Usualis* labels the last unit "sole ending" instead of "termination." This is because the psalm tones for some of the other modes have multiple terminations.

16. "Dominus regit me" is numbered as Psalm 22 in the *Liber Usualis*, in accordance with the Greek numbering used by the Latin Vulgate Bible (most Protestant Bibles use the

The psalm tone formula can be broken down into the following parts, as illustrated in Example 4.11:

1. The first two or three syllables of the first line of the entire psalm begin with the intonation, which usually consists of two or three notes, in this case F–A–C.
2. After the intonation, the rest of the text of the first half of the verse is sung on the reciting note, also called the reciting tone, tenor, or dominant (not to be confused with the dominant in tonal harmony). Each mode has a designated reciting note. If the first half of the verse is too long to sing in one breath, it is divided into two parts, with a descending note called a *flex*.[17]
3. At the end of the first line of each individual verse, there is a cadence at the mid-point of the psalm verse, which is called the *mediation*. This is where the first choir pauses and lets the second choir take over (the switch to the second choir is indicated by the asterisk).
4. The second choir then continues with the second half of the verse ("in loco pascuae ibi me").
5. At the end of the psalm verse, there is a cadence called the *termination*. (Other terms for the termination are final cadence, difference, or differentia.)

Example 4.11: Intonation, mode 5

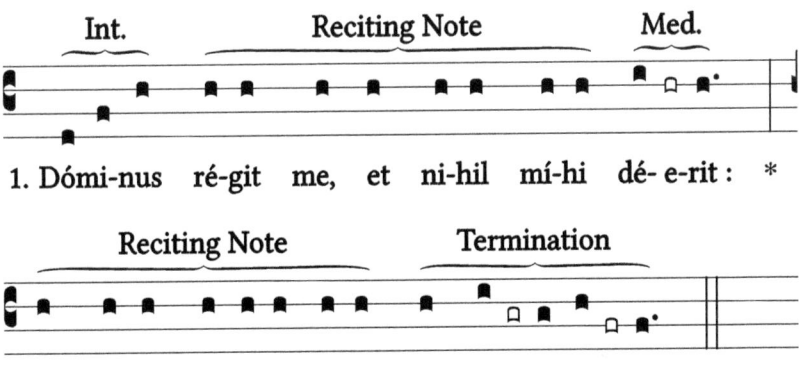

Hebrew numbering). This English is taken from the 1952 Revised Standard Version of the 1611 King James Bible. In the *Liber Usualis*, an example of "Dominus regit me" in mode 5 can be found after the second matins antiphon during the Feast of Corpus Christi.

17. See Example 4.10. The flex note is used if the first line is extremely long and the singers will need to breathe. In that case, the singers would end the first phrase with the *a*, take a breath, and then continue with the rest of the phrase on the reciting note. Our example does not require a flex. (In the *Liber Usualis*, lines that require the use of the flex are marked with a cross.)

If more than one verse of the psalm is going to be recited, all subsequent verses begin on the reciting tone and not the intonation (there are some exceptions to this, depending on the liturgy of specific feasts).

These modal formulas were useful for several reasons: they made it easier to set text; they helped to imprint the general sound of a particular mode; and they facilitated memory of the psalm text and a specific pattern for that particular mode.

Some of the psalm tones (1, 3, 4, 7, and 8) give multiple options for the "termination" portion of the formula. These are supplied in order to provide options for the smoothest possible melodic transition to the repetition of the specific antiphon. For example, you would expect the mode 1 psalm tone to end on D. But what if a D would sound awkward or jarring if juxtaposed against the beginning of the antiphon that follows? Here is the psalm tone for mode 1 as shown in the *Liber Usualis*. Notice the large number of possible endings shown in Example 4.12.

Plainchant singers were expected to know and memorize these psalm tone patterns and to be able to apply them to psalm verses by rote. In order to know which psalm tone to use after a particular antiphon or other type of chant, however, one had to be able to recognize and identify the mode of the chant. This led to the development of a number of mnemonic patterns used to help singers recognize and memorize modal patterns and characteristics. We will consider these next.

Intonation Formulas

The intonation formulas, or *echemata*, as they are called in Greek, are short melodic formulas sung to syllables such as *no-na-no-e-a-ne* or *n-o-e-a-gis*.[18] They are found in a number of manuscripts from as early as the ninth century and are similar in function to formulas used for Byzantine chant, exemplifying the melodic characteristics of each mode. The memorization of these formulas would ostensibly help the singer learn the pattern of tone and semitone that characterize each mode and become able to recognize those patterns by ear. Example 4.13 shows the intonation formulas for the eight modes as they appear in the tenth-century manuscript known as the *Commemoratio brevis*:[19]

---

18. These should not be confused with the intonation that is the beginning of a psalm tone.

19. See Bailey, *Intonation Formulas*, 12, where these are shown in juxtaposition with analogous formulas from Byzantine chant.

Example 4.12: Mode 1 psalm tone with terminations

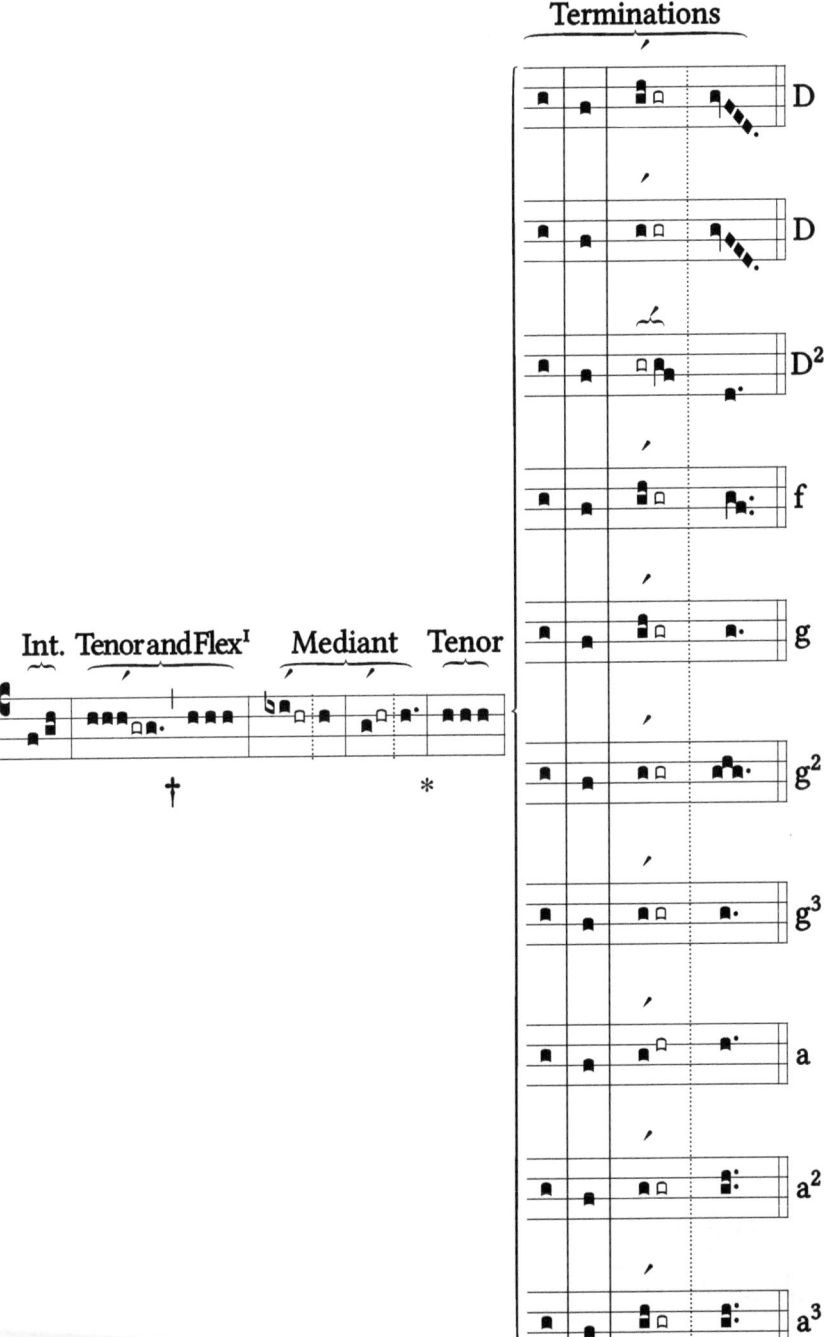

Example 4.13: Intonation formulas

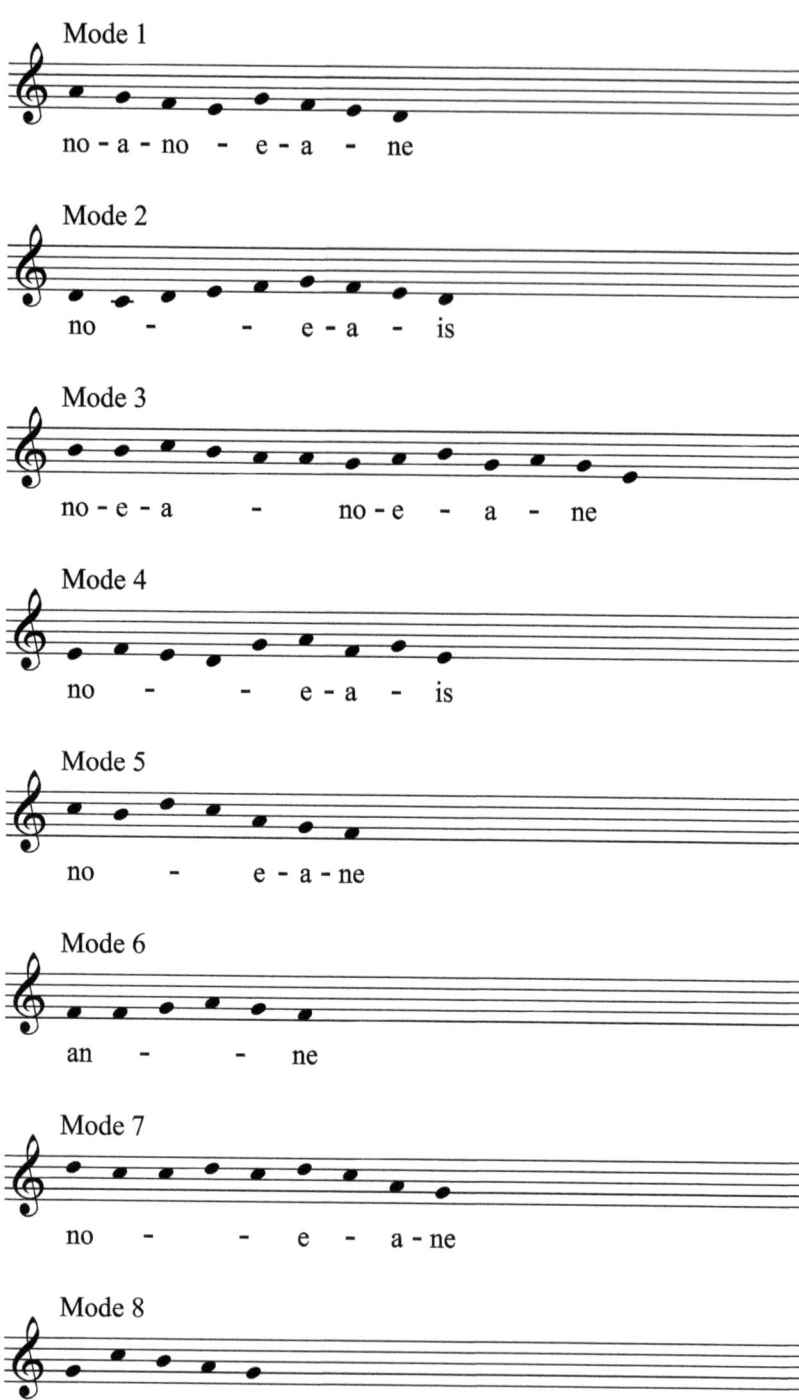

These formulas appear in a number of medieval manuscripts with quite a bit of variation, although their basic melodic shape remains fairly stable, as demonstrated by the variations on the intonation for mode 1 in Example 4.14.[20]

Example 4.14: Variants of the intonation formula for mode 1

In chapter 3, I discussed some of the prevailing ideas about the oral transmission of chant and the relevance of those ideas to issues of improvisation and fluid composition in medieval music. The fact that there are multiple variations of each

20. The manuscript provenance of each of these variations is identified in Bailey, *Intonation Formulas*, 48.

intonation tells us something about the way these formulas were taught and transmitted from one person to another. Even though there was room for variation, there is a certain stability to the patterns. In all six variants in Example 4.14, the notes are the same over the first two syllables; however, while the note over the third syllable is in the first two cases, in the other four it is replaced with F–E. The note over the fourth syllable is G in all cases except the last, where it is F–G. The fifth syllable has the most variation, ranging from F to F–E to F–E–D, and the last syllable is the final D in every case. Bailey is at pains to remind us that some of these variations are approximations based on his best reading of the sources; some of the intonations were compiled from manuscripts in which the neumes indicated melody shape but not specific pitch, and in some cases the underlay of the syllables was unclear.[21] Even with these caveats, we can see that certain parts of the patterns remain stable, and in turn we can deduce that the parts of the intonation formulas that remain stable from one source to the next have the most to tell us about the repertoire of melodic gestures that characterizes that particular mode. The very existence of psalm tones suggests that it was extremely important to memorize and transmit modal patterns with a certain amount of stability; in a liturgical context even the variations themselves are strictly prescribed, and the medieval theorists were adamant that singers memorize the psalm tones and the chants exactly. This does not take away from the fact that there was a great deal of orality in the transmission of chant and medieval song; it simply shows the oral transmission of material still takes place within certain parameters.

Neumae

In some medieval sources, each intonation formula was followed by a long melismatic phrase called a *neuma*. These *neumae* served as additional models for the characteristics of each of the eight modes and also varied slightly from one manuscript source to another. Example 4.15 illustrates the eight *neumae* as they appear in the *Commemoratio Brevis*.[22] By comparing an antiphon to the *neumae*, one could ascertain the mode of the antiphon, which in turn enabled one to choose the correct psalm tone to be used in conjunction with that particular antiphon's corresponding psalm verse. In some cases, it would appear that the appropriate *neuma* was sometimes even sung in the liturgy after certain antiphons.[23] Much later, some of the *neumae* take on a non-liturgical life of their own, showing up as motet tenors (such as Philippe de Vitry's *Garrit Gallus / In nova fert / Neuma*).

21. Bailey, *Intonation Formulas*, 45.
22. See *Commemoratio brevis de tonis st psalmis modulandis*, trans. and ed. Terence Bailey (Ottawa: University of Ottawa Press, 1979), 31–45. Bailey also includes these, along with *neumae* from other manuscripts, in his *Intonation Formulas*.
23. Bailey, *Intonation Formulas*, 16.

Example 4.15: *Neumae*

The Latin Formulas

Another mnemonic device for memorizing the modal characteristics, shown in Example 4.16, is a series of eight Latin formulas, also found in numerous manuscripts. Each consists of a short Latin phrase taken from scripture, beginning with the Latin word for a cardinal or ordinal number (*primum, secundum, tertia, quarta,* and so on).[24]

Example 4.16: Latin formulas

Mode 1
Primum quaerite regnum dei
"First seek ye the kingdom of God"

Mode 2
Secundum autem simile est huic
"And the second is like unto it"

Mode 3
Tertia dies est quod haec facta sunt
"Today is the third day since these things were done"

Mode 4
Quarta vigilia venit ad eos
"In the fourth watch of the night he went unto them"

24. These are from Reichenau (Bamberg, Staatsbibliothek, Ms. Lit. 5); they can also be found in Bailey's *Intonation Formulas* and are cited in Berger, *Medieval Music and the Art of Memory*, 69.

Example 4.16: *(Continued)*

Mode 5
Quinque prudentes intraverunt ad nuptias
"And the five wise ones went to the wedding"

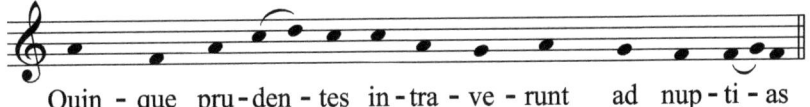

Quin - que pru - den - tes in - tra - ve - runt   ad nup - ti - as

Mode 6
Sexta hora sedit super puteum
"It was the sixth hour he sat on the well"

Sex-ta   ho   -   ra se - dit   su - per pu - te - um

Mode 7
Septem sunt spiritus ante thronum dei
"Seven were the spirits before the throne of God"

Sep - tem sunt spi - ri - tus   an-te   thro - num de - i

Mode 8
Octo sunt beatitudines
"Eight are the Beatitudes"

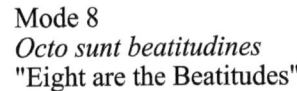

Oc - to   sunt   be   -   a - ti - tu - di - nes

All of these intonation formulas, *neumae*, psalm tones, and Latin formulas are an excellent place to begin an exploration of medieval mode, and a very good way to integrate them into one's memory. In an article on the Aquitanian eleventh-century monk and music scribe Adémar de Chabannes, medieval music scholar James Grier pointed out that Adémar used these very same formulas in a tonary assembled by Adémar and his assistants. For each mode, Adémar first places the *noeane* intonation, *neumae*, and Latin formula for that mode, followed by examples of psalm-verse terminations in that mode and a corresponding example of how each termination would lead into a particular antiphon in that mode.[25] We can do the same thing, using sources such as Bailey's *Intonation Formulas* as indicated in Practice 4.1 and engage in the same process followed by musicians who were working in this earlier context of oral/aural transmission.

Practice 4.1

USING BAILEY'S INTONATION FORMULAS

This practice requires the use of Terence Bailey's book *The Intonation Formulas of Western Chant*. Part 2 of Bailey's *Intonation Formulas* (41–95) contain the noeane/noeagis intonations, the *neumae*, and the Latin formulas as they appear in no fewer than thirty-eight different manuscripts.
- Read through the variants for each mode from an analytical point of view and compare them.
- Where do the patterns remain stable from one variant to another? For example, the mode 1 noeane formulas in every manuscript begin with the notes A–G–F, and the mode 1 Latin formulas in every manuscript begin with a rising fifth from D to A.
- Look for areas of stability within variation.

OBSERVING MODAL CHARACTERISTICS IN MELODY

Having considered modal formulas, the next step in internalizing the language of mode is to encounter that language in the context of existing melodies. Once again the *Liber Usualis* can be used as an easily accessible source for the examination of plainchant melodies, following a process outlined in Practice 4.2.

In their original context, it is unlikely that the modal formulas, psalm tones, and intonations would have been presented sequentially in a pedagogical setting. While the intonations certainly had a pedagogical and mnemonic function, in actual practice it is most likely that young singers would be exposed to the intonations at some point in an ongoing process of memorizing hundreds of chants by ear and would learn the workings of the psalm tones gradually through aural exposure in the liturgy. In addition, singers in a particular location would have most likely learned one set of formulas and would have been instructed to memorize them exactly. Any variant or deviation would have thus been heard in relation to the original model.

---

25. James Grier, "Adémar de Chabannes (989–1034) and Musical Literacy," *Journal of the American Musicological Society* 66, no. 3 (Fall 2013): 614–15.

> *Practice 4.2*
> # USING THE *LIBER USUALIS* AS A SOURCE FOR MODAL MODELS
>
> Note: As a prerequisite for this practice, one should procure a copy of the *Liber Usualis* or download it from the Internet. If you are not familiar with the *Liber Usualis* notation, consult its introductory chapters, which contain a comprehensive explanation of the *Liber*'s notation, abbreviations, and symbols.
> - Choose at least five or six chants in each mode. The mode of each chant is indicated in the score by the Arabic numeral just above the initial capital.
> - Beginning with first mode chants, sing or play through your chosen examples simply, without attempting any analysis, intending only to engage with the sound of the mode through a nonverbal process.
> - Now examine the same pieces from a more analytical point of view. Notice patterns, particularly at the beginnings of the chants and at cadence points, and compare them with the intonations or Latin formulas discussed in this chapter.
> - Examine the chants for internal cadences (especially at points of punctuation) that fall on the steps of the mode other than the final or the reciting tone. Notice which other tone or tones are used most often as the last note of a phrase and which are never used.
> - Repeat this procedure with selected chants in each of the eight modes.

As one compares the intonations, *neumae*, and Latin formulas to actual examples of chant, it becomes clear that the actual melodies are often close to the formulas, but not exactly the same, just as the formulas themselves differ slightly from one source to another. In some cases, a chant melody will not conform to any of the modal formulas at all but will nevertheless contain a particular incipit, cadence, or melodic gesture that is typical of that mode. Eventually it becomes apparently that the process of familiarizing oneself with modes is most effective when the practices offered in this chapter are employed in tandem with each other and not in isolation. In order to facilitate that practice, a series of eight "mode models" is included in the appendix (see pages 197–214). For each mode, one example each of an intonation, *neuma*, Latin formula, and psalm tone is placed before an example of a specific plainchant in the same mode. Practice 4.3 outlines a system for implementing the mode models.

Practice 4.3
USING THE MODE MODELS (SEE APPENDIX)

1. Without attempting any kind of analytical process, sing or play through the intonation, Latin formula, *neuma*, and a sample chant melody for a given mode.
2. Repeat the process in no. 1 using an instrument, voice, or some kind of tone generator to play the final of the mode as a long, sustained note against which you will listen to the melody. This can be done one of several ways:
   - with a second musician playing the sustained tone, so that you focus your complete attention to the sound of the melody against the final
   - by playing the long sustained note on an instrument and singing the tune
   - by singing the final and playing the tune on an instrument.

   Hearing a modal melody against its final sensitizes the ear to the pitches that create the most tension/resolution in each mode. Note also the sound of the reciting tone against the final; this is the tone that would have been used in plainchant to intone long sections of text.
3. Commit the noeane or noeagis intonation to memory. Experiment with playing/singing it slowly, quickly, in different rhythms. Try amplifying or abbreviating this small intonation without actually changing its basic melodic structure, in the following ways:
   - Where there is one pitch per syllable, retain that pitch. Try adding others: passing tones, neighboring tones, and so on.
   - Where there are multiple pitches per syllable, experiment with removing one or more. Retain at least one of them.
   - Experiment with repeating pitches.

   Do the above practice aurally, and resist writing out the variations.
4. Play or sing through the *neuma* that follows this mode's Latin formula, with the intention of committing it to memory. Note how the *neuma* relates to the intonation or the melody of the Latin formula and if it repeats or expands on any of its melodic material. Experiment with breaking the long *neuma* into shorter phrases, noting patterns or internal cadences, and even rearranging the short phrases. Commit the intonation to memory.
5. Repeat no. 4 above with the Latin formula for that mode.
6. Proceed to the plainchant example. Experiment in the following ways:
   - Sing or play the intonation first, and then the plainchant.
   - Sing or play the *neuma*, and then the plainchant.
   - Sing or play the Latin formula first, and then the plainchant.

- Sing or play some combination of the above, or all three, then begin the plainchant.

Repeat the above procedure, but against the sound of the sustained final.

7. Using the *Liber Usualis* or some other source of plainchant, gather a number of chants in the same mode and repeat the above process with each one. (You do not have to be able to identify the mode by ear yet; many modern sources of chant, including the *Liber Usualis*, show a number at the beginning of each chant that indicates the mode. The number is usually right above the initial letter of the text incipit.) Notice common phrases, melodic gestures, cadence formulas, reciting tones used in the psalm verses, and other characteristics.

It may be useful to think of each of the mode models as a mental folder in which you store formulaic information about each of mode; or if you are using one of the mnemonic techniques discussed in chapter 3, as a physical location in a memory "storehouse" of some kind. It may also be helpful to work on the mode models together with a small group of musicians, preferably with an instructor or group leader who has some experience with improvisatory musics. The practices and mode models can also be employed in the context of an immersive course in medieval mode.

MODE MODELS AND SECULAR OR VERNACULAR REPERTOIRE

Continued observation of the modal characteristics of multiple examples of both plainchant and secular medieval melody will reveal that some melodies conform to modal patterns, rules, and formulas more precisely than others. This is even more apparent in medieval secular song than in plainchant; some songs may reflect the formulas very well, while others seem to go from one mode to another, or at the very least appear ambiguous.

Discrepancies often exist between theory and practice, and it is often the case that theoretical systems are created after the fact in order to explain an already-existing paradigm. Systematic models, therefore, do not always account for every variation on the paradigm. Many of the theoretical treatises of the ninth and tenth centuries were written in light of the Carolingian initiative to unify chant repertoire and practice throughout the Holy Roman Empire. Chants written before the Carolingian reforms (Mass Proper chants, for example) may not conform to the modal rules as neatly as the ones written after the Carolingian reforms (such as many of the later Mass Ordinary chants). In terms of secular music, there was no such unifying initiative, and although medieval secular song uses the same basic modal language as plainchant, composers of secular music were not under any kind of pressure to conform to liturgical mode formulas at all.

In fact, it is quite likely that a number of medieval secular melodies were created by musicians who could not even read. Mode was their musical cradle language, absorbed aurally by the time they were toddlers, much as children of diverse ethnicities and origins in the latter half of the twentieth century aurally absorbed the pentatonic patterns of blues, gospel, rhythm and blues, rock, and hip-hop. It is probable that many medieval composers of secular song—and almost certainly of instrumental music, most of which was orally transmitted and is lost to us—depended on their ears and their musical intuition when composing and improvising melody, and they were unlikely to have been aware of or concerned with modal rules and formulas. (The poetic and rhetorical aspects of the lyric, on the other hand, would have concerned them much more).

When studying formulas and patterns, therefore, we should not become attached to a set of rigid expectations, but rather strive to create and develop points of reference for ourselves as performers to recognize and identify aspects of modal language present in medieval monophonic music.[26] If you have reached a point at which you can tell by ear that a particular chant or medieval secular song does not follow a particular formula or stay strictly in a particular mode, you may at least feel confident that you are succeeding in the establishment of your modal memory archive.

Practice 4.4 contains suggestions for expanding your exploration of medieval mode from plainchant to secular or vernacular monophonic repertoire. The distinction between "secular" and "vernacular" is important; while there is a large repertoire of secular Latin song, there are also monophonic songs in vernacular languages, such as the Italian *laude spirituali*, that have texts related to sacred topics.

MODAL IMPROVISATION AND INVENTION

The technical aspects of improvisation on one's instrument, including the voice, cannot be conveyed by a book. While a written resource such as this can supply the reader with insights into historical processes, languages, and tools that are relevant to a particular repertoire or idiom, the actual act of hands-on playing must be learned from a living model.

---

26. It is also worth noting that the modal system would change a great deal during the Renaissance, and that mode as it relates to Renaissance polyphony is another subject entirely. Later modal music cannot necessarily be expected to adhere to the patterns and formulas of the tonaries discussed here.

> *Practice 4.4*
> # EXPLORING MODE IN SECULAR OR VERNACULAR REPERTOIRE
>
> Examples of repertoire appropriate to this practice would be Latin song, sequence, *lai*, *laude spirituali*, *cantigas*, *Minnesang*, troubadour and trouvére repertoire, and Middle English lyric song.
> - Mode is most easily ascertained by cadences and short melodic patterns.
> - The last note of a song is not always the final arbiter of modal identification. In some strophic songs, the last note of one strophe often leads into the return of the first line of the next strophe. Look for internal cadences as well.
> - Some songs do not stay in the same mode throughout. (That is also true of some plainchant.) Also, the range of many songs makes it difficult to tell whether it is, for example, mode 1 or 2, or mode 5 or 6. Aim for the identification of *protus* (d), *deuterus* (e), *tritus* (f), or *tetrardus* (g). Keep in mind that the mode might be transposed (Dorian mode 1 on *a*, for example).
> - As an exercise, sing or play the song over the sustained tone of the final that you have identified, listening for dissonance and resolution. Notice if the points of tension and resolution appear to have any relation to the meaning of the text.
> - Observe whether multiple examples of the genre in question make repeated use of the same mode(s).
> - Having examined a specific song, invent or improvise a melody that stays in the same mode but also borrows a couple of the song's prominent melodic themes, patterns, or cadences. Try to do this without utilizing any kind of writing, if possible.

The demonstration-imitation-critique model described in chapter 2 must involve a living musician (particularly in terms of the "critique" element in that particular triad).

With that proviso, Practice 4.5 offers a sequential "first steps" procedure for improvising within the eight medieval modes. Readers who are already proficient at improvisation may find it elementary, but it may be a useful introduction for a student. If you are an accomplished musician who has never improvised, the practice may also prove to be of benefit. The best possible scenario would be to work through it with a teacher who specializes in historical performance practice, with a small group of music colleagues, or both.

Practice 4.5
MODAL IMPROVISATION

- Dorian (1 or 2) or Mixolydian (7 or 8) are often the best modes to explore first, particularly if most of your musical experience has either been in Western classical music, Anglo-Celtic folk musics, or rock and roll, as they will be more easily internalized.
- It is easier to initiate the process of learning to improvise in a mode if the final of the mode is audible and sustained. This can be done using a bowed-string instrument, organ, piano with the pedal down, hurdy-gurdy, shruti box, someone else's voice, or any other kind of instrument or electronic device.
- Sing the intonation, then the *neuma*, then the Latin formula of your chosen mode.
- Singing or playing against the sustained final, try using only the first three notes of the mode, inventing as many variations of those first three notes as you can. It is permissible to use repeating notes, free rhythm, metered rhythm, or some of both. The intent is to see how much you can do with only three notes.
- Repeat the previous step, adding the note BELOW the final.
- Repeat the previous step, adding the fourth note of the mode.
- Proceed as above, adding one note at a time into your set of "allowed" tones. Note carefully if, and at what point, you hear one of the modal intonations or formulas making its presence heard in your improvisation. Try to include a formula consciously; then try consciously to avoid doing so.
- This practice may be expanded by choosing a short phrase of text (no more than ten syllables or so) and singing your improvisation on a text. It is not necessary to use a medieval text. Observe any changes in the process that come about as a result of adding text, noting particularly whether the use of text automatically creates structure in your improvisation.

As with all of these exercises, it is helpful to practice with a teacher or partner, or in a small group. Members of the group may suggest text phrases for each other or be designated to identify phrases that stray out of a given mode. The activity should be done in a spirit of exploration and enjoyment, as should any foray into the world of improvisation.

In closing this chapter, we have reached the end of the portion of the book that deals with the abstract and theoretical aspects of our process: models, notation, memory, and mode. We now progress to the direct and concrete application of *inventio* to musical performance, beginning in chapter 5 with instrumental music, and then moving in subsequent chapters to polyphony and the performance of monophonic song.

CHAPTER 5

Inventing Melody

Old Instruments, New Voices

Iconographic and literary sources from the medieval period abound with evidence of both instrumental performance and collaboration among singers and instrumentalists, as exemplified in this passage from the thirteenth-century *Romance of Flamenca*:[1]

> After [the meal], the minstrels arise; each one wished to make himself heard. There you would have heard strings resounding in many tunings. He who knew some new fiddle-tune or a *canso* or *descort* or *lais* pressed forward as best he could. One plays the *lai* of Cabrefoil on the *viola*, and the other the *lai* of Tintagoil; one sang the *lai* of the Fins Amanz, and another the *lai* which Yvain composed. One brought the *arpa*, another the *viula*; one plays the *flaütella*, and another whistles; one brings the *giga* and another the *rota*; one gives out the words and another puts the music to them.

Despite the existence of such vivid descriptions of the interaction of instruments and voices, we cannot say with any certainty exactly what was being played by the instruments, as written accompaniments either did not survive

---

1. English translation by Christopher Page, in his important and substantive *Voices and Instruments of the Middle Ages: Instrumental Practice and Songs in France, 1100–1300* (Berkeley: University of California Press, 1987), 172. In addition to extensive information about repertoire, instruments, and performance practice, Page's main text and the appendices contain a collection of passages about voices and instruments from medieval literary sources.

or did not exist in the first place. Some descriptions say that the instruments played "the melody," but not always; others describe preludes, alternations of instruments with voices, or instrumental pieces used as interludes. Ascertaining the specific nature of both medieval instrumental music and vocal-instrumental collaboration therefore requires detective work, historical imagination, and a willingness to invent and improvise. Our performance decisions must contain a certain amount of well-informed conjecture, as the sound of our models must forever exist only in our imagination.

Some questions regarding the use of instruments have even become somewhat contentious, and others are unlikely to be definitively answered. The one exception is the obvious use of instruments for dance music; on that there is universal consensus, since there are many surviving examples of instrumental pieces identified by title with specific dances. As for the rest, however, there are widely divergent opinions about the use of instruments to play an untexted line in a polyphonic piece; the addition of preludes, interludes, or postludes to medieval pieces, either instrumental or vocal; the instrumental accompaniment of medieval song; the ornamentation of, or improvisation upon, an already-extant melody; or the creation of new instrumental pieces with the style and structure of medieval dances.

Lack of consensus notwithstanding, every single one of the abovementioned uses of instruments has been employed at some point by professional performers of medieval music. The purpose of the current chapter is not to espouse a particular point of view; those who wish to undertake a serious study of medieval music will benefit from reading discussions about medieval instrumental performance practice with diverse approaches, opinions, and conclusions.[2] Nor is this chapter a compendium of medieval instruments or their characteristics, physical technique, tunings, or history; an extensive discussion of all the extant repertoire for medieval instruments; or an argument for or against the aforementioned instrumental performance of untexted polyphonic voices. These are all addressed in the extensive literature of organological scholarship, performance practice, and technique pertaining to medieval instruments.

Instead, the intention of this chapter is to address the strong probability that an instrumentalist who tackles medieval music will at some point be called upon to provide something that was never written upon a page, and it

---

2. A comprehensive list of literature on the use of instruments and voices is beyond the scope of this document, but this subject is addressed in considerable detail and depth in Page's *Voices and Instruments*. See also Thomas Binkley's article "The Work Is Not the Performance," in *Companion to Medieval and Renaissance Music*, ed. Tess Knighton and David Fallows (New York: Schirmer, 1992), 36–43. An extensive discussion of the diverse views on the use of instruments and voices in medieval music performance can also be found in the first two chapters of Leech-Wilkinson, *Modern Invention of Medieval Music*.

is with that eventuality and that process that we are engaged. Focus is placed on examples of instrumental processes that require some degree of improvisation or invention in the context of medieval performance practice: preludes, interludes, postludes, ornamentation, and creating instrumental pieces on the models of extant medieval dances (song accompaniment is addressed from a rhetorical point of view in chapter 7).

Pedagogical emphasis in this chapter will be placed on procedures and processes rather than complete notated examples of specific musical realizations (the one exception being the creation of a new *estampie*). This is quite deliberate. Experience suggests, particularly with new students, that it is difficult to resist the temptation to simply incorporate an example from a book, or a clone thereof, into one's own performances, while greater integration of process and procedures fosters a deeper and more integrated understanding, confidence, and originality.

"PLAY WHAT THE INSTRUMENT WANTS TO PLAY"

The groundbreaking medieval music performer and scholar Thomas Binkley often told his students, "Play what the instrument wants to play." It is most likely the case that instruments were played in a way that was in concord with their natural physical and sonic properties. In other words, in the process of musical invention, medieval players would take advantage of the natural characteristics of their instruments rather than employ extended techniques. If the instrument has a crisp, short attack and decay, like a lute, it is not an ideal choice for a part that requires sustained notes, one more suitable for a bowed string instrument such as a vielle.[3] On the other hand, a lutenist might very well be called upon to ornament the melody of a dance tune or invent a set of variations on a vocal piece. The characteristics of the instrument determined, to a degree, what one would play. In a 1992 radio interview, Binkley explained that this was true whether you were playing a pre-composed piece or improvising:

> In the case of improvisation, the idea is not to impress with the fluency of one's playing. Rather, the idea is to find a union of melody with instrument: what can this instrument play that *it* wants to play, with this sort of a melody that really best suits it? And that was combined with the particular instrumental technique that this particular player may have. In the Middle Ages, the playing

---

3. The word "vielle" as used in this book refers to the medieval fiddle found throughout Europe and is not to be confused with the French hurdy-gurdy known as the *vielle à roue* (although a hurdy-gurdy also produces a sustained tone).

of instruments was not schooled as it is today, with only two or three violin schools in the whole world—you play the Russian way, or you play this way or that way. That isn't the way things were. They were individual in terms of technique, and sometimes they were somewhat regional in their musical instincts, so that a German lutenist wouldn't play like an Italian lutenist, but nor would two instrumentalists, let's say from Nuremberg, play quite the same way. So finding one's *own* way was as important then as it is now.[4]

When beginning one's inventive journey with a medieval instrument, playing something that is idiomatic to the instrument is also simply practical. While internalizing the idiomatic characteristics of a particular musical genre or repertoire is one of the most important requirements of improvisation or fluid composition, that process is complicated in medieval music because of the lack of audible models from the time period itself. The alternative involves research, experience with many pieces in a given repertoire, awareness of regional styles and genres, and a knowledge of mode, to name only a few factors. This is complicated by the lack of consensus mentioned above. One must also discern the difference between the style and performance choices of a certain ensemble or mentor with the idiomatic characteristics of a particular repertoire. Before one becomes immersed in these more complicated issues, an inquiry into the nature of the instrument itself provides a place to begin, as in Practice 5.1.

The considerations outlined in Practice 5.1 can assist in choosing an instrument for a particular piece, in making decisions about the role of an instrument in accompanying song, or in determining what role an instrument might play in any improvised, pre-composed, or fluid arrangement ("fluid" in this case meaning pre-composed but subject to change in the course of performance).

In the following pages, we will consider several roles that instruments have taken in the historical performance practice of medieval music: the addition of preludes, interludes, and postludes to an extant piece; the complicated issue of ornamentation; the sometimes overused technique of using instrumental drones; and the use of extant medieval dances as models for invention.

PRELUDES, INTERLUDES, POSTLUDES

Medieval music performers from multiple musical lineages have made effective use of improvised and prearranged preludes, interludes, and postludes in their performances. The rationale for the insertion of invented or improvised

---

4. Thomas Binkley, interview on the radio program *Harmonia*, WFIU-Bloomington, 1992.

Practice 5.1

WHAT DOES THE INSTRUMENT "WANT" TO PLAY?

This series of questions may help to identify characteristics of an instrument that will determine what kind of melodic or harmonic invention will be idiomatic to that instrument.

- Can the instrument play more than one note at a time, or is it limited to a single melody?
- What is the melodic range of the instrument?
- If it is a bowed string instrument, does it have a string that extends beyond or outside of the fingerboard, and if so, what is the purpose of this "drone" string?
- Can the tone of the instrument be changed or manipulated?
- Can the instrument play sustained notes (like a bowed string or wind instrument), or does it have a quick attack and decay (like a plucked string)?
- It is easy or difficult to articulate long passages of fast notes on this instrument?
- Is the instrument constructed so that the pitch is fixed (keyboards, fretted strings), or can the pitch be manipulated by the breath (like a recorder) or with the fingers (like a fretless string instrument)?
- What is the dynamic range of the instrument? Is this an "indoor" instrument (lute, recorder, vielle, rebec, harp, sinfonia) or an "outdoor" instrument (shawm, sackbut, trumpet, bagpipes)?

---

musical content before, during, and after a piece of medieval music has included the expression of rhetorical principles, perceived or assumed commonalities with oral music traditions of the same region and/or culture, and, most importantly, descriptions found in the primary sources themselves. A didactic example of the latter would be the much-quoted statement from Johannes de Grocheio's *Ars Musice* that singers sometimes added a melodic phrase or *neuma* to the end of an antiphon, "just like on the vielle after a *cantus coronatus* or a *stantipes*, the ending of which vielle players call *mode*," and his declaration that "the good artist introduces every *cantus* and *cantilena* and every musical form on the vielle."[5] For a literary example, also quoted

---

5. Johannes de Grocheio, *Ars musice*, ed. and trans. Constant J. Mews, John N. Crossley, Catherine Jeffreys, Leigh McKinnon, and Carol J. Williams (Kalamazoo, MI: Medieval Publications, 2011), 105, 73.

frequently, we might consider this famous passage from the twelfth-century Anglo-Norman *Roman de Horn*:

> Then he takes up the harp, for he wants to tune it. God! Whoever then watched him, seeing how he knew how to handle it, how he touched the strings, how he made them vibrate, sometimes he made them sing, other times play a counterpoint. . . . When he had done his tune, then he takes it up. And he makes the strings sound with all different tones. Everyone marvels that he knows how to manage it like that. And when he had done so, he begins to play the lai that Orains composed about Batolf, loudly and clearly, just as those Bretons are accustomed to doing it.[6]

Since we cannot listen to a recording of this Breton paragon, and we have no idea how Grocheio's vielle player executed the final flourish of his *cantus coronatus*, where do we begin?

Our first instinct as players is often to turn instantly to the instrument at hand and start playing. However, there are several prior steps that should be taken in order to form a coherent concept in the mind, thus avoiding the ever-present possibility of random modal peregrinations posing as medieval melody. First and foremost, if one's prelude, interlude, or postlude is going to be part of an arrangement of a texted piece, one *must* know the text—and the melody of the song—as well as the singer must know it. The musical content the instrumentalist provides must be relevant to the extant piece and in concord with the intentions of the other performers. If that content departs in some way from the rhythm, affect, mode, or character of the piece, it must be intentional. Thus, when pondering the inclusion of preludes, interludes, and/or postludes, it is important for a performer to ask not only "What shall I add," but also "Why am I adding this?"

Critical thinking and artistic expression need not be mutually exclusive, and added material that develops out of a specific, clearly articulated expressive or rhetorical intention will be much more convincing than content that is added because it conforms to the way a player has heard other performers do it. This is as true for an actor, artist, speaker, or poet as it is for a musician in the process of creating a performance. Rhetoric and music were both among the seven liberal arts that constituted the prevailing paradigm of medieval education, along with grammar, logic, arithmetic, geometry, and astronomy. The basic principles of rhetoric are very relevant to music, as we will discuss in more detail in chapter 7; for our

---

6. Quoted from Sylvia Huot, "Voices and Instruments in Medieval French Secular Music: On the Use of Literary Texts as Evidence for Performance Practice," *Musica Disciplina* 43 (1989): 78. Christopher Page also includes this passage from *Roman de Horn* on page 4 of *Voices and Instruments* and discusses *Horn* at length in pages 103–7.

purposes here, it is enough to say that preludes, interludes, and postludes are effective when they contribute to the intention, structure, and delivery of a piece of music. In this passage from the thirteenth-century *Poetria Nova* of rhetorician Geoffrey of Vinsauf, one could easily replace the word "poetry" with "music:"

> Let the poem's beginning, like a courteous attendant, introduce the subject with grace. Let the main section, like a diligent host, make provision for its worthy reception. Let the conclusion, like a herald when the race is over, dismiss it honourably. In all of its parts let the whole method of presentation bring credit upon the poem, lest it falter in any section, lest its brightness suffer eclipse.[7]

Preludes

A prelude functions as a rhetorical *exordium*, or introduction. Intention is paramount; not all introductions have the same set of goals or intentions, and the performers must decide what they are trying to accomplish.[8] For our purposes, we will look at three different possibilities.

First, and most simply, a prelude may be created for practical reasons: the establishment of a tempo or the introduction of a particular section of the melody or refrain. It may be beautiful and very pleasing to the ear, but there is not much subtlety involved—the instrumentalist plays the refrain, the singer gets the pitch from the refrain, and off we go.

Second, a prelude may allow the musical content of the piece to unfold. It may be used to establish the sound of the mode or to highlight or manipulate particular phrases in the melody or patterns in the rhythm. This can happen slowly or quickly, depending on your intent. For example, a player may play phrases that suggest the melody without actually revealing it until the singer enters.

---

7. Geoffrey of Vinsauf, *Poetria Nova*, trans. Margaret F. Nims (Toronto: Pontifical Institute of Mediaeval Studies, 1967), 18.

8. In his influential article "Zur Aufführungspraxis der einstimmigen Musik des Mittelalters," Thomas Binkley described four ways in which an instrumental prelude might function in European medieval music: (1) a short prelude whose function is to "announce" that a piece is about to be performed; (2) a prelude that employs elements of that melody or "significant qualities of the accompaniment"; (3) A "character" prelude, which "attempts to establish a mood for the song or portray the dramatic development of the text"; and (4) a "conceptual" prelude, which "attempts to reveal bit by bit the elements of the song or its melody." All except the first, according to Binkley, have one thing in common, and that is "the element of permitting something to emerge from a collection of notes, moving towards clarity and meaning slowly, and allowing the song itself to emerge as the final step in revealing the clarity and meaning." See Thomas Binkley, "Zur Aufführungspraxis der einstimmigen Musik des Mittelalters," *Basler Jahrbuch für historische Musikpraxis* 1 (1977): 19–76. (The above quotes are taken from Binkley's unpublished English translation of the article, which has circulated widely amongst Binkley's medieval music students for decades.)

A third possibility is to create a prelude to convey something about the mood of a piece. This is a subtler and more subjective task, and its execution is to some degree also more culturally specific to your audience than to the audience's medieval counterparts. The cultural element is an important consideration for a performer—the parallel fourths that might have suggested "organum" to a medieval audience might vaguely suggest "Asian traditional music" to a modern Western audience that has rarely heard music earlier than Bach. Only you can decide how you will evoke "sadness" or "yearning" or "anxiety" to your audience and how much you are willing to push the boundaries of what you consider to be historical performance practice in order to accomplish that.

Interludes

An interlude is either an elaboration of the musical and textual content of the song or an intentional diversion from it. As is the case with the prelude, therefore, the most important consideration is need and intent: What purpose does this interlude serve, and what does it contribute to the performance? The answer to that question does not have to be complicated, but there must be an answer to the question in order to create a musically and/or rhetorically integrated and convincing performance.

An interlude itself can take many forms. The most basic can be as simple as a short phrase between strophes to allow the singer to recover his or her breath. Short phrases such as this can also give the audience a moment of mental breathing space as well, particularly in a piece that features multiple strophes. The short phrase itself can vary in any way the performers choose; it can be exactly the same every time, or can be ornamented or improvised.

A longer interlude can be pre-composed or improvised. For example, it might be a long improvisation, perhaps based on the melody of the song, played without accompaniment or over a static pattern or drone (more on drones below). An interlude could consist of a basic musical pattern, melody, or rhythm that is subject to ornamentation and variation and therefore differs slightly in each performance. It might incorporate borrowed melodic material, perhaps as an allusion to another medieval piece. Alternately, one might create newly composed music for an interlude, introduced for some specific artistic or expressive purpose.

Postludes

The intent of a postlude is to provide a rhetorical *conclusio*; it is a closing statement. As with the prelude and the interlude, the music can be taken directly from the content of the piece or be improvised or newly composed. It can be brief or quite extended. Of the various roles that a postlude might play, the most straightforward is a simple signal: a short cadential phrase, the repetition of a final line, or an additional repetition of a final refrain. Any of these signal "Our story is finished."

A longer postlude may have a more complex purpose. It may, for example, provide the listener with an opportunity to contemplate the piece that has just ended, rather than racing on to the next one. This can be especially effective in the case of a piece with deep philosophical or emotionally intense textual content. Like an interlude, this could be improvised, composed, or a longer reiteration of previous musical material.

Postludes may also provide a sense of resolution. The additional repetition of a final refrain can do this quite effectively, but so can a longer postlude, coda, or even a segue into another piece (an example of this would be a narrative piece that ends with a segue into an instrumental dance that expresses a particular affect or mood).

Finally, if one does decide to employ interludes, preludes, or postludes, it is important to acknowledge that *inventio* happens within a continuum ranging from free improvisation to note-for-note composition. It is highly likely that musicians in the Middle Ages moved along that same continuum, the specifics of any given performance being determined by genre, skill, and regional practice. Those elements might be part of our consideration as well. Is this a piece that would have likely been performed by a single singer and one instrument for the amusement of an Aquitanian queen sitting in a chilly English castle, or by musicians in an Iberian court famous for its multicultural roster of international players? Would the original audience for a Latin conductus have been fluent in Latin and able to recognize all the classical and Biblical references? Perhaps most importantly, how do each of the above scenarios relate to the audience with whom you are expecting to communicate? These are the questions we must ask ourselves. Practice 5.2 offers some suggestions for experimenting with the process of adding preludes, interludes, or postludes to a performance of medieval music.

TO DRONE OR NOT TO DRONE

The use of drones in medieval music most often results from the idiomatic nature of a particular instrument or the desire to emphasize a particular tone such as the final of a mode. There are a number of medieval instruments whose construction suggests that one of the desirable qualities of that instrument was its ability to produce a long sustained tone, or drone, and we also find in medieval repertoire the occasional presence of long sustained tones in various types of vocal music, such as organum. Long sustained tones are part of the sound production of sinfonias (medieval hurdy-gurdies), bagpipes, and organs. We may also consider medieval fiddles or vielles as instruments that

> *Practice 5.2*
> ## PRELUDES, INTERLUDES, POSTLUDES
>
> If you have decided to add preludes, interludes, or postludes to your performance of a given medieval piece, the following steps may be useful.
>
> Step 1. It is critical to learn and memorize the melody, even if you are not going to be the person playing or singing the melody. An awareness of mode is also important. Note whether the melody stays in the same mode throughout the piece; not all do, particularly in secular music.
>
> Step 2. If the piece has text, it is also important to learn and memorize it whether or not you will be singing it. Knowing the meaning of each word and where the word falls in the melody is also crucial.
>
> Step 3. Ask if the piece and the performance will be served by preludes, interludes, or a postlude. What is the intention? What rhetorical purposes are being served? Consider the different approaches detailed in this chapter.
>
> Step 4. Plan and construct the framework of your arrangement. How will you determine the form? What role does text play in this decision? How much predetermined material will there be, and will it be written down for the purpose of learning it, or will it be planned in the mind? Will there be improvised sections or transitional passages? The more one plans ahead, the more productive the rehearsal.

could in some circumstances be used to produce a drone. Jerome of Moravia, in his *Tractatus de Musica* (ca. 1280), gives us tuning options that feature two adjacent strings tuned to the same note. Christopher Page cites both Jerome's treatise and other evidence for the use of drones in *Voices and Instruments in the Middle Ages*:

> Jerome's tunings suggest that as late as the final decades of the thirteenth century, *viellatores* used drone-accompaniments to their own playing and generally conceived of their own technique in terms of simultaneously sounding strings. We have found similar signs of polychordal thinking (often involving drones) in relation to plucked fingerboard instruments, the harp and psaltery. In all probability, therefore, drones were a resource used by medieval string-players of all levels of attainment.[9]

9. Page, *Voices and Instruments*, 136.

Some vielles had strings placed outside the fingerboard (sometimes referred to by modern players as "outrigger" strings, to borrow a nautical term). There are a number of ways to take advantage of the outrigger string and the adjacent unisons; for example, one might sustain the note of the drone string for a certain amount of time while simultaneously sounding a melody on a different string.[10]

From a purely expressive standpoint, the sustained sounding of the final in a particular mode can also highlight the consonances and dissonances that are part of the character of a particular mode. If one sings through the notes in a particular mode while sustaining the final, it will become evident that points of tension occur when different notes in the mode are sounded against that final. This can be used to enhance the rhetorical expression of a particular passage. To illustrate this with a concrete example, let us consider the phrase that closes each verse of troubadour Girault de Bornelh's "Reis glorios." Example 5.1 contains the melody with the text of the first strophe.[11]

The lyric of the refrain is *et ades sera l'alba*, "and soon it will be dawn." The song is sung from the point of view of a loyal companion who is standing guard all night while his friend has a tryst with the wife of "the jealous one." His vigil has lasted a long time, and he is getting anxious about the fact that it will soon be dawn. The song is in mode 1 on D. If the song is being accompanied by a bowed string player and he or she chooses to sustain that D while the last phrase is sung, we would get dissonance as in Example 5.2 (read as written or an octave lower, depending on the range of the singer).

The C, E, and to some degree the G in that sung phrase will produce points of tension when heard against the final, especially the major second interval between the sustained D and the penultimate E in the melody. This can have a powerful rhetorical effect, especially if the singer takes advantage and "leans into" the dissonance (perhaps with a slight crescendo, *messa di voce*, or change in intensity of tone quality).

On the other hand, a drone should not necessarily be regarded as the default setting of a medieval bowed string instrument. Had the vielle player

---

10. In his *Tractatus de Musica* (ca. 1280), translated by Christopher Page, Jerome of Moravia uses the word *bordunus* to describe a string that is "fixed outside the body of the viella." Page points out that despite the temptation to translate *bordunus* as "drone," that use was "not actually implied in the treatise." An outrigger string such as this certainly could have been used in multiple ways for various effects, a sustained note being only one of them. For more information, and a description of Jerome's vielle tunings, see Christopher Page, "Jerome of Moravia on the Rubeba and Viella," *Galpin Society Journal* 32 (May 1979): 77–98. See also Margriet Tindemans, "The Vielle Before 1300," in *A Performer's Guide to Medieval Music*, ed. Ross Duffin (Bloomington: Indiana University Press, 2000), 297–99.

11. "Glorious King, true light and brilliance; all-powerful Lord, if it should please you, be a loyal help to my companion, for I have not seen him since night has fallen, and soon it will be dawn" (translation mine).

Example 5.1: "Reis glorios"

Example 5.2: "Reis glorios" refrain with drone

sustained nothing but a long D note through the entirety of all the strophes of "Reis glorios," there would be little change in affect to heighten the tension of the last line (or anything else). While the judicious use of occasional long sustained tones can serve a rhetorical purpose, emphasize the final of a mode, and provide a desired sound texture, there is no evidence whatsoever that the standard practice of a medieval bowed string player involved the playing of only one long sustained note while a singer executed an entire monophonic song.

Perhaps the best rule of thumb once again involves intention: the use of a drone should be intentional, either for a particular desired effect (or affect) or because it is a natural characteristic of the instrument, as in the case of the aforementioned sinfonia or bagpipe. Certainly those two considerations might be taken in combination; a desired effect may be achieved by using an instrument that naturally "wants" to drone.

ORNAMENTATION: A PATH FOR INQUIRY

Ornamentation is a crucial element of musical style. A flute player using a simple-system wooden flute may memorize five hundred Irish jigs and reels, for example, but if the player does not learn the cuts, taps, and rolls associated with the style, he or she is not really playing Irish traditional music. In modern times, players of the Irish tunes have tutorial books and videos to supplement transmission by way of a living model, but in the previous centuries, the ornaments could only be learned through demonstration by another human being, learned by ear and observation, and held in the memory.

In the case of earlier music such as Baroque and to some degree Renaissance music, the survival of a certain number of primary-source primers and tutorials gives us a fairly specific idea of how certain kinds of ornamentation were employed. Such tutorials were also usually written in the context of a particular repertoire, which helps us draw further conclusions regarding style according to genre and region.

In the case of medieval music, however, written descriptions of ornamentation appear in the context of chant or other ecclesiastical music, and it is not always clear whether ornaments described in the context of plainchant would extend into secular vocal practice. We also cannot assume in every case that ornaments described in the context of vocal music would extend into instrumental practice.

It is entirely possible, therefore, that if musicians from the thirteenth century could hear our performance of a *lauda spirituale* or one of the *Cantigas de Santa Maria*, they would find it lacking in some critical aspects of style, both vocally and instrumentally. These stylistic gestures would have been understood in the original context, and therefore not deemed necessary to write down. Many modern performers have sought to address this dilemma by observing modern traditional music that corresponds geographically and culturally with a particular medieval repertoire. While this can be illuminating and informative, and at least acknowledges the existence of regional differences, it is also the case that the styles and idioms of folk and traditional music also change with time. The practices of today may bring us a bit closer to the mark, but they are unlikely to be identical to the practices of a thousand years ago.

The fact that we cannot produce an exact replica of a medieval performance with all its ornamentations and musical gestures does not mean, however, that we should cease our attempt to discover what kinds of ornamentation may have applied to different genres of medieval music. Creating music that is the combined result of our research and our historical imagination is the very heart of the quest that is medieval performance practice. The resulting music—moving, beautiful, relevant, thoughtful—draws upon the past, but still belongs to us; this is not science fiction, and we are not "channeling" a performance from the twelfth century.

I would like to suggest five different paths of inquiry for investigating ornamentation in medieval music: (1) the nature of neumatic notation itself; (2) descriptions of ornamentation in primary sources; (3) the existence of variants in monophonic song melodies; (4) observation and analysis of repeating patterns and figures in the melodies of a given genre of medieval music; and (5) examples of written music that appear to reflect an improvisatory practice. An exhaustive study of any of the five would be enough for an entire book on its own; the intent in the following pages is to offer an example of each, in the hope that this will point the reader to his or her own individual path of inquiry. The first was discussed in chapter 3; we will now consider examples of the other four.

Descriptions of Ornamentation in Primary Sources

Theoretical treatises from the Middle Ages have provided us with some information about medieval ornamentation. Sometimes the information is contained in relatively short passages from larger works, and sometimes the descriptions are frustratingly vague and ambiguous. Descriptions of shakes, repercussions, vibrations, tremolo, and "stormy" ornaments can be subject to multiple interpretations, and sometimes we are left feeling as though we are involved in a treasure hunt in which all the clues are riddles. Ultimately, there is no guarantee that when we translate these primary source descriptions into our own vocalizations, we are in fact making the same sound that the writer of the treatise was describing, but there is nothing to stop us from trying to further our understanding.

One of the clearest descriptions of medieval ornamentation is from chapter 25 of Jerome of Moravia's thirteenth-century *Tractatus de musica* and concerns the *flos harmonicus*, or "harmonic flower." This ornament that can be either vocal or instrumental (*vocis sive soni*) and is a "quick and stormy" (*procellaris*) vibration. Most unusually, Jerome explains the ornament's execution in the context of a specific instrument, the organ, and then clearly describes what modern musicians would call a trill, executed by holding down the key of the pitch to be ornamented while repeatedly pressing the note above it. (Jerome very specifically indicates that the ornamental is the note *above* the written pitch, and not the note below). He also says that the player may vary the ornament in three ways: "long" trills, which feature a steady vibration not to exceed (*non excedit*) a semitone; "open" trills, also characterized by a steady vibration, but not to exceed a whole tone; and "sudden" (*subiti*) trills, which begin with a steady vibration that then speeds up at the end (*in fine est celerrima*).

Other descriptions of medieval ornaments, unfortunately, are not always as clear. For example, in contrast to the *flos harmonicus*, Jerome (and others) also describes an ornament that he calls *reverberatio*. Depending on the context of the individual passage and on how you interpret and translate the original Latin, it would appear that this word sometimes describes a note repeated quickly on the same pitch, sometimes vibrato, sometimes a trill, and other times an appoggiatura. The point here is that the while the treatises offer us invaluable information about ornamentation, they require very close readings and interpretations; the information is not something that one can distill into a one-page practice exercise containing examples that can be memorized and applied randomly to any monophonic song regardless of regional considerations.

The prospect of gathering information about ornamentation from all of the medieval sources is obviously mind-boggling, but we are in luck: it has already been done by Timothy J. McGee in his 1998 Oxford monograph *The Sound of Medieval Song: Ornamentation and Vocal Style according to the Treatises*. In addition to his discussion of "ornamental" neumes cited previously, McGee classifies the ornaments described in forty-six medieval treatises in two different ways: first as either graces or *passaggi* and then in a concluding chapter in terms of placement, function, and purpose. For those who wish to make a thorough study of the topic of ornamentation in the context of improvisation and invention in medieval music, this extensively researched and authoritative examination of medieval ornamentation is required reading.[12]

Variants in Monophonic Song Melodies

While many monophonic medieval songs survive as *unica*, there are a few repertoires in which individual songs survived in multiple manuscripts. The

---

12. McGee, *Sound of Medieval Song*. The section on placement, function, and purpose on pages 129–53 organizes ornaments into cadential function, phrase beginnings, internal placements, quantity, application to the repertory, and geographical stylistic differences.

songs of the troubadours and trouvères fall into this category, and more often than not the different manuscript versions of both the melodies and the texts vary quite a bit. This provides us with a number of excellent examples of variation arising as a result of oral transmission. These variations within the different versions of a single song are not mistakes; they are variant versions of the same song. They can also be considered the product of "oral" transmission even when there is a scribe involved; the extent of the variants suggests that the scribe was writing down something that he or she heard and not copying from a previously written source.

The study of these variants has been part of the extensive scholarship on the music of the troubadours and trouvères and its performance practice. At this particular point in our inquiry into improvisation and invention, however, let us narrow our focus to the topic at hand, which has to do with ornamentation, which can include the concept of varying a melody. What can the variants in troubadour song tell us about this process? One thing is clear: there was not a definitive version of a song that needed to be memorized and repeated in every detail, either in writing or in performance. In her comprehensive study *The Music of the Troubadours*, Elizabeth Aubrey discusses the transmission process:

> "Memorization" should not necessarily be understood as exact imprinting on the mind of details from which one must not waver, as we tend to think of it today. A singer could retain the important features of a song that gave it its identity, while allowing some details to change. For the poem, its features of versification (rhyme, verse length and number) were the most compelling elements and allowed for little modification. But individual words, short phrases, and order of stanzas could diverge without losing the essence of the text. For the music, there must be similar elements—perhaps the contour, range, tonal orientation, intervallic structure—that a singer retained in the memory, while allowing details to change. ... The singers received a song, either by ear or by eye, and they appropriated that song into their own repertoires, retaining its essence, but reconstructing it according to their own performing style.[13]

So much for performing a piece of music "exactly as it was done." If reconstructing or interpreting a song according to one's own performing style is "what was done," then that process is the essence of its performance practice. The process of making a piece of music "one's own" also applies to the

---

13. Elizabeth Aubrey, *The Music of the Troubadours* (Bloomington: Indiana University Press, 1996), 33–34. The quoted passage occurs within a chapter about transmission. Aubrey's closing chapter, "Performance," and indeed the entire book, is highly recommended reading for anyone undertaking the performance of medieval music.

performance practice of dozens of other musical genres, including but not limited to Baroque arias, ballads, dance tunes, traditional airs, and rock and roll covers.

This does not mean, of course, that we are reinventing the entire melody of the song. As Aubrey states, a singer or player could "retain the important features of a song that gave it its identity, while allowing some details to change." How do we determine the important features? Let us begin with an examination of the variant melodies in one of the most famous troubadour songs, Bernard de Ventadorn's "Can vei la lauzeta mover." Example 5.3 gives us a comparison of three different versions of the melody found in three different manuscripts.[14]

Considering other aspects of musical and textual analysis as given, let us now imagine that we are either about to sing it (having already chosen one of the three versions of the text indicated here) or that we are holding the vielle and pondering this piece while preparing to play it with a singer. It is often the case in modern performance that the singer simply chooses which versions he or she wishes to sing and follows it exactly. But that is not at all the process that was just described.

Here is an alternative process to consider. We may note that the melody, when viewed across all three manuscript versions, shows very obvious places of stability (where it is the same or at least very close in all three) and places of instability (where the melody differs markedly across the three versions). It can be surmised that the places of stability reflect the "important features of a song that gave it its identity." Note that there is strong stability at the beginning of each verse (the term "verse" here being used to refer to one line of a stanza). That stability extends farthest in the first and last verses. There is also stability in the final notes of most verses, the exceptions being four and six, and yet some of the greatest instability occurs just before a cadence. The places of instability are points at which the performers put "themselves" into the song, where the ornamental characteristics of regional vocal technique would have manifested, where it might have been difficult for a scribe to remember exactly what was sung at that spot, since it might have been different every time the song was sung.

Points of instability such as this are "invitations" to improvise, and to put ourselves into the song as well. However, I also offer two caveats. First, it is important to observe the nature of the melodic gestures, specific figures, and phrases that characterize the variants.[15] Are they mostly stepwise,

---

14. Paris, Bibliothèque nationale, f. fr. 22543 [R]; Paris, Bibliothèque nationale, f. fr. 844 [W]; and Milan, Biblioteca Ambrosiana, S.P. 4 (olim R71 sup.) [G]. For a complete edition of all of the works of the troubadours arranged in this same comparative fashion, see Hendrik van der Werf, *The Extant Troubadour Melodies: Transcriptions and Essays for Performers and Scholars* (Rochester, NY: published by author, 1984).

15. I am using the word "gesture" to convey a characteristic melodic movement or expression encountered in the context of either a mode, repertoire, style, or particular composer's works. When referring to a specific sequence of notes in a musical example, I use "figure."

Example 5.3: Bernard de Ventadorn, "Can vei la lauzeta mover," three variants

(continued)

Example 5.3: (Continued)

Example 5.3: *(Continued)*

ascending, descending, groups of two, three, four notes, or more? Are there similar melodic shapes that recur? Do they stay within the mode that appears to predominate in the song? In this way, we combine what variants can teach us about both the object and the process. Second, the effective use of variants as a model for improvisation requires that the process described

Example 5.3: (*Continued*)

above and in Practice 5.3 be repeated with many pieces from the same repertoire (for example, two dozen troubadour songs, not just one or two). Going through the steps with only one or two pieces will not provide enough stylistic vocabulary to produce confident and consistent improvisation.

Practice 5.3
MELODIC VARIANTS AS "INVITATIONS" TO IMPROVISATION

Begin this practice by choosing a monophonic song that has survived in at least two manuscripts, and preferably more. (Critical editions of monophonic song will usually contain information about the existence of multiple sources.) If you cannot find a critical edition in modern notation, it is not difficult to compare the primary source manuscripts themselves, especially as a great many manuscripts are now available to view online.

Step 1. Prepare a written version of the song with the variant versions of each line or verse are arranged vertically, one above the other (see Example 5.3). If you are using a secondary source article or book, it is quite possible that your example may already be arranged in this way.

Step 2. In some cases, there will be alternate versions of the text; you will need to decide which one you are going to use. Many vernacular songs have been the subject of study by scholars of lyric poetry, and the lyrics have been rendered into standardized or corrected versions free of idiosyncratic spellings and more obscure dialectal features.

Step 3. Sing or play through all of the variant melodies.

Step 4. Compare the alternate melodies, and note places where the melody is exactly or almost exactly the same in each. These are places of stability, an identifying part of the melody that stayed relatively constant through the process of oral transmission.

Step 5. Sing or play through these stable parts of the melody.

Step 6. Next, compare the alternate melodies again, and note places where the melody varies from one version to the other. This is a place of instability, part of the melody that did not stay constant through the process of oral transmission. These are the places that invite invention and improvisation.

Step 7. Sing or play through the unstable areas of the variant melodies as they are written—no improvising yet.

Step 8. Observe the nature of the melodic gestures, specific figures, and phrases that characterize the variants, particularly the unstable areas. Look for characteristics such as conjunct/disjunct motion, the frequency of certain intervals, the predominance of ascending or descending passages, the number of notes present in groupings, and so on. Note also whether the mode remains constant in these places of instability.

> Step 9. Now experiment with your own vocal ornaments and melodic variations at the places of instability, remaining aware of the characteristics mentioned in the preceding step. Vocal ornaments that work beautifully in another kind of music may not necessarily work. If your additions sound jarring, or if you think you are hearing an abrupt change in melodic character, mode, or style, you may have retrieved your ornaments from another "room" in your storehouse of musical memory (the rock and roll room, the Giulio Caccini room, etc.). If that is the case, re-examine the characteristics of the unstable parts of the melodies in your medieval examples.
>
> Step 10. To make the most of this exercise, the procedure should be followed with multiple songs from a given repertoire (for example, go through the procedure with two dozen troubadour songs). Musical style cannot be absorbed through just one or two examples; it does not give us enough vocabulary to improvise convincingly.

Repertoire-Specific Patterns and Gestures

As stated in Practice 5.3, musical style cannot be absorbed through just one or two examples. However, when we work with a particular body of repertoire over a period of time, we being to notice certain melodic, rhythmic, modal, or structural characteristics that are common to a large number of pieces. These features tell us something about the musical language of that repertoire and can inform all the points in performance that call for invention or improvisation.

Suppose, for example, that you are presenting a concert of music by Guillaume de Machaut, and there are certain points in that concert where you will be "inventing" some musical content—perhaps short instrumental interludes within a very long piece, an instrumental accompaniment to a monophonic *virelai*, or something similar. It would make sense that one might try to incorporate aspects of Machaut's own musical language. I chose Machaut as my example because his music is rife with certain characteristic melodic gestures. For example, many Machaut pieces include multiple instances of a figure characterized by three notes that descend stepwise, followed by a stepwise ascent and then a descending third. Several examples of this pattern are shown here in Example 5.4a. The first two figures are identical; in the third, Machaut treats the figure with some rhetorical *repetitio*.

Example 5.4a: Machaut-style melodic figure, alone and with *repetitio*

In Example 5.4b, from Machaut's rondeau "Rose, liz, printemps, verdure," we see two examples of this figure occurring in the cantus part, followed by the last phrase of the cantus part in the B section of the rondeau, in which Machaut treats the same figure with a rhetorical *amplificatio*:

Examples 5.4a and 5.4b merely scratch the surface; there are many more such characteristic gestures that occur repeatedly in Machaut's compositions. If

Example 5.4b: Machaut-style melodic figure, with *amplificatio*

we seek to employ invention and improvisation within a particular repertoire, searching for and identifying these characteristic figures and phrases is part of the inquiry and process of performance practice. The inclusion of only one example here is quite intentional: experience suggests that the internal integration of such identifiable musical vocabulary units is best accomplished experientially. Anyone can memorize someone else's list of "figures employed by Machaut over and over again," but it is much more effective if medieval music performers themselves work through a number of pieces in a given repertoire and identify these figures, both in the scores and by ear, and absorb them in context, as described in Practice 5.4. It is at that point that we are able to invent new musical content that is stylistically, rhetorically, modally, and melodically consistent with the original.

Practice 5.4

WORKING WITH REPERTOIRE-SPECIFIC PATTERNS AND GESTURES

Step 1. Gather at least five or six pieces from a specific medieval repertoire. It is important to limit your examination to one style, region, composer, or genre. "Medieval song," for example, will not work; more specific choices would be trecento *ballate*, Machaut secular vocal pieces, Hildegard von Bingen's works, the monophonic conductus from the Notre Dame repertoire, etc.

Step 2. While singing or playing through the pieces, notice patterns that occur frequently within the repertoire. It might be short phrases or figures, rhythmic patterns, particular sequences of pitches, or other characteristics. Writing them down may be beneficial.

Step 3. Once you have identified some of these patterns, notice whether they also occur in hidden or manipulated ways: lengthened or shortened, ornamented, etc.

Step 4. If you were to add, invent, or improvise material in the process of creating a performance of this repertoire, how might you use some of these characteristic patterns? (Possibilities: in the context of preludes, interludes, postludes, creating a collaborative instrumental part with a singer; writing a completely new piece to juxtapose against the old one in the context of a performance.)

Step 5. The last is a reflective question. To what degree might these patterns and ornaments reflect something about the style or vocal technique of that particular era or region? Are they the product of a particular composer's style, or does the composer's style reflect some kind of common use? These are not questions that necessarily have a definitive answer, but they may subtly affect your own performance or interpretation.

Written Manifestations of Improvisatory Practice

Another source of repertoire-specific information about improvisatory patterns and gestures occurs in written pieces that seem to reflect an improvisatory practice. This phenomenon is encountered frequently in later Renaissance music, but examples in extant medieval music are rarer and generally manifest in the form of ornamented instrumental versions of a pre-existing piece. Two notable examples are the Robertsbridge Codex (ca. 1360) and the Faenza Codex (ca. 1415). Robertsbridge, the earliest example of notated keyboard music, contains dance music plus three pieces that might be described as florid elaborations on *ars nova* motets. The Faenza Codex also contains florid instrumental pieces, including highly ornamented arrangements of both chant and songs by Machaut, Landini, and others. The pieces in Faenza are scored in a way that suggests keyboard performance, although the pieces can be realized by two instruments. Example 5.5 contains the first part of one of two Faenza pieces based on the *Kyrie cunctipotens genitor* chant.

It is highly likely that the pieces in both Robertsbridge and Faenza represent an improvised tradition, and therefore it provides us with a model, as Richard Taruskin eloquently put it, "for historian-sleuths to interpret."[16] While it is clearly unwise to assume that two manuscripts present a model for "all late medieval instrumental improvisation on polyphonic vocal models," the sources still contain valuable information. First of all, looking at the "big picture," they confirm that elaboration on a pre-existing vocal piece was part of the improviser's toolbox and that the skill of improvising over plainchant was included in that category. We can also note consistent characteristics in the pieces: the florid part is the upper part, with the original melody retained in the lower; stepwise motion prevails in the florid parts; the structure of the original piece is usually retained at least to some degree; and a great deal of rhythmic freedom and variation occur in both parts.[17] This tells us something, perhaps, about the improvisatory process, at least in that region, with that repertoire, in that particular time. However, in order to experiment with the improvisatory paradigm hinted at in the Faenza Codex and apply it to other pieces or to pieces of one's own invention, it would be necessary for a player to experience some immersion in the repertoire contained within, analyzing and ideally performing multiple pieces in the collection, as described in Practice 5.5. Attempting to build an improvisatory paradigm on the basis of only one piece from a particular source would be akin to a jazz student attempting to master bebop by transcribing one Charlie Parker solo.

---

16. Taruskin, *The Earliest Notations to the Sixteenth Century*, 306.

17. A more detailed discussion of the improvisatory characteristics of the Robertsbridge and Faenza intabulations can be found in Timothy J. McGee's *Medieval Instrumental Dances* (Bloomington: Indiana University Press, 2014), 30–34. As is the case with *The Sound of Medieval Song*, *Medieval Instrumental Dances* is another indispensable contribution to the practical application of medieval performance practice scholarship. Originally published in 1989 and reissued in 2014, it contains transcriptions of all the extant medieval dances.

Example 5.5: Faenza Codex, "Kyrie cunctipotens genitor," after Richard Taruskin, *The Earliest Notations to the Sixteenth Century* (New York: Oxford University Press, 2005); with permission

Example 5.5: (*continued*)

> *Practice 5.5*
> ## A MODEL OF IMPROVISATORY PRACTICE: THE FAENZA CODEX
>
> Note: Two prerequisites for this practice are access to transcriptions of all the pieces in the Faenza Codex and sufficient lead time to immerse oneself in the repertoire through both analysis and performance. The practice looks very compact on the surface, but will actually require a great deal of time and study.
>
> Step 1. Having examined the scores/transcriptions and played through as many of the pieces in the collection as possible, note and write down musical characteristics that are common to most or all of the pieces in the collection. Here are examples of some of these characteristics:
>   1. Upper voice is more florid than lower voice.
>   2. The lower voice usually contains melodic material from the original piece or chant.
>   3. The rhythm of the original musical material has often been changed or altered in some way.
>   4. The florid upper voice favors stepwise motion.
>   5. (Add your own observations.)
>
> Step 2. Note any frequent melodic or rhythmic patterns, especially in the upper voice.
>
> Step 3. Choose a simple monophonic song or plainchant. On the basis of the information gathered in steps 1 and 2, experiment with using the song or chant as the lower voice and improvising a florid upper voice in the style of the pieces in Faenza. You may wish to compose instead of improvise; it can be illuminating to try both and see how one process informs the other.

INVENTING DANCES

Most examples of extant medieval instrumental music are dances, and most dances were notated as a single melody. The repertoire of surviving pieces is very small; in contrast to the hundreds of extant medieval songs, we have fewer than fifty medieval dances. They have been transcribed and discussed in many sources and extensively performed and recorded.

The limited amount of extant notated instrumental repertoire, combined with the lack of prescriptive information included in that notation, suggests that instrumental music in the medieval period was by and large an orally transmitted repertoire. Kenneth Zuckerman calls the dances "excellent written examples of what may be taken as essentially a non-written, improvised tradition."[18] Analogues exist to the present day; a variety of still-thriving global dance music genres also come from non-written traditions, and a copious amount of repertoire is held in the players' and dancers' memory. As for improvisation, if the choreography of a particular medieval dance necessitated an invariable musical structure, it is still conceivable that improvisation may have been employed within that structural framework, while a dance that contained improvised movement may or may not have required a static form. The fact is, we know very little about the actual choreography of medieval dances, which suggests that the movement itself was also an orally transmitted art.

While the notation of medieval dance does give us information about form, structure, and rhythm, it tells us nothing about instrumentation or tempo. It also tells us nothing specific about ornamentation and variation, but it is highly likely that both ornamentation and variation existed in dance music just as it did in vocal music. It is also the case that in many non-classical music genres, natural differences in idiomatic articulation and ornamentation occur as a matter of course when several instruments are playing the same melody together; from the Middle East to Ireland, musicians "play what their instruments want to play." This is the sound texture that is sometimes described as *heterophonic* and is characteristic of many types of global instrumental music. However, recovering the specifics and the subtleties of ornamentation that would have characterized the regional differences in the playing of European dance melody is a tall order and involves the same considerations as those mentioned previously in the area of vocal music.

In addition to the purely instrumental dances such as the estampie, nota, and possibly ductia, there appear to have been dances in which singing and dancing happened simultaneously, such as the rondellus and the carole.[19] Despite all that we have learned, and despite the survival of some stunning pieces of music, we most likely do not have a comprehensive "big picture" of dance repertoire throughout medieval Europe.[20] It is possible that there may be descendants of these medieval dances that live on in European traditional folk music and dance, but it would be difficult to prove that conclusively, and we would have no way of knowing the extent of divergence between the originals and their later counterparts.

---

18. Zuckerman, "Improvisation in Medieval Music," 140.

19. Zuckerman, "Improvisation in Medieval Music," 6–7. An extensive study of the *carole* can be found in Robert Mullaly's *The Carole: A Study of a Medieval Dance* (Abingdon, UK: Routledge, 2011).

20. Albert Seay, *Johannes de Grocheo Concerning Music* (Colorado Springs: Colorado College of Music Press, 1973).

A number of performers of medieval music have used the forms and structures of medieval dances as a model providing a framework for the invention of new pieces in the style of their medieval antecedents. The resulting pieces, while based on a medieval model, are undeniably new music, but the employment of the considerations and processes of historical performance practice and the creation of new music are not mutually exclusive. In addition to providing a creative outlet for improvisation and invention, I would argue from a pedagogical standpoint that creating new pieces modeled on the structures of medieval dance is an excellent way to internalize the style and character of those dances, and thus to add more content to our storehouse of musical memory.

The Estampie: A Template for *Inventio*

The estampie (in Italian *istampitta*) is by far the most well-represented medieval dance form, constituting nearly half of the surviving instrumental dance melodies from the Middle Ages. It is characterized by sections, each of which contains its own melody (*punctum*), which is repeated twice. The cadential phrase that completes the first iteration of each melody ends on a note other than the final and is described as the "open" ending (*aperto* in the Italian manuscripts and *ouvert* in the French). The cadential phrase that completes the repeat of each melody ends with the final and is called the "closed" ending (*chiuso* in the Italian manuscripts and *clos* in the French). The open and closed endings often share some melodic or rhythmic material, or both. In the Italian istampitta, each *punctum* ends with a common refrain that precedes both the open and closed endings.[21] This is illustrated in Table 5.1.

A simple version of a French estampie can be seen in Example 5.6, which comes from the thirteenth-century manuscript known as the *Chansonnier du Roi*.

The French and Italian estampies differ from one another in the structure and length of their *puncta*. The Italian istampitte, for example, tend to be longer and have more *puncta* sections than the French version. Example 5.7 contains a transcription of "Ghaetta," one of the late fourteenth- and early fifteenth-century Italian istampitte contained in a manuscript now housed at the British Library.[22]

---

21. There are two Italian istampitte, "In Pro" and "Parlamento," in which the last two *puncta* share a different refrain and open and closed ending from the previous *puncta*.

22. London, British Library, Additional 29987, f. 55v–56r.

Table 5.1. COMPARATIVE STRUCTURES OF THE FRENCH AND ITALIAN *ESTAMPIE/ISTAMPITTA*

The French estampie

Punctum 1 + open	Melody A followed by "open" ending
Punctum 1 + close	Repeat of melody A followed by "closed" ending
Punctum 2 + open	Melody B followed by "open" ending
Punctum 2 + close	Repeat of melody B followed by "closed" ending
Punctum 3 + open	Melody C followed by "open" ending
Punctum 3 + close	Repeat of melody C followed by "closed" ending

(pattern repeats with remaining puncta)

The Italian istampitta

Punctum 1 + R + open	Melody A followed by refrain with "open" ending
Punctum 1 + R + close	Repeat of melody A followed by refrain with "closed" ending
Punctum 2 + R + open	Melody B followed by refrain with "open" ending
Punctum 2 + R + close	Repeat of melody B followed by refrain with "closed" ending
Punctum 3 + R + open	Melody C followed by refrain with "open" ending
Punctum 3 + R + close	Repeat of melody C followed by refrain with "closed" ending

(pattern repeats with remaining puncta)

Other medieval dances share the structure of the Italian istampitta (with *punctum*, refrain, and open and closed cadences) but differ in some other way. The saltarello, for example, is generally more varied in length and structure than the Italian estampies, with some being quite short and others quite complex. The trotto and the rotta occur as the second dance in a set of paired dances. Both are shorter than the first dance of the pair, and tend to be written in smaller note values. The ductia is described by thirteenth-century theorist Johannes de Grocheio as having the same basic form as the estampie, an

Example 5.6: "La Septime Estampie Real"

INVENTING MELODY (121)

Example 5.7: "Istampitta Ghaetta"

(continued)

Example 5.7: (continued)

Example 5.7: (*continued*)

Example 5.5: (*continued*)

Example 5.7: (*continued*)

untexted dance with paired *puncta* and open and closed refrains.[23] (There are actually no surviving examples of a medieval dance whose title includes the word *ductia*.)

There are various ways in which the form and structure of a dance such as the estampie/istampitta can be used as a template for invention. Practice 5.6 offers a suggestion for inventing a new section, or *punctum*, for an extant medieval dance.

Practice 5.6

INVENTING A NEW SECTION FOR AN EXTANT MEDIEVAL DANCE

Before starting the following process, it is important that you are already able to play the dance on your instrument, preferably from memory.

Step 1. Mode: Identify, if possible, the mode of the piece. This may be difficult to ascertain, as some of them have a large range, some are rather ambiguous, some change mode midstream, and some have quite a few accidentals. However, it is usually possible at least to identify the final (in an estampie, this will generally be the last note of the closed ending). Modal consistency with the other extant *puncta* will contribute to a sense of musical cohesiveness.

Step 2. Structure: Note the structural characteristics of the *puncta* of this dance. Is there a refrain section that repeats at the end of each *punctum* just before the open and closed ending, as in most of the Italian istampitte? Again, strive for consistency within the existing form.

Step 3. New material: Invent a new *punctum* (or two or three) for the estampie. Keep in mind that the *puncta* of an estampie do not tend to be all the same length; in fact, variation in the length of *puncta* is characteristic of the genre.

Practice 5.7 offers options for varying the sections of an extant medieval dance with ornaments, additional instruments, or added polyphonic lines.

---

23. McGee, *Medieval Instrumental Dances*, 11. McGee suggests that the ductia and the carole may have been the same thing. Mullaly identifies the carole as a specific dance with simple repeated steps executed repeatedly in a circle that moved to the left, taking place simultaneously with the singing of a series of songs by the dancers—songs that existed independently of the dance. (See the chapter "A Reconstruction of the Choreography," in Mullaly, *Carole*, 41–50.)

> *Practice 5.7*
> ## OPTIONS FOR VARYING THE SECTIONS OF AN EXTANT MEDIEVAL DANCE
>
> As in Practice 5.6, it is important that you are already able to play the dance on your instrument, preferably from memory.
>
> Option 1. Ornament the individual lines with passing tones, neighboring tones, trills, or any other kind of embellishment that is idiomatic to your instrument. When considering this option, note also the nature and character of florid passages and embellishments present in the piece itself.
>
> Option 2. Assign different instruments to different *puncta* or to the refrains. An alternate to this would be to arrange the piece so that the refrains or the open and closed endings are the only place at which everyone plays *tutti*.
>
> Option 3. Add polyphonic passages: for example, it is possible to choose a section to which organum-style parallel intervals may be added. (Caveat: when using this option, in most cases less is more.) Inventing a countermelody to an extant *punctum* is another polyphonic alternative.
>
> Option 4. If you have multiple players, it can be effective to have one instrument play only a simplified version of the tune melody while the others play the quick ornamental notes. The most practical way to achieve this is to use instruments that naturally sustain (bowed strings, winds) for the pared-down or reduced melody and to use for the faster ornamental notes either instruments with a quick attack and decay (plucked strings) or instruments whose sound naturally is foregrounded in the texture (high winds, for example).

Modern Clothes from Medieval Cloth: Creating an Estampie

Table 5.2 and Example 5.8 illustrate the way in which an extant medieval tune can be used as melodic material for the creation of a new tune using the structural form of an estampie.[24]

---

[24]. In addition to the example given in this chapter, Margriet Tindemans created an excellent guide to the process, contained in her chapter "Improvisation and Accompaniment before 1300," in Duffin, *Performer's Guide to Medieval Music*. On pages 458–61, Tindemans gives step-by-step instructions on how to use the melodic material from a trouvère song (Gace Brulé's *Quant voi reverdir*) to create a series of instrumental dances, including an *estampie*, *rondellus*, and *rondeau*.

Table 5.2. MELODIC MATERIAL FROM ORDO VIRTUTUM USED IN A COMPOSED ESTAMPIE

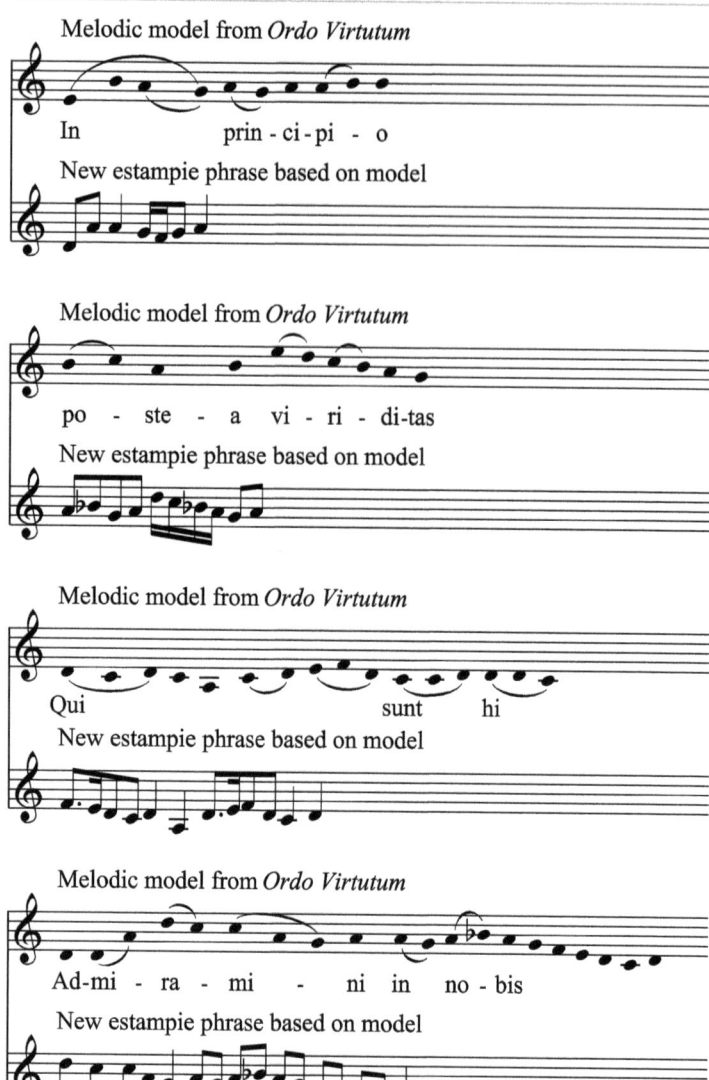

Table 5.2. (continued)

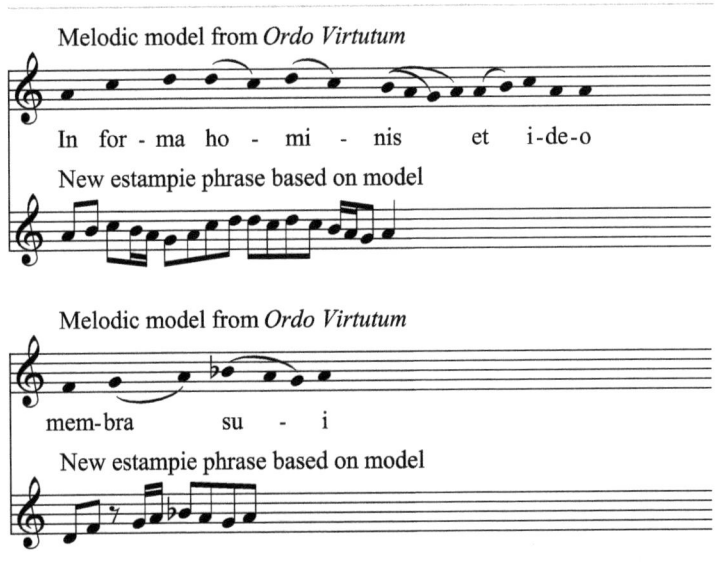

Several years ago, my early music ensemble at Texas Tech University presented a performance of Hildegard von Bingen's *Ordo Virtutum*. We decided to create an introductory piece from which we could also draw excerpts for dramatic interludes. We decided on an estampie form in a stately tempo that could serve as an entrance for the Virtues and the Patriarchs at the beginning of the play, using melodic phrases from the *Ordo* itself. We chose to follow the form of the Italian istampitta, ending each *punctum* with a common melodic phrase preceding its open and closed ending. Each member of the instrumental group contributed melodic material for the various *puncta*. Table 5.2 shows some examples of the process whereby melodic material from the *Ordo Virtutum* was used in the invention of the *puncta*. Example 5.8 contains the score of the completed istampitta.

Ultimately, the final version of the piece shown in Example 5.8 was the result of a number of revisions, as is often the case when invention happens in a group situation involving what one might call "composition by committee." Most notably, our original version contained *puncta* of equal length in order to coordinate consistently with the staging of the movement of the singers as they processed on and off during scene changes, while the typical Italian istampitta would have puncta of varying lengths.[25]

---

25. A distinction must be made here between a composition that is revised after the fact and "fluid composition," which I have used in this book to refer to an arrangement or composition that allows for variation or improvisation in the course of performance. The *Ordo* dance is not an example of fluid composition.

Example 5.8: The *Ordo* dance

Example 5.8: *(continued)*

Practice 5.8 offers a sequential process for creating a new dance using the structure of the medieval estampie and melodic material from an extant medieval piece.

Practice 5.8
CREATING AN ESTAMPIE

The following steps constitute a suggested sequential process for creating a new estampie using melodic material from an extant medieval piece.

Step 1. Because it is easier to arrange and compose over a predetermined framework, structural decisions should be made first, followed by decisions about meter and mode.

Step 2. Considerations involving the organization and arrangement of pre-existing melodic material would happen at this point. For example, you may choose to use particular melodic phrases verbatim from the original, or choose particular phrases and reworking them in a different meter, or vary them. The use of rhetorical techniques can be useful in this process, such as *amplificatio* (adding material to elongate a particular phrase) or *abbreviatio* (a reduced or shortened version of a phrase or theme from the original). (See chapter 7.)

Step 3. Composing the open and closed endings first will further provide structure and cohesion.

Step 4. Play the open and closed endings a few times. If you are working in a group, it can be useful at this point to improvise a few *puncta* together. If you are all comfortable improvisers, it is conceivable that this could be the sum total of performance: structure and open and closed endings pre-composed, and the rest improvised. However, a caveat: the form of an estampie requires that each *puncta* be played twice, once with the open and once with the closed ending; this requires a sharp memory and a certain degree of in-the-moment mindfulness. Will you remember what you just played? This exercise can be further developed in a group setting by having one person improvise a short *punctum* and play the refrain with the open ending and then pass the baton to the next person, who attempts to remember the improvised *punctum* and play it back, ending with the closed refrain. Recording this exercise can also be effective, especially of you think you may want to save some of these spontaneous *puncta* to use in a final composed version of the dance.

Step 5. This is the point at which *puncta* will composed, unless you are going to rely completely on improvised *puncta* in your performance. The music may be written down or memorized in the process of its creation. Since you are working with material that was most likely

> learned through the process of oral transmission, you might also have the composer of a particular puncta teach the others by ear, assuming that you are working in a group. If you have composed the music yourself and are teaching it to other musicians, consider teaching it to them by ear—a process that requires you to memorize it yourself.
>
> Step 6. If you are working through this process without writing down the music, at the end of your session I suggest that you record it or write it down—but do not listen to the recording or look at the music in the time that elapses between this rehearsal session and the next. It is extremely informative, and an effective memory practice, to see how well the group remembers the piece at the next session. While we are trying to develop our memory storehouses, it does not always happen overnight, and if you have a recorded or written record of the music, you will not risk losing all of your good work if everyone has forgotten the music at the next rehearsal.

The opportunities for improvisation and invention described in this chapter—preludes, interludes, postludes, variants, ornaments, and dances—have mostly fallen into the category of monophonic music. In some cases, however, the addition of invented material creates polyphony: countermelodies, instrumental/vocal collaborations, a florid improvised line placed above a pre-existing melody. Chapter 6 expands upon the process of adding a second voice to an already-existing voice as we examine the role of improvisation and invention in some of the most complex and fascinating vocal music of the Middle Ages: organum.

CHAPTER 6

Inventing Organum

Memoria *and* Formula

Bach left us the *Well-Tempered Clavier* in the form of musical scores, and yet he was also known for his skill at improvising fugues. Church congregations, having intuitively internalized the chordal characteristics of hymnody, are able to burst into spontaneous harmony even when a large percentage of them are not able to read the notes in the hymnal. New Orleans jazz players simultaneously improvise multiple melodies over the chord changes of pre-composed songs. Players of rock and folk music often work out arrangements with no paper involved, committing the structures and parts directly to memory, often leaving space in the arrangement for improvisation in the context of performance. If we wish to explore the topic of improvisation in the context of medieval polyphony, and particularly organum, it is important to reflect upon the fluidity of the distinctions between written and oral transmission, and between composition and improvisation.[1]

Leo Treitler, in his article "Medieval Improvisation," points out that composition and performance in the Middle Ages were not necessarily viewed as two different processes:

> Even in the late Middle Ages composing and performing could be thought of as a single act. A music master of the thirteenth century writing a handbook instructing singers in the invention of counterpoints to be sung along with traditional chant melodies states his purpose as teaching how "to compose and

---

1. See chapter 1, in the section "Improvisation versus Composition," pages 4–7.

perform discant *ex improviso*"—the last two words of that can be rendered "extemporaneously," "spontaneously," or "in an impromptu manner."[2]

In addition, written and oral transmission are not mutually exclusive. While the mathematically complex isorhythmic motets of the fourteenth century are still viewed as composed creations that, as explained by Anna Maria Busse Berger, "need to be transmitted intact in order to make sense" and thus are dependent upon writing, there are strong arguments for concluding that other polyphonic repertoires were sometimes improvised, particularly within the area of medieval repertoire associated with the organum of the Notre Dame school.[3] In her article "Mnemotechnics and Notre Dame Polyphony," Busse Berger states:

> We no longer need to assume that the introduction of writing necessarily replaced the hitherto "mental" and "oral" composition and transmission. Not only are we now aware of the central importance of "orality" in the classical and medieval cultures. We also begin to realize that these cultures remained to a very significant extent "oral" long after the introduction of writing, that writing and orality do not necessarily exclude one another, whether in the process of composition, or in that of transmission of texts. So far as the latter is concerned, it is now increasingly clear that written texts may be used to aid the memory instead of replacing it. The fact that something was written down does not have to mean that it was not transmitted orally as well. Written texts and oral transmission may well co-exist.[4]

There are a number of medieval treatises that give directions in how to invent or improvise organum. This chapter takes as its basic premise the idea that modern musicians can use these treatises as models that assist in the organization, understanding, and memorization of formulaic patterns and rules for improvising and inventing music in the style of medieval polyphony. Through an examination of a few representative models, we can observe what these patterns and rules can tell us about the *organista*'s inventive process and identify elements of that process that are common to invention in advance of performance (composition), in the act of performance (improvisation), or some combination thereof. Our inquiry, in the interest of manageability, will be limited to selected representative examples based on models that have come down to us from the Middle Ages, with the intention of offering a few practical suggestions for experimenting with the process of inventing polyphony.

    2. Treitler, *With Voice and Pen*, 12. The theorist referenced here is Anonymous II, quoted from Edmund de Coussemaker, ed. *Scriptores de musica medii aevi nova series a Gerbertino altera*, vol. 1, (Paris, 1864), 311.
    3. Berger, *Medieval Music and the Art of Memory*, 254
    4. Anna Maria Busse Berger, "Mnemotechnics and Notre Dame Polyphony," *Journal of Musicology* 14, no. 3 (1996): 264.

EARLY EXAMPLES OF POLYPHONIC PRACTICE

The earliest written description of polyphony is in the anonymous ninth-century *Musica Enchiriadis*. This is also where we first find the term "organum" used to describe a musical texture in which two or more voices are simultaneously sounding different notes, resulting in the creation of multiple independent melodies that interact together in time. In these early examples, one of the voices consists of a pre-existing melody; this is the *vox principalis*, or principal voice. The second, added vocal line is called the *vox organalis*. (These terms are abbreviated in this chapter and some of the musical examples and practices as VP and VO.)

Of the several different methods of creating organum described in *Musica Enchiriadis*, the simplest is *parallel organum*, in which the VO sings either a fifth or a fourth below the VP. This is extremely easy to improvise, since both voices sing the exact same melody, only at different pitch levels, as shown in this example from *Musica Enchiriadis* that uses a phrase from the chant "Te Deum laudamus."[5] (See Example 6.1.) In practice, each voice could also be doubled at the octave, producing four parts.

Example 6.1: Parallel organum from *Musica enchiriadis*

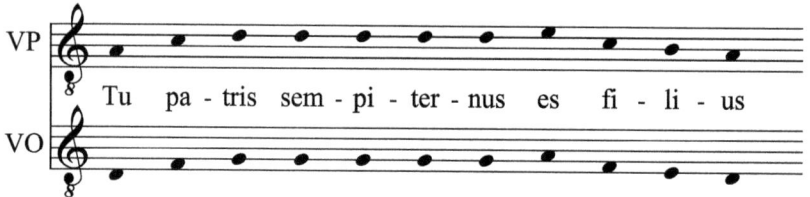

Parallel organum at the interval of a fourth is also described in *Musica Enchiriadis*. However, if one stays strictly within a particular mode, a problem arises, because augmented fourths will occur. For example, if the VP moves from G to A to B, and the VO moves from D to E to F, an augmented fourth (tritone) occurs between F and B, which was not acceptable. In practice, while singing by ear, it is possible that singers both then and now would have simply corrected the augmented fourth to a perfect fourth; however, the resulting accidentals would not work within the theoretical parameters of the system described in *Enchiriadis*. Instead, to avoid the tritones, the author of the treatise tells the singers of the *vox organalis* to stay on the same note until the *vox principalis* has moved to a pitch location that allows the *vox organalis* to proceed in parallel fourths again. This

---

5. "You are the eternal Son of the Father."

results in a mixture of both oblique motion and parallel motion between the two parts.

Since the point of the exercise in this chapter is to view these medieval instructions as models for improvisation, let us apply these procedures to a specific chant. Example 6.2 shows the first line of the requiem communion chant "Lux aeterna."[6] The addition of a *vox organalis* a fourth or fifth below is in itself a simple matter, easily done by ear. However, if we are using fourths, an F natural will occur below the B natural in the *vox principalis*. This is an augmented fourth that has to be adjusted, as shown in Example 6.2.

Example 6.2: Parallel organum, "Lux aeterna"

If we were to proceed on the basis of our modern musical instincts, we would simply make the F an F♯. However, that introduces a note that is outside the mode, and it will not work in the system on which *Musica Enchiriadis* is based. Instead, the issue is solved through the use of oblique motion, as shown in Example 6.3:

Example 6.3: Tritone in 6.2 avoided through the use of oblique motion

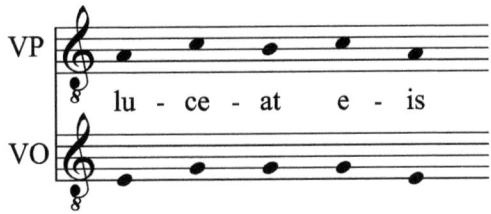

6. "Let eternal light shine on them, Lord." The entire chant is contained in the appendix, Mode Model 8.

It is perhaps the case that a medieval singer of a *vox organalis*, having heard these tritone-avoiding adjustment hundreds of times, would have instinctively moved to oblique motion at such a moment. This may not be the case for modern singers, who might need to work through the exercise a few times either by ear or in writing, and to look at primary sources for models. *Musica Enchiriadis* offers an example of mixed parallel and oblique motion as applied to the sequence "Rex caeli domine." Example 6.4 contains a modern transcription.[7]

Example 6.4: "Rex caeli domine," from *Musica enchiriadis*

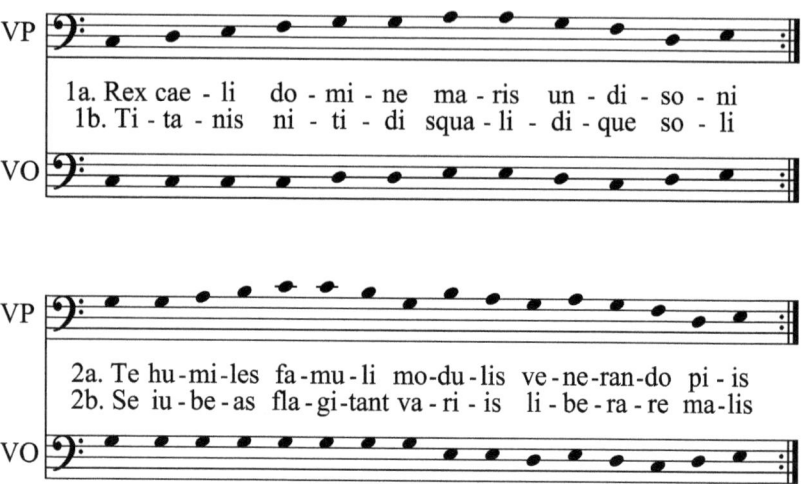

The procedure described here—the use of examples in a medieval treatise as models for one's own invention and improvisation—can be applied to any didactic source. Early treatises that postdate *Musica Enchiriadis*, such as Guido d'Arezzo's *Mikrologus*, the *Winchester Troper*, and *Ad organum faciendum*, expand the possibilities for the *vox organalis*, which can now rise above the *vox principalis* in pitch, repeat a pitch, or occur at an interval other than a fourth, fifth, or unison with the *vox principalis*. A detailed study of the rules in each of these early sources is beyond our scope, but the procedure is the same for the musician seeking to use these early sources as models, as described in Practice 6.1.

---

7. "King of the heaven and the roaring sea surge, of the bright Titan and the parched land; your humble servants, piously worshiping you with song, entreat you, as you command, to free us from various evils."

> *Practice 6.1*
> # ADDING A *VOX ORGANALIS*, USING A MEDIEVAL SOURCE AS A MODEL
>
> For this exercise, you will need to find a good translation of a medieval treatise that describes early polyphonic practice, such as *Musica Enchiriadis*, Guido's *Mikrologus*, *The Winchester Troper*, or *Ad organum faciendum*.[a] Many music history textbooks also contain concise summaries of the contents of these treatises, with modern transcriptions of the musical examples.
> 1. Study the rules that are set out in a particular treatise, and examine their application as shown in the musical examples given.
> 2. Using these given musical examples as a model, and observing the rules demonstrated therein, choose a monophonic chant or song as your *vox principalis* and add a second voice.
> 3. Try working out the process described in (1) and (2) above by both written and oral/aural methods. It may be easier to write out the solutions the first few times, and then try creating a *vox organalis* "by ear." It may also be beneficial to record your "ear" version and then transcribe it, checking to see how closely you followed the model.
> 4. When applying these techniques to performance, it is important to note what kind of repertoire is being described in the treatises, and consider whether the techniques would be used outside of that repertoire, with an awareness that a definitive answer to that question may not be available.
>
> [a]See Raymond Erickson, trans., *Musica Enchiriadis and Scolica Enchiriadis*, ed. Claude V. Palisca (New Haven, CT: Yale University Press, 1995); for the *Micrologus*, see Warren Babb, trans., *Hucbald, Guido and John on Music* (New Haven, CT: Yale University Press, 1978); for the Winchester Troper, see Alejandro Planchart, *The Repertory of Tropes at Winchester*, 2 vols. (Princeton, NJ: Princeton University Press, 1977), and a facsimile in Susan Rankin, *The Winchester Troper* (London: Stainer & Bell, 2007); for *Ad organum faciendum*, see Jay A. Huff, ed. and trans., *Ad organum faciendum and Item de organo* (Brooklyn: Institute of Mediaeval Music, 1969).

ORGANUM AND DISCANT

Later models for our exploration of medieval polyphonic invention can be found in the more florid ornamental style of Aquitanian polyphony (twelfth century) and the larger corpus of twelfth- and thirteenth-century polyphony associated with Notre Dame in Paris. Because our purpose is to examine ways in which didactic sources can provide models for improvisation and invention, the remainder of this chapter will focus on the process of creating Notre Dame polyphony described in the Vatican Organum Treatise.

There are two primary types of polyphonic texture associated with Notre Dame polyphony. *Organum* (sometimes *florid organum*, sometimes *organum purum*) is characterized by a polyphonic texture in which the lower voice (the *tenor*) sings the original plainchant in long sustained tones while the upper voice sings long, florid, non-metered melismatic phrases of irregular length. In *discant* style, the tenor is still singing the notes of the original plainchant, but regular measured rhythm has been applied to the chant, following a system of "rhythmic modes" characterized by repeating rhythmic patterns in which the basic unit of duration (*tempus*) occurs consistently in groupings of three units (later called a *perfection*). The upper voice is also in measured rhythm but moves in a faster and more florid fashion, usually with one to five notes for each note of the tenor.[8]

While it is generally accepted that organum purum may have arisen from an improvised tradition, Busse Berger argues in *Medieval Music and the Art of Memory* that entire "compositions" of Notre Dame organum may have been worked out in the memory and transmitted orally. Citing a scholarly consensus that dates the bulk of the composition of the Notre Dame repertoire between the second half of the twelfth century and the beginning of the thirteenth, she points out that the very earliest written manuscripts containing this repertoire date from the 1230s, with most of them dating from the 1250s.[9] She makes an additional argument for the existence of improvisation and oral transmission of material in the Notre Dame repertoire based on "markers of style" in music treatises (the presence of verse, tables, melodic formulas, and other such mnemonic devices) that correspond to instructional works in areas of grammar and arithmetic that were definitely meant to be memorized.[10] Since medieval poets learned poetry orally from memory or "systematically memorized phrases by reading and memorizing poetry" and then often incorporated these phrases into their own work, Berger poses the possibility that a similar process was true for performers and composers of polyphonic music.

In his book *Music and Ceremony at Notre Dame of Paris, 500–1550*, Craig Wright also discusses the dearth of earlier polyphonic source manuscripts and suggests that the "organum, discant and counterpoint of the church" was performed either through the art of improvisation, the memorization of

---

8. A third texture, *copula*, can be described generally as a combination of organum and discant. More specifically, it occurs as a transitional passage between sections of organum and discant in which the tenor retains the sustained notes of organum texture, while the upper voice continues in modal rhythm of discant.
9. Berger, *Medieval Music and the Art of Memory*, 163n.
10. Berger, *Medieval Music and the Art of Memory*, 118–19.

formulas, or a mixture of the two.[11] Wright also cites the absence of books of polyphonic vocal music for the choir of Notre Dame until late in the sixteenth century, while written liturgical books containing monophonic plainchant abound. While admitting the possibility that the written sources of polyphonic church music may have "gone undocumented before this time because they were owned by individual singers," he concludes that "taking the absence of polyphonic sources at face value, we must conclude that much of the organum, discant, and counterpoint of the church, whether sung by memory, by improvisation, or by some combination thereof, was performed without the assistance of written notation." He then presents an impressive list of documented accounts containing directives for specific performances of polyphony at Notre Dame, several of which indicate that the singers who were to "discant" the chants or "sing them in organum" would receive a higher payment. The specific numbers of singers mentioned in these directives also suggests that Notre Dame organum was "a soloist's art," and that the only line that would have called for multiple voices was the tenor consisting of long, sustained notes.[12]

THE VATICAN ORGANUM TREATISE

The Vatican Organum Treatise (VOT) is one of the clearest and most highly organized and formulaic instructional sources of the medieval period, dated to the late twelfth or early thirteenth century.[13] The VOT contains a theoretical section plus a practical pedagogical manual on how to invent organum, which is composed of a set of thirty-one "rules." Each of these rules is written out in Latin text and then followed by several musical examples that illustrate how the rule may be put into practice. The rules are sorted according to intervallic movement between two notes in the chant, or *cantus*, line of a two-part organum, and they give guidelines for the intervallic movement of the upper organum line.

For example, here is rule no. 1: *Si cantus ascenderit duas voces et organum incipiat in dupla, descendat organum 3 voces et erit in quinta.* (If the chant ascends by a second and the organum begins at the octave, let the organum descend by a third, and it will arrive at a fifth.) We can summarize the intervallic progression in rule no. 1 as shown in Example 6.5:

11. Craig Wright, *Music and Ceremony at Notre Dame of Paris, 500–1550* (Cambridge, UK: Cambridge University Press, 1989), 333–34.
12. Wright, *Music and Ceremony at Notre Dame of Paris, 500-1550*, 335–42.
13. Rome, Biblioteca Apostolico-Vaticana, Ottob. Lat. 3025. A modern edition with critical notes can be found in Irving Godt and Benito Rivera, eds., "The Vatican Organum Treatise—A Colour-Reproduction, Transcription, and Translation," in *Gordon Athol Anderson: In Memoriam*, ed. Irving Godt and Hans Tischler (Ottawa: Institute of Medieval Music, 1984), 2:264–345.

Example 6.5: Diagram representing rule no. 1, Vatican Organum Treatise.

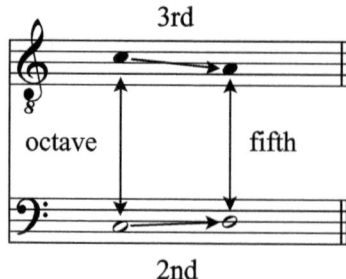

In his extensive article "The Vatican Organum Treatise Re-examined," Steven Immel provides a table that condenses all thirty-one rules into one model for each rule, as shown in Table 6.1.[14]

Table 6.1. IMMEL'S MODEL OF THE THIRTY-ONE VOT PROGRESSIONS, FROM IMMEL, "VATICAN ORGANUM TREATISE RE-EXAMINED"

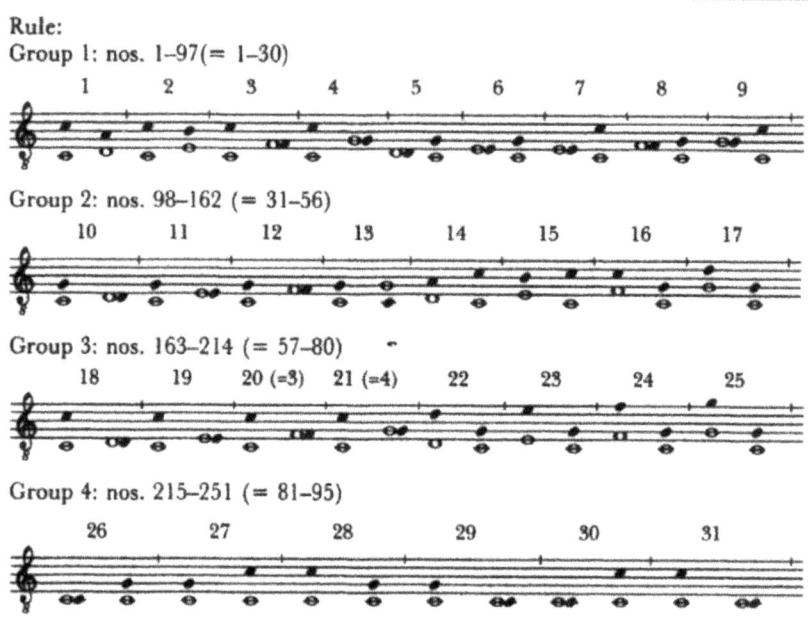

It is important to note here that Immel's study, which is critical to any examination of the Vatican Organum Treatise, also includes a set of "supplemental" rules that are not named as such in the VOT but appear in the

---

14. Steven C. Immel, "The Vatican Organum Treatise Re-examined," *Early Music History* 20 (2001):125.

examples included in the treatise. Immel also includes charts of progression formulas from other treatises associated with this repertoire that are not included in the VOT, and some in the VOT that are not in the other treatises. Those who wish to engage seriously with the models in the VOT should consult these additional charts of Immel's, as users of the VOT-related practices in this chapter may find that the progressions in the VOT alone will not cover every possibility.

In the VOT, each of these thirty-one rules is followed by notated examples, each of which show the beginning and ending interval and a melismatic passage in the upper voice connecting the two (See Example 6.6). These melismatic formulas illustrate ways in which the connective melismatic passages can be added to the upper voice between the initial and final notes and thus may serve as models for composing or improvising. This is remarkable, because not all didactic treatises provide models for a florid upper voice. In many cases we must turn to the extant repertoire itself as a model for relative note values, conjunct or disjunct motion, articulations and ornamental gestures, and so on, but the VOT offers us many models within the treatise itself. Example 6.6 shows, in modern notation, the examples given for rule no. 1.[15]

Note that the author of the VOT gives examples that begin on C (mm. 1–4), D (mm. 5–8), and E (mm. 9–11)—the first, second, and third notes of the natural hexachord. As a result, although the lower voice in each case moves "a second," in measures 9–11 the lower voice moves a semitone rather than a tone. The rule concerning the upper voice still applies; the point is that the interval between the two voices ultimately moves from an octave to a fifth.

Immel describes these melismatic formulas as "ordered by the compiler in progressive stages of elaboration, with the formulas becoming longer and their structure more isoperiodic."[16] Immel's article also provides an extensive table with typical examples of these progressive elaborations and shows via a number of concordances that they are drawn directly from the Notre Dame corpus. Immel's thesis is that the VOT's extensive concordance with the Notre Dame repertoire identifies it as "a 'grammar' for the Notre Dame organum duplum" and "a conscientious attempt at bringing together a generous sampling of Notre Dame formulae and organising them in a systematic way." He suggests that it would "not be an exaggeration" to consider it part of

---

15. The transcription in Example 6.6 is after f. 46r of the VOT manuscript. Another transcription of this model plus all of the other melismatic models for each rule in the VOT can be found in Godt and Rivera, *Gordon Athol Anderson*.

16. Godt and Rivera, *Gordon Athol Anderson*, 130. "Isoperiodic" is described in *Grove Music Online* as having "successive phrases of equal length but not necessarily the same rhythm." Margaret Bent, "Isorhythm," in *Grove Music Online*, http://www.oxfordmusiconline.com/subscriber/article/grove/music/13950.

Example 6.6: Musical examples pertaining to rule no. 1, Vatican Organum Treatise

(*bracket = ligature*)

Example 6.6: (*continued*)

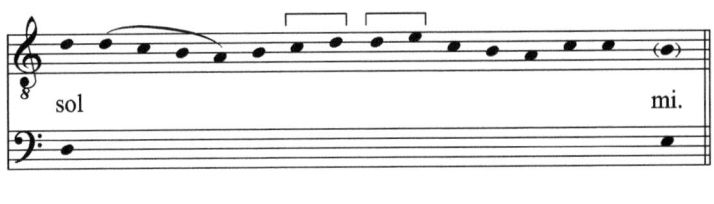

the same corpus as the rest of the *Magnus liber organi*.[17] Immel's point is well taken; it is completely plausible that someone connected with the Notre Dame school may have created a pedagogical guidebook specifically for that repertory and borrowed musical material from that repertory for the purposes of demonstration.

In terms of the relevance of the VOT to the practice of improvisation or oral composition, it is interesting that Immel, at least at the time of his article's publication, concluded that these extensive concordances with the Notre Dame repertoire of the Magnus Liber proved that the orientation of the Vatican treatise was "written composition based on written models."[18] Craig Wright questions this conclusion:

> These concordances are too numerous and too lengthy to be mere coincidences, but it is not apparent whether the tradition of the treatise influenced the

---

17. Immel, "Vatican Organum Treatise Re-examined," 166. The *Magnus liber organi* (Great book of organum), was attributed to the composer Leoninus (fl. 1150s–ca. 1201) by the thirteenth-century theorist known as Anonymous IV. In actual fact, this "great book" has come down to us as a body of repertoire located in several sources rather than as one single volume.

18. Ibid, 155.

compositional process of Leoninus or whether it reflects a later distillation of formulae extracted from his *Magnus Liber Organi*. Although the precise relation between the *theoria* and the *practica* remains to be defined, the treatise certainly would have been concordant with the general method of learning music for the choir of Notre Dame where much of the plainsong was sung by memory and much of the polyphony generated *ex tempore* by improvising over a given chant.[19]

Anna Maria Busse Berger, although she identifies Immel's work as being "the best article on the Vatican Organum Treatise," argues that the VOT was meant to be committed entirely to memory, and she agrees with Wright:

> While it is entirely possible that that author of the Vatican treatise had access to some manuscript version of the Magnus Liber and copied his formulas from there, it is also possible that he learned the formulas from a teacher and wrote them down himself. The classification of the formulas is strikingly similar to that encountered in tonaries and grammars. Both the tonaries and the Vatican treatise rely on an analysis of the music that probably could not have happened without musical notation. To this extent, at least, Immel is right. Where I disagree with him is in the function of the treatise. . . . It is important to understand that the performers or composers who had memorized the formulas in the Vatican treatise were able to use them in unwritten performances as well as in written-out compositions. Thus, the evidence in the treatise allows us to conclude that there was not necessarily a difference between the performer and the composer—both relied on the same practice. One person might choose to notate their version, while another one might perform it.[20]

Berger argues further that "the note-against-note counterpoint is not distinguished from diminished counterpoint [two or more notes against one] and thus all formulas were memorized and made their way in the Notre Dame repertory," adding more weight to the hypothesis that "the *Magnus liber organi* was transmitted orally since oral cultures are typically formulaic."[21]

A Mnemonic Model Based on the Vatican Organum Treatise

What follows is a suggested method for developing the ability to improvise organum duplum in the Notre Dame style, using the Vatican Organum Treatise as a sort of primer. In offering this, I am joining with Wright and Berger in concluding that the VOT is indeed a compendium of formulas that would be committed to

---

19. Wright, *Music and Ceremony*, 338.
20. Berger, *Medieval Music and the Art of Memory*, 126, 128.
21. Berger, *Medieval Music and the Art of Memory*, 156.

memory, that organum was at least in some cases an improvised art, and that the improvisatory practice may have extended to discant as well as organum purum. If one wishes to memorize the VOT rules, I suggest a system of mnemonic models based on the condensed rules from Immel's article shown previously in Table 6.1. In the model shown in Figure 6.1, the left side illustrates the rule from the VOT, with a representation of that rule in notation, with the tenor written in white notes and the organum in black. The right side of the model duplicates the notated illustration of the rule but omits the second note of the organum, and thus requires the person using the model to fill in that second note from memory.

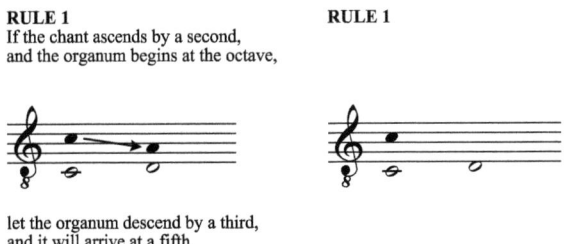

Figure 6.1: VOT mnemonic model

It is important to recall here that, as mentioned, the VOT contains a number of musical examples containing intervallic motion that is not covered by its specific rules, and that there are rules in contemporary treatises that do not appear in the VOT. One can apply the VOT mnemonic model in Figure 6.1 to any of these rules.

The format of Figure 6.1 can also be used to create an entire set of examples, one representing each rule in the VOT. If desired, the examples can be printed or written onto individual cards as a mnemonic aid. (The practice exercises that follow in this chapter would be facilitated by such a set, but are not dependent upon having one.) Practice 6.2 is designed for a group of participants, and provides instructions for an exercise in improvisation in the style of Notre Dame organum.

Applying the VOT Rules to a Plainchant Tenor

Once a basic familiarity with the rules has been established, one can put the rules into practice by applying them to a plainchant tenor. Before looking at a specific example, however, it is important to note that the singing of polyphony, and the invention thereof, was the job of the trained soloists in the chant choir. Therefore, if one wishes to apply polyphony to liturgical plainchant, it is

Practice 6.2

AN IMPROVISED ORGANUM "RELAY"

This exercise requires a group of singers, and access to the rules in the Vatican Organum Treatise. Recommended, but not required, is a compiled set of the VOT mnemonic models as shown in Figure 6.1—one model for each rule.

Step 1. The singers will be arranged in two groups.

Group 1: the chant tenor group (*vox principalis*)
Group 2: the duplum group (*vox organalis*)

For example, if there are ten singers, divide into two groups of five, numbered accordingly:

Group 1 (tenor, *vox principalis*): VP1 VP2 VP3 VP4 VP5
Group 2 (duplum, *vox organalis*): VO1 VO2 VO3 VO4 VO5

Step 2. Proceed in the following manner:

a. VP1 and VO1 are given an image of the same VOT rule. It can be on a card, piece of paper, blackboard, etc. They may look at the rule, but it is best to memorize it.
b. VP2 and VO2 are given an image of the VOT rule that begins with the interval on which the VP1/VO1's rule ends.
c. VP3 and VO3 are given an image of the VOT rule that begins with the interval on which the VP2/VO2's rule ends. . . . and so on. The exercise can be done with any number of singers.

Step 3. By consensus, choose a mode (a church mode, not a rhythmic mode). Mode 1 (Dorian), mode 5 (Lydian), and mode 7 (Mixolydian) are probably the best choices to begin.

Step 4. VP1 will begin with the first of the two lower notes in their assigned rule and sustain it. VO1 will begin on the first of the two upper notes of their assigned rule and connect it to the second of the upper notes of the assigned rule by improvising a melismatic passage that begins on the first note and ends on the second. The improvised melisma may contain as many notes as VO1 is comfortable with, but there should be more than two. Do not add rhythm or meter. VP1 must watch VO1 carefully and not move to the second note until VO1 arrives at the final pitch of their melisma. VO1 should be prepared to provide a clear and visible cue.

Step 5. If VP1 and VO1 have done the exercise correctly, they will end on the same interval that begins the VOT rule assigned to VP2 and VO2. At that point, VP2 and VO2 will begin, overlapping with the sound of the final interval sung by VP1 and VO1.

> Step 6. Repeat this sequence. In other words, if VP2 and VO2 have done the exercise correctly, they will end on the same interval that begins the VOT rule assigned to VP3 and VO3. At that point, VP3 and VO3 will begin, overlapping with the sound of the final interval sung by VP2 and VO2. As each pair of singers ends their assigned internal and the next pair of singers begins on the same interval, a line of improvised organum will be created.
>
> The goal of this practice is not to replicate the sound of an actual piece of Notre Dame organum, but rather to start the process of creating organum with the rules of the Vatican Organum Treatise in mind. It would also be possible for two singers to set up a sequence of VOT rules in the same fashion and move from one to the other together. Ideally, it should be done in the spirit of experimentation and good humor.

important when choosing a tenor line to look for a portion of chant that would have been performed by soloists (this could mean anywhere from one to four singers, depending on the liturgical occasion). While many chants include a short intonation that would be sung by a soloist, more substantial solo sections are found in the more ornate and melismatic Graduals and Alleluias and the similarly melismatic Responsories found in the various offices.[22] Soloist material appropriate for polyphonic settings can also be found in troped ordinary chants. There are many examples of troped Kyries, and the "Benedicamus Domino" chant that replaces the closing "Ite, missa est" at certain seasons was often a candidate for troping and polyphonic setting.

Keeping the role of the soloist in mind, here is a suggested procedure for inventing polyphony on an extant plainchant tenor, beginning with a small fragment of plainchant. Since the Notre Dame repertory includes two famous polyphonic settings of "Viderunt omnes," one attributed to Leoninus and the other to Perotinus (fl. ca. 1200), we will use the "Viderunt omnes chant," an Easter gradual, for our model. Example 6.7 shows the first phrase of "Viderunt omnes" as it is found in the *Liber Usualis*.

Example 6.7: First phrase of "Viderunt omnes"

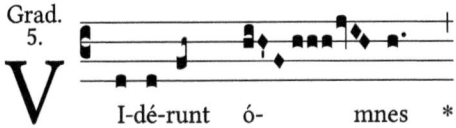

22. In the *Liber Usualis*, solo sections of a chant are marked off by asterisks. The rubrics explaining the use of these asterisks are included in the preface of most editions of the *Liber*.

The incipit of a Gradual would be performed by soloists and is therefore a good candidate for polyphonic elaboration. In the *Liber Usualis*, the end of this incipit will be marked by an asterisk, as in Example 6.7. Using the plainchant melody as the tenor, one may apply the VOT rules to create an upper voice, producing intervals that will be used to create the organum line, as has been done in Example 6.8 (limited for the sake of brevity to just the notes corresponding with the text "Viderunt").[23]

Example 6.8: Opening phrase, "Viderunt omnes," with upper voice following VOT rules

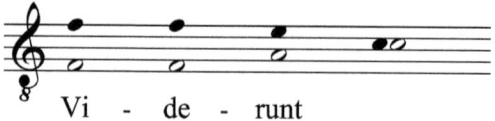

Having built this framework, it is now possible to add smaller note values to the upper voice between the syllables, as shown in Example 6.9, using either extant pieces from the Notre Dame organum repertory or the melismatic examples in the Vatican Organum Treatise (see Example 6.6, "Musical Examples Pertaining to rule no. 1, Vatican Organum Treatise," as a model).

Example 6.9: "Viderunt," with organum

Practice 6.3 summarizes the procedure of applying the VOT rules in a step-by step fashion.

To experiment with inventing polyphony using a discant texture, one must choose a soloistic section of chant that contains a melismatic passage, since discant happens where there is a melisma in the original chant. This could be a long passage, or it could be as simple as the "omnes" in "Viderunt omnes," as shown in Example 6.10.

---

23. The first two intervals, an octave followed by an octave, follow one of the rules described by Immel as "supplemental rules drawn from the musical examples in VOT." The other intervals follow VOT rules no. 2 and 11, respectively. It is also worth noting that Leonin's setting of "Viderunt omnes" uses the same sequence of intervals, corresponding to the VOT rules exactly.

Example 6.10: The "Omnes" melisma from "Viderunt omnes"

ó-   mnes   *

Practice 6.3
CREATING ORGANUM ON A PLAINCHANT TENOR, USING VOT RULES

This exercise is most effective when done with two or more musicians.

Step 1. Begin by choosing a small fragment of plainchant that would be sung by a soloist or soloists, such as the opening words of a Gradual, Alleluia, or Great Responsory (up to the asterisk in the *Liber Usualis*), or part of the verse of the same types of chant (again, up to the asterisk, when the choir joins for the last word of the verse). This will produce the tenor line (*vox principalis*).

Step 2. It is ideal to memorize the chosen chant fragment immediately, but for practical purposes one may also write out the melody to facilitate working with the VOT rules and then commit it to memory. All the musicians taking part in this practice should memorize the resulting tenor line (*vox principalis*), even if they will eventually be singing the upper voice (*vox organalis*).

Step 3. Begin the upper voice at either a unison, fifth, or octave higher than the tenor. Not every interval option will work equally well; it may be necessary to try a couple of different options. For instance, if the chant immediately rises, it is probably best to start on a fifth or octave above to allow room for both voices to move in contrary motion. If the chant immediately falls, start on a unison or fifth.

Step 4. Following the VOT rules, move from one interval to the next. It can be beneficial to write down the number of each rule just above the staff, for future reference. You may notice that certain rules are implemented more often than others.

Step 5. When you have completed your sequence of intervals, one singer (or player, if this exercise is being done with instrumentalists) will fill in the top voice with melismatic passages. These passages can range from two or three notes to any number. If you are working in a group, take turns providing the improvised upper voice. If you have access to a translation and transcription of the entire VOT, it can be very instructive to try using the melismas included in the treatise as a model. You may find it easier to use the melismas if you have had some basic training in hexachord solmisation, but you can experiment with them even if you have not.

Instead of expanding the chant into a tenor line comprised of long sustained notes, as in organum duplum, the chosen tenor line will now have one of the *rhythmic modes* applied to it. Characteristic of certain types of Notre Dame polyphony, the rhythmic modes are a system of rhythmic patterns comprised of combinations of long notes ("longs," from the Latin *longa*) and short notes (breves, from the Latin *brevis*). The modes are based on poetic meters, which are defined according to pattern of syllable length within the metrical foot: trochee, long-short; iamb, short-long; dactyl, long-short-short; anapest, short-short-long; spondee, long-long; and tribrach, short-short-short. In medieval notation, the rhythmic modes were not expressed in terms of single note shapes but were instead written as groups of attached notes called "ligatures." Each rhythmic mode had a characteristic ligature pattern.[24]

In modal rhythm, the basic unit of duration is called the *tempus*. This is represented by the breve, which in modern transcriptions of modal rhythm is usually expressed as an eighth note. A group of three *tempora* is defined as a "perfection," which is analogous to the metrical foot of poetry described above. A longa can be "perfect" (equal to three breves) or "imperfect" (equal to two breves). A perfection, therefore, may be expressed in terms of three breves (1 + 1 + 1); a single "perfect" long that is equivalent in duration to three tempora; an "imperfect" long that is equal in duration to two tempora, followed by a single breve (2 + 1); or a single breve, followed by an "imperfect" long that is equal in duration to two tempora (1 + 2). When two breves follow or precede a perfect long, the second breve is "altered" to be twice as long as a tempus (1 + 2, but written as two breves rather than as breve-long), so that the two breves together fill out a perfection. Table 6.2 shows the six patterns known as the rhythmic modes; they are expressed here in modern notation. Note that rhythmic modes 3, 4, and 5 contain two perfections.

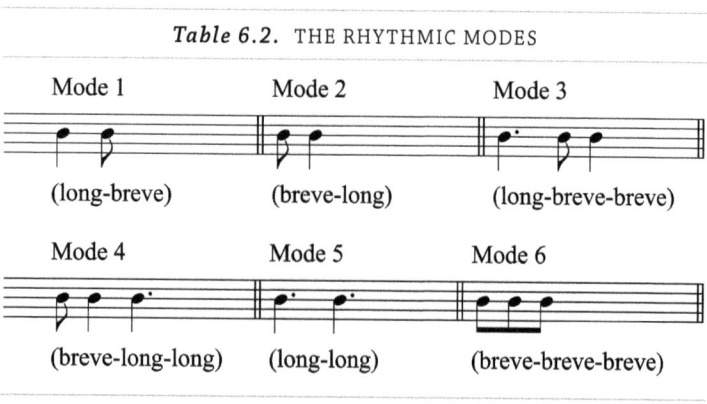

Table 6.2. THE RHYTHMIC MODES

24. This very basic introduction to the concept of the rhythmic modes is intended to provide the reader with a very basic explanation of the modes, and does not venture into a discussion of the notation. For a detailed discussion of modal rhythm that

In the actual practice of the Notre Dame repertoire, the notes could be broken into smaller units or combined into a longer unit, as long as a triple grouping was maintained. It was also standard practice to end a phrase with a rest that would replace the last eighth note or dotted quarter of the pattern.

The most commonly used rhythmic modes were 1 and 5, which are also thought to be the oldest. It is also very common in the Notre Dame repertoire to find mode 5 in the tenor and mode 1 in the upper voice, or duplum. Let us therefore apply mode 5 to the melisma on the syllable "om" in the chant "Viderunt omnes." In music based on the rhythmic modes, the modal units are grouped into phrases, or *ordos*, that generally end with a rest. In this case, the pattern also contains a double-long (two perfect longs combined). At the end, the last note is held in order to provide the possibility of a transition back to organum duplum texture on the syllable "nes." (See Example 6.11.)

Example 6.11: "Omnes" melisma as tenor, with rhythmic mode 5 applied

Now that we have our tenor line, expressed in modal rhythm, we can invent a second part (duplum) above it as in Example 6.12, using the long-short pattern of rhythmic mode 1. Note that once you have settled on a rhythmic mode, you should not change modes in the middle of a phrase, although you may express a triple unit of duration as three eighth notes (for example, in mode 1 you may sometimes use three eighth notes for one unit instead of a quarter followed by an eighth). You may also combine units (for example, a dotted half note may represent two units).[25] You will notice a passage at the end in which the tenor holds the penultimate note while the duplum part moves from modal rhythm back into organum purum to cadence on the last syllable of "omnes." This kind of transition is common in Notre Dame repertoire and provides a transition back to either more organum purum or unison chant.

---

also includes more extensive excerpts of "Viderunt omnes" settings, see Taruskin, *The Earliest Notations to the Sixteenth Century*, 175–91.

25. In addition, you should not shift between rhythmic modes 1 and 2 or between rhythmic modes 3 and 4, and mode 1 should never be combined melodically or in counterpoint with modes 2, 3, or 4. When in doubt, stay as close as possible to the patterns in Table 6.2.

Example 6.12: Discant on "Omnes" melisma from "Viderunt omnes"

The sample of discant in Example 6.12 is fairly short; in practice such discant sections were often longer. This could be accomplished by using a longer melismatic passage for the tenor line or by repeating the segment of chant on which the discant is based. (Indeed, in actual Notre Dame practice, the sections of organum purum and copula were generally longer than any of the examples shown above.)

Practice 6.4 outlines a step-by-step procedure for creating discant on a plainchant tenor, using the rules in the VOT.

Practice 6.4

CREATING DISCANT ON A PLAINCHANT TENOR, USING VOT RULES

This exercise is most effective when done with two or more musicians.

Step 1. Begin by choosing a melismatic section of chant that would have been performed by soloists. Good sources for examples are Graduals, Alleluias, Benedicamus Domino chants, and troped Mass Ordinary chants. It is best to choose a short passage in order to facilitate memory, and go through as much of the process as possible without writing anything in score.

> Step 2. Create a tenor line by applying one of the rhythmic modes to the notes in the melisma. If you are working in a group, it may be most effective to have one person do this and then teach it to the others. It may also be most effective to begin by planning to use mode 5 for the tenor and mode 1 for the duplum (upper voice).
> Step 3. The resulting tenor line may be written down in order to facilitate the use of the VOT rules. However, all the musicians taking part in this practice should memorize the resulting tenor line, even if they will eventually be singing the upper voice.
> Step 4. Next, one by one each singer or player should improvise an upper line in discant rhythm, with one voice or instrument at a time adding the upper line while the rest sing the invented tenor line in unison.
> Step 5. You may wish to combine Practice 6.3 with Practice 6.4 and create sections of organum alternating with sections of discant and sections of chant as one finds in the Notre Dame repertory.

Once you have created a piece of discant in the Notre Dame style, you have also unlocked the door to composing a medieval *ars antiqua* motet. As mentioned, the tenors of the discant sections were rhythmicized versions of a melisma on a particular word in the original chant. Later composers/inventors of organum would often rework the same discant section, using the same rhythmicized discant tenor but adding a new upper voice. The resulting new discant section could then replace the original one within the same larger piece. These reworked discant sections were called "substitute clausulae." Over time, these substitute clausulae became independent works, and the upper voices were set with text (words, or in French *mots*), yielding a new genre called the *motet*, with a chant tenor as the lower voice and a more florid, rhythmic upper voice with text in either Latin or French. In short, if you set a text to the upper voice of the discant piece that you created in Practice 6.4, you will have in effect created a medieval motet.

A CONCLUDING THOUGHT: THE BEGINNING BEFORE THE BEGINNING

This chapter began with the image of Johann Sebastian Bach improvising fugues. In closing, we may reflect on the fact that as modern musicians attempting to create polyphony in the context of medieval music, we begin our inquiry having already read the last few chapters of the book of Western polyphony before reading the first chapter. We cannot "unhear" *The*

Well-Tempered Clavier, Palestrina, Brahms's Requiem, Webern, progressive rock, and countless other examples of polyphonic music from the last five hundred years. In most cases, the more recent music found its place in our musical storehouses of memory before we ever heard of Perotin, Leonin, or Notre Dame polyphony.

Therefore, it is not possible to come to this exercise *tabula rasa*. Later polyphonic music is part of our collective story as modern musicians, and our musical training did not begin at the beginning of polyphony. But this need not discourage us from inventing organum and discant, or from bringing forth new music through the use of medieval formulas, "historically informed" procedures, and historical imagination. It is not necessary, or even desirable, to conceive the development of polyphonic music as a linear phenomenon that requires us to obliterate all memory of later counterpoint, voice-leading, and the avoidance of parallel intervals in order to be "authentic." We merely use different tools, materials, and processes in the context of performing medieval music, much as we would use different tools, materials, and processes if we were going to learn to play North Indian classical music or sing the blues. In the next chapter, we will explore more deeply the tools, materials, and processes of rhetoric, a highly prized art in the Middle Ages, and examine how rhetorical concepts can inform *inventio* in the interplay of text and melody.

CHAPTER 7

༜ུ

Playing Poetry

The Rhetoric of Invention

The interrelationship of words and music is an important consideration in the study of any vocal music, but in medieval repertoire it is critical. Musicians trained to take interpretive and expressive cues from harmonic function, rhythmic pattern, and periodic phrase structure, however, are often at a loss when they first encounter chant and monophonic song. I repeatedly encounter music history students who opine that plainchant "all sounds alike" and voice students who wish to engage with medieval repertoire but say they "do not know where to begin." With no knowledge of the linguistic, poetic, or liturgical context, no background in poetic structure, no exposure to the concepts of rhetoric, and no visual cue other than the modern practice of rendering medieval melodies into rhythmically ambiguous noteheads, how can we expect them to react otherwise?

Barbara Thornton clearly articulated the importance of understanding the deep interrelationship between text and music in the monophonic song repertoire:

> There is significance in the number of syllables per poetic line, how the lines combine to make a strophe, and how strophes march along in time to command attention and memory. A performance cannot communicate these essential things in a composition if it is ignorant of them, or, more importantly, if it is unmoved by them. The creator shows the way into the space of the piece, the living interpreter must make the journey. In its day, all this was achieved without notation. Having never or rarely seen a text or notes written in separate form, the medieval musician was never obliged to think of them as two separate things.[1]

---

1. Barbara Thornton and Lawrence Rosenwald, "Poetics as Technique," in Duffin, *Performer's Guide to Medieval Music*, 269.

Using the precepts of grammar and rhetoric as tools for understanding the interrelationships of musical and textual structures informs our understanding of the lyric or narrative text of a piece. Rhetoric itself also informed the process of invention for the composer-poets of the Middle Ages, and can do so for us; it is therefore essential to include its consideration in any study of invention in the performance of medieval music.

Consider, for example, a long melismatic passage. How differently we might view a modern transcription's stream of "rhythmically ambiguous noteheads" if we place it in the context of Geoffrey of Vinsauf's description of *amplificatio*: "Since a word, a short sound, passes swiftly through the ears, a step onward is taken when an expression made up of a long and leisurely sequence of sounds is substituted for a word."

Most of the scholarly material concerning the relationship of rhetoric to early music is presented in the context of late Renaissance and Baroque repertoire, but rhetoric was also one of the seven liberal arts that constituted a medieval education, and its rules would have been known at least to literate musicians in the Middle Ages. In addition, there is a certain amount of universality to rhetorical skill: storytellers, actors, lecturers, lawyers, writers, politicians, and poets learn to use these skills by close observation and imitation of teachers and models. The ancient Greek and Latin writers codified the observed characteristics of successfully persuasive speech, and they drew a strong connection between music and rhetoric. Quintilian, in Book 1 of his *Institutio Oratoria*, tells us that "Timagenes asserts that music is the oldest of all literary arts, and this is confirmed by the evidence of the greatest poets, in whom the praises of heroes and gods were sung to the accompaniment of the lyre at royal banquets."[2] Quintilian goes on to say that although music has been "abandoned by orators and taken over by philosophers, it once belonged to our work, and eloquence cannot be perfect without the knowledge of all such things."[3] He argues further that "*Grammaticē* and music were once united," and he speaks eloquently in defense of that connection in the two extended passages quoted below. Note in the first passage that Quintilian compares oratory with musical composition, and that he includes instrumental music in his comparison:

> Music has patterns of two kinds, in sounds and in the movements of the body, for both need proper control of some kind. The musical theorist Aristoxenus divides what concerns sounds into rhythm (*rhythmos*) and melody (*melos*), the former comprising the "modulation," and the latter the tone and quality of the

---

2. Quintilian, *The Orator's Education*, Books 1–2, trans. Donald A. Russell (Cambridge, MA: Harvard University Press, 2001), 219. Quintilian's passages on music are in 1.10.9–33.

3. Quintilian, *Orator's Education*, 219.

sound. Now are not *all* these essential to the orator? One point is relevant to gesture, the second to word arrangement, and the third to the inflexions of the voice, many of which are also involved in making a speech. Or do you imagine that some kind of structure and euphonious combination of sounds is necessary only for poetry or the sung parts of plays, and not essential in pleading? Or that oratory does not employ various kinds of Composition and sounds according to the needs of the subject just as music does? Music indeed employs sound and modulation, to express sublime thoughts loftily, pleasing thoughts with sweetness, and ordinary thoughts with easy grace; it uses all its skill to accord with the emotions required by the words it accompanies. Yet in oratory too, raising, lowering, or inflecting the voice is a means of affecting the hearer's feelings; we use one "modulation" (if I may use the same term) of phrasing and of voice to arouse the judge's indignation and a different one for arousing pity; why, we even feel that mental attitudes are affected in various ways by instruments which are incapable of articulate speech.[4]

In this second passage, Quintilian offers a *confutatio* to those who may disagree with his assessment that music is a useful skill for both the orator and the poet. His rhetorical question "Do poets exist without music?" is particularly striking:

I should like, for the sake of some persons who are less well instructed and have a "coarser Muse" (as the saying is), to remove all doubts about the usefulness of this art. They are bound to admit that the reading of the poets is of use to the future orator; but do poets exist without music? If anyone should be blind enough to be doubtful about the others, this must at least be true of those who wrote songs for the lyre.[5]

Once again, Quintilian emphasizes the importance of the connection between rhetoric and musical performance that involves an instrument. While the importance of rhetoric is obvious for singers and those who would "write songs for the lyre," I suggest that the ability to apply rhetorical analysis to a piece is equally important to the person playing that lyre. Too often one hears performances of medieval repertoire in which the singer is accompanied by an instrumentalist "doodling" away in Dorian or Mixolydian mode, playing material that has little relation to either the song or the singer. I recall hearing someone describe this as "playing two different songs in two separate rooms." In all, it is an unsatisfying experience for player, singer, and audience. The material in this chapter will present an alternative to that scenario. After a

---

4. Quintilian, *Orator's Education*, 225–27.
5. Quintilian, *Orator's Education*, 227.

brief discussion of the precepts of *inventio* and the use of rhetorical figures, I will offer a rhetorical analysis of a specific song, the *Planctus cygni*, followed by a series of practical exercises to guide the preparation of such a rhetorical analysis and its realization in performance.

INVENTIO AND THE *RHETORICA AD HERENNIUM*

There were a number of sources used to teach rhetoric in the medieval period. The works of Cicero (first century BCE) and Quintilian (first century CE) were popular, as was a work called *Rhetorica ad Herennium* (ca. 90 BCE), once attributed to Cicero but now of disputed authorship.[6] These works were also interpreted by medieval authors such as Geoffrey of Vinsauf (*Poetria Nova*), who is particularly important for performers of medieval lyric because his treatise focuses on the delivery of poetry. His treatment of rhetorical structure and his concise but detailed commentary on rhetorical ornament has a direct application to medieval song.

The *Rhetorica ad Herennium* tells us that a speaker should "possess the faculties of Invention (*inventio*), Arrangement (*dispositio*), Style (*elocutio*), Memory (*memoria*), and Delivery (*pronunciatio*)."[7] Everything on this list can be applied to the art of musical composition and performance.

The *Rhetorica*'s author further divides the art of *inventio* is into the "six parts" of a discourse. These are based on the art of persuasion, and at first glance they may seem to be more applicable to a lawyer's closing arguments than a musical composition. However, I have suggested a few analogies.

1. The *exordium*, or introduction, which prepares the listener, gets his or her attention, and provides a beginning
2. The *narratio*, in which the facts of the issue are stated or the narration of events is given
3. The *divisio*, in which the speaker outlines the different views on the issue at hand or the main points that he or she is going to present
4. The *confirmatio*, in which the speaker builds his or her argument and bolsters it with convincing corroboration
5. The *confutatio*, in which the speaker refutes all opposing arguments
6. The *conclusio* or *peroratio*, which provides an artful end to the discourse, or, in our case, to the song or instrumental piece

Exordium, narratio, and *conclusio* have straightforward musical analogues. We can compare the *exordium* to a prelude, or any introductory verse, stanza,

---

6. Harry Caplan, trans., *De Ratione Dicendi (Rhetorica ad Herennium)* (Cambridge, MA: Harvard University Press, 1964).
7. Caplan, *De Ratione Dicendi*, 7.

or section. The *narratio* can be the stanzas that provide the background, topic, or theme of the lyric, or, in later instrumental music, the full statement of the theme or fugue subject. (A prelude comes before a fugue for a reason, just as the opening adagio sections in some early symphonies are followed directly by the statement of the first theme in the allegro.) The musical *conclusio* can take many forms; in medieval music, we often get a cadence that is very typical of the song's mode, a consonant fifth or octave cadence, or a lyric "punch line," such as the two-line *tornada* that ends a troubadour *canso*.

It is a bit more challenging to assign musical analogues to the *divisio, confirmatio*, and *confutatio*; the resulting interpretations can be highly subjective, although in later music it is tempting to draw parallels with certain aspects of functional harmony and sonata form. In terms of medieval music, one can find examples in "dialogue" songs such as the troubadour *tenso* and in lyric in which a particular point is being argued; however, the rhetoric in these cases may be much more closely tied to the lyrics, while the music may simply be strophic. In the musical example given below, I am most concerned with the *exordium, narratio*, and *conclusio*, and with the ways in which the music is crafted to match some of the rhetorical figures in the lyric.

The rhetoric of a speech, story, or argument has to do with the way in which it unfolds over time. An *exordium* by definition is an introduction, and therefore it is first. Music's units, phrases, expressive gestures, and larger structures also unfold in time, and the rules of rhetoric can apply to a musical composition as well. Matching the rhetorical characteristics of a text to a melody was (and is) an important skill for a composer of song or chant, but in fact a melody itself can be crafted to follow the *Rhetorica*'s guidelines as it unfolds. If we apply rhetorical analysis to both the texts and the melodies of the medieval pieces that we are performing, it will not only inform how we present the pieces vocally, but it will also inform the choices we make in terms of instrumental additions (e.g., preludes, interludes, phrases that may be used to connect one line of verse or one stanza with another, and concluding instrumental material).

EXAMPLE FOR RHETORICAL ANALYSIS: THE *PLANCTUS CYGNI*

The *Planctus cygni*, or *Lament of the Swan*, is a ninth-century Latin planctus found in a number of insular and continental manuscripts. The notation in Example 7.1 is based on a transcription by musicologist Bruno Stäblein; Table 7.1 includes the *Planctus cygni* text, with its English translation and syllable count.[8]

---

8. Bruno Stäblein, "Die Schwanenklage, Zum Problem Lai-Planctus-Sequenz," in *Festschrift Karl Gustav Fellerer: Zum sechzigsten Geburtstag am 7. Juli 1962*, ed. Heinrich Hüschen (Regensburg, Germany: Gustav Bosse Verlag, 1962), 491–502. The *Planctus cygni* is one of the oldest, most famous, and most often analyzed of the medieval Latin sequences. John Stevens points out the *Planctus cygni*'s "complex use of small

Example 7.1: *Planctus cygni*

Example 7.1: (*continued*)

Table 7.1. PLANCTUS CYGNI

	Latin text and translation [a]	Syllable count
1	*Clangam, filii, ploratione una* I will cry out, O children, with a lamentation	12
2a	*Alitis cygni, qui transfretavit aequora* Swans, cherish the one who crossed over the seas;	13
2b	*O quam amara lamentabatur, arida* O how bitterly it wept for the dry land	13
3a	*Se dereliquisse florigera, et petisse alta maria,* because it had deserted flower-bearing lands and sought the deep seas,	10/9
3b	*Ajens: "infelix sum avicula, heu mihi, quid agam misera* saying: "I am an unhappy little bird, alas for me,	10/9
4a	*Pennis soluta inniti lucida non potero hic in stilla* Weakened in my wings, I will not be able to stay afloat here in this clear element;	19
4b	*Undis quatior, procellis hic intense allidor exulata.* I am battered by waves and winds; here I am tossed about and beaten unceasingly.	19
5a	*Angor inter arta gurgitum cacumina, gemens alatizo intuens mortifera, non conscendens supera;* Anguish amid the close peaks of the whirling waves! Groaning, I beat my wings anticipating what brings death, since I do not rise to the regions above.	13/13/7
5b	*Cernens copiosa piscium legumina non queo in densos gurgites assumere alimenta optima.* I perceive an abundant crop of fish, but in the dense waves I can find no fitting sustenance.	13/13/7
6a	*Ortus occasus plagae poli administrate lucida sidera.* "Bright stars, control the rising and falling of the region of the pole!	20
6b	*Sufflagitate Oriona, efflagitantes nubes occiduas.* Raise up Orion while blowing away the western clouds!"	20
7a	*Dum haec cogitarem tacita, venit rutila adminicula aurora.* While I thought these things in silence, rosy dawn came as my helper."	21
7b	*Oppitulata afflamine coepit virium recuperare fortia.* With a desired breath of wind, the swan began to recover its strength.	21
8a	*Ovatizans jam agebatur inter alta et consueta nubium sidera.* Rejoicing, it was then borne up among the high and accustomed stars of the clouds.	24
8b	*Hilarata ac jucundata nimis facta penetrabatur marium flumina.* The seas' currents, which had been made agreeable and kind, were traversed.	24
9a	*Dulcimode cantitans volitavit ad amoena arida.* Singing sweetly, the swan flew to the welcome dry ground.	18

Table 7.1. (continued)

	Latin text and translation [a]	Syllable count
9b	*Concurrite omnia alitum et conclamate agmina:* Rush together and shout, all you throngs of birds:	18
10	*Regi magno sit gloria. Amen.* Glory be to the great King. Amen.	8/2

[a]Translation by Dr. Byron Stayskal, Western Washington University, for Altramar medieval music ensemble.

The medieval planctus shares the formal structure of a sequence, which means that its form is composed of couplets, or double verses (sometimes called paired versicles). Despite its liturgical provenance, sequence structure also appears extensively in medieval secular song, particularly in the planctus and lai repertoire. The text of a sequence is usually mostly syllabic—that is, a syllable for each note or neume. Note also that the two lines of a paired versicle almost invariably have the same syllable count, which is indeed the case with the *Planctus cygni*. In many medieval sequences and planctus, the first and last versicle are single, as is the case with the *Planctus cygni* (see Table 7.2).

Next, let us consider the rhyme scheme and metric characteristics of the text. This particular planctus is also a *prosa*; its lines and versicles do not make use of word rhyme, with the exception of a couple of internal rhymes (*hilarata, jocundata*). It does rely heavily on assonance, or the use of a repeating vowel sound; note that every line ends with the sound of the vowel "a" and that the same sound is used internally to end phrases within a poetic line as well. In terms of accent, there is a strong emphasis on words that have an accent on the antepenultimate (third to the last) syllable: *fí-li-i, é-quo-ra, lú-ci-da, ca-cú-mi-na, óp-ti-ma,* etc.[9]

The *Planctus cygni* offers us a brilliant example of rhetorical principles reflected in the composition of melody. In terms of rhetorical *inventio*, the text of the first line is a classic example of *exordium*, containing a general summation of what is to come ("I will cry out, O children, with a lamentation"). In terms of melody, two important rhetorical "building blocks," shown in

segments," suggesting that these "link the *planctus* with the music of the lai" and that "traditions other than Gregorian chant are alive and working in the imagination of the poet." See John Stevens, *Words and Music in the Middle Ages* (Cambridge, UK: Cambridge University Press, 1986), 110–14. In *The Performer's Guide to Medieval Music*, Barbara Thornton cites the *Planctus cygni* in her discussion of the sequence as an "entirely new poetic form . . . superimposed upon the old and beloved chant formulae" (269). Thomas Binkley also used the *Planctus cygni* to illustrate rhetorical analysis in his performance practice classes at Indiana University.

9. Stress on the antepenultimate syllable is called *proparoxytone* rhythm.

Table 7.2. SEQUENCE FORM

Versicle 1	
Line 1 of text	Melody A
Versicle 2	
Line 2 of text	Melody B
Line 3 of text	Melody B
Versicle 3	
Line 4 of text	Melody C
Line 5 of text	Melody C
Versicle 4	
Line 6 of text	Melody D
Line 7 of text	Melody D
(double versicle pattern continues according to number of verses)	
Final versicle	
Last line of text	Melody X

Example 7.2, appear right at the beginning of the song: the melodic figure over *clangam, filii* and, second, the figure over *ploratione*. Both melodic figures recur in various permutations through the remainder of the piece.

Example 7.2: "Clangam" and "Ploratione" motives

Unlike the above recurring figures, verse 2 also includes a descending fourth on *cygni* in 2a, which recurs on *amara* in 2b. This descending fourth is placed at a very important rhetorical moment, highlighting the long syllable of *cygni* (swan) on D. This D will be the final note of the song, but that is not clear yet, since there has not actually been a cadence on D.

The *exordium* continues into verse 3b, when the text changes in to the first person, handing the narration over to the swan himself (Example 7.3):

Example 7.3: *Planctus cygni*, strophe 3b, first line

As the narration continues, these melodic "seeds" are cultivated into a number of rhetorical flowers. The three descending notes of *filii* recur in different guises throughout the piece; indeed, some variant of it is found in literally every single versicle. In Example 7.4, we see several examples of the repetition, amplification, and abbreviation of the entire *clangam filii* figure. In verses 2 and 7, the figure is transposed; in verses 5 and 7, it is amplified; in verses 8 and 9, it is abbreviated; and verses 5, 7, and 8 include exact or varied repetition.

Example 7.4: Rhetorical treatment of "Clangam filii" figure

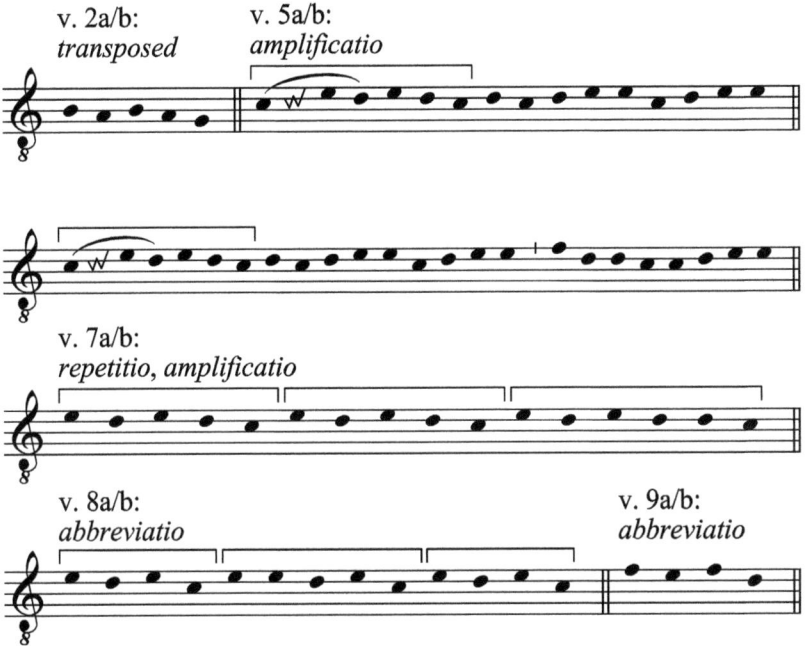

Both amplification and abbreviation are important rhetorical devices and are discussed at length in treatises such as Geoffrey of Vinsauf's *Poetria Nova*. Here he speaks of *amplificatio*:

> Although the meaning is one, let it not come content with one set of apparel. Let it vary its robes and assume different raiment. Let it take up again in other words what has already been said; let it reiterate, in a number of clauses, a single thought. Let one and the same thing be concealed under multiple forms—be varied and yet the same.[10]

---

10. Geoffrey of Vinsauf, *Poetria Nova*, 24.

The descending *filii* third is also treated with *amplificatio* in a number of places, as shown here in Example 7.5:

Example 7.5: *Amplificatio* on "filii"

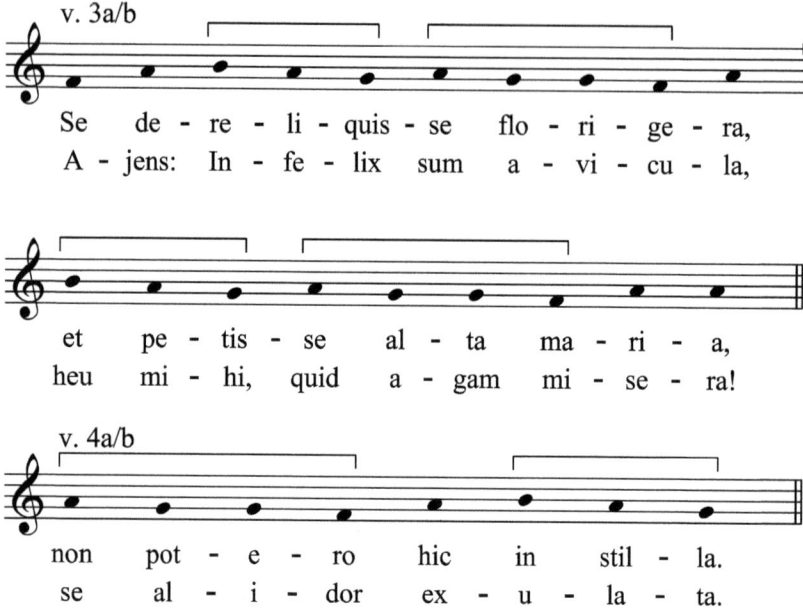

Abbreviation, as was previously shown in Example 7.4, is the opposite of *amplificatio*:

> Compress it in accordance with the following formula. Let *emphasis* be spokesman, saying much in few words. Let *articulus*, with staccato speech, cut short a lengthy account. The *ablative*, when it appears alone without a pilot, effects certain compression. Give no quarter to *repetition*. Let skillful implication convey the unsaid in the said. ... Let the craftsman's skill effect a *fusion of many concepts in one*, so that many may be seen in a single glance of the mind. By such concision you may gird up a lengthy theme; in this bark you may cross a sea.[11]

(Interestingly, the model of abbreviation that Geoffrey offers, while not identified by Geoffrey, is based on a song: "Advertite, omnes populi," part of the eleventh-century lyric collection known as the Cambridge Songs.)[12]

---

11. Geoffrey of Vinsauf, *Poetria Nova*, 40–41.
12. Cambridge University Library MS Gg.v.35. A complete text edition of the Cambridge Songs can be found in Jan Ziolkowski, ed. and trans., *The Cambridge Songs (Carmina Cantabrigiensia)*, Garland Library of Medieval Literature 66 (New York: Garland, 1994). Vinsauf shows off his skill at *abbreviatio* by condensing this very lengthy Latin sequence into one short paragraph.

The *ploratione* motive, three notes ascending stepwise followed by a descending leap, is also found throughout the piece. In some cases, such as Example 7.6 below, it is extended by the descending three-note motive or some variant thereof:

Example 7.6: "Ploratione" motive

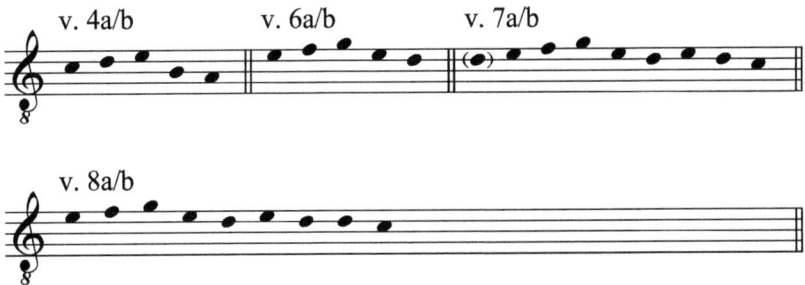

In the example cited from verse 7 above (Example 7.6), we see that the *ploratione* motive also overlaps with something new: a four-note figure ascending from D to G, the highest pitch in the song so far. This phrase is the first to begin on a D, and occurs after a series of melodic phrases in verses 5 and 6 in which D is used repeatedly as a pivot point between C and E. Verse 7b is the point at which the narration of the text changes back into the third person and is the beginning of the *conclusio*. The swan ends his prayer and begins to contemplate silently and recover his strength, and the sun rises: "Rejoicing, it was then borne up among the high and accustomed stars of the clouds. / The sea's currents, which had been made agreeable and kind, were traversed." Meanwhile, despite beginning on the note D, the melody has headed off again into the territory of C and E, and continues there in verse 8, with D still occurring as a pivot point between the C and E, further building the suspense as the swan ascends into the heavens and then dives down through the waves.

As we see in Example 7.7 below, Verse 9 begins with the full expression of the new phrase that was promised to us in verse 7: an arc-shaped melody on the words *Dulcimode cantitans*, "sweetly singing."

This time the second half of the phrase does not echo the *ploratione* figure, as in verse 7, but descends stepwise through the interval of a fourth, recalling the descending *cygni/amara* fourth in verse 2, and provides the convincing cadence on D that was promised in the melodic figure D–E–F–G–F–E–D that begins verse 9 at *Dulcimodi cantitans*. Overlapping with this is a descending stepwise third F–E–D on *cantitans*, reiterated in verse 7b on *omnia*, which echoes the *filii* figure (although it moves semitone-tone rather than tone-tone). It is repeated again, only to overlap with the abbreviated *clangam filii*

Example 7.7: *Planctus cygni*, verse 9

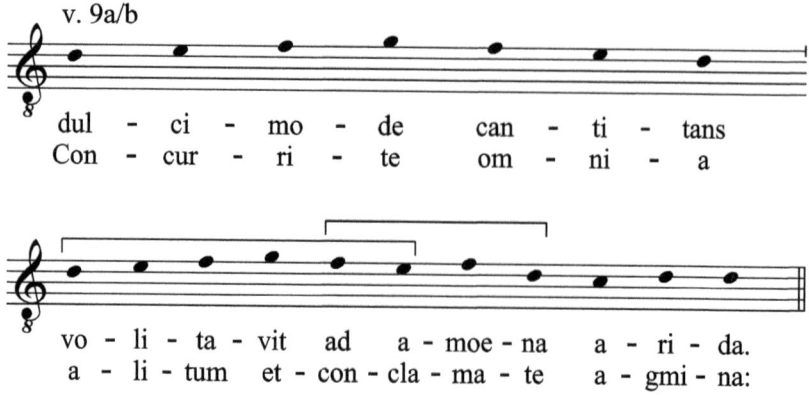

(lament) theme. The swan is "singing sweetly," has "traversed the sea's currents," and has flown "to welcome dry ground," but let us not forget the metaphorical meaning of the term "swansong." Is there another deeper meaning to *penetrabatur marium flumina*? Does our swan live or die? Perhaps it does not matter, since in either case it is still a poem about redemption.

It is worth noting at this point that the *Planctus cygni* does not fit easily into the system of church modes. (It is a very old piece, dating from the ninth century at the latest, and it is not liturgical, so it is not necessarily surprising that it does not conform completely to the modal system described in the tonaries.) Its structure, however, is quite clear, and based on a shift of range that is directly related to the text. The first four verses lie in a relatively low range from F to E, with cadences on G and A. The later verses fall in a considerably higher range, from high C to high G, with cadences on high E in verses 5–8 and on high D in the last two verses. Even taking into consideration the fact that pitch in the Middle Ages was relative and not constant, any singer would have to begin the piece in the low part of his or her range and move gradually higher, an effect that admirably matches the rhetoric of the poetry.

It would seem, then, that while the *Planctus* contains some melodic gestures characteristic of certain modes, the rhetorical aspect of the piece was far more important to the anonymous composer than the adherence to the rules of church mode. I would suggest, however, that regardless of modal assignation, there are a few hints that foreshadow an ending on the note D. The melodic figure D–E–F–G–F–E–D that begins verse 9 at *Dulcimodi cantitans*, in addition to providing a strong feeling of resolution, as noted above, is also identical to the last seven notes of the mode 2 *noeagis* intonation formula that resolves on D (see appendix: Mode Models, mode 2) even though the range of the *Planctus* would be highly unusual for mode 2. In addition, it is not far-fetched to hear the back-and-forth movement between C, E, and D in verses 5 and 6 (and later in 8) as a long *amplificatio* of the C–E–D cadence figure found frequently in the D modes and prominently featured in the cadence of the Latin intonation formula for mode 2 at *simile et huic*. Geoffrey of Vinsauf describes this rhetorical figure as *circuitio*, a subcategory of *amplificatio*. In this case, the *circuitio* between *c* and *e* points us toward the D, anticipating the resolution by way of delay:

> Do not unveil the thing fully, but suggest it by hints. Do not let your words move straight onward through the subject, but, circling it, take a long and winding path around what you were going to say briefly. Retard the tempo by thus increasing the number of words. This device lengthens brief forms of expression, since a short word abdicates in order that an extended sequence may be its heir.[13]

The concluding single verse of the *Planctus cygni* (Example 7.8) begins with the descending *filii* third, directly followed by the arc-shaped melody: *Regi magno sit gloria*, "Glory be to the great King." At *sit gloria* we end with G–F–E–D, the transposed descending fourth of *cygni/amara*; taken alone, the *gloria*'s descending stepwise third echoes the *filii* figure, followed by a rhetorical *repetitio* of the cadence on D at *Amen*.

Example 7.8: *Planctus cygni*, verse 10

Thus, through an examination of these intricately overlapping patterns, we discover that our planctus begins (*filii*) with its end (*cantitans, regi mag-, gloria*). Vinsauf tells us that the poet "travels the pathway of art" if he does not begin at the beginning:

> The material's order may follow two possible courses: at one time it advances along the pathway of art, at another it travels the smooth road of nature. Nature's smooth road points the way when "things and "words" follow the same sequence, and the order of occurrence. The poem travels the pathway of art if a more effective order presents first what was later in time, and defers the appearance of what was actually earlier. ... Deft artistry inverts things in such a way

---

13. Geoffrey of Vinsauf, *Poetria Nova*, 24.

that it does not pervert them; in transposing, it disposes the material to better effect. The order of art is more elegant than natural order and in excellence far ahead, even though it puts last things first.[14]

It should be clear at this point that monophonic song is far from "simple." What may appear to the novice as a meandering stream of noteheads actually contains a huge amount of information, and understanding the rhetoric of a piece helps us unlock that information and gain insight into how we may use improvisation or fluid composition in a piece such as this. The above analysis, while not exhaustive by any means, is sufficient to help us begin to make performance choices.

PERFORMANCE ISSUES: VOICES, INSTRUMENTS, AND ARRANGEMENTS

One of the first issues to be determined by an individual performer concerns the musical forces that will be used for the performance. While the *Planctus cygni* can be performed beautifully and powerfully a cappella, there is no reason to believe that a skillful performer could not also create an effective performance with the addition of an instrument. That said, there is one caveat: any musical material one adds to a medieval monophonic song other than doubling the melody—even reconfigured melodic material taken from the piece itself—will result in *newly composed or improvised music*. If one adds something, it is important to be clear about the reasons for doing so and to maintain an awareness of whether these additions contribute to the rhetoric of the piece or might possibly be working at cross-purposes. For example, one of the effective suspense-building rhetorical devices used in the *Planctus cygni* is the long amplification of motives around the notes *c* and *e* that lead to a strong feeling of resolution when the melody cadences on D, which ultimately proves to be the final note of the melody. If a player were to start right in at the beginning of the *Planctus* with instrumental motives that resolve on a D, it would work against the rhetoric of the song; in effect, one would be giving away the end of the story.

Another issue in the *Planctus* might be the use of a prelude, or a "beginning before the beginning." The first line of the *Planctus* is a beautifully crafted *exordium*, containing the melodic seeds of the most of the rest of the piece, and in fact the material in the beginning "contains the end," which would have certainly delighted Geoffrey of Vinsauf. Therefore, even if the piece is

---

14. Geoffrey of Vinsauf, *Poetria nova*, 18–19.

performed by voice and a small harp, for example, the harpist must think carefully about what he or she will add that will support that *exordium*. It may not need anything added to it; it is not necessary (or desirable) to fill every pause with instrumental sound. On the other hand, he or she may decide to add transitional phrases leading from one verse to the next, or, in purely practical terms, to use the instrument to provide a place for the singer to rest or breathe. The performer may be planning to begin this piece directly after another piece, and the so-called prelude may actually be a transition between the two.

Yet a third consideration might arise from regional characteristics. The *Planctus cygni* can be found in a variety of manuscripts from different regions. If you have decided to use historical Latin pronunciation from, say, the region around Limoges in France, will this regional specificity also affect your choice of instrumentation?

Performance Issues: An Example

Here is an example of a hypothetical performance of the first three verses of the *Planctus*. Our imagined performance situation includes a singer and a player of a bowed-string instrument, such as a vielle. The programming is such that the *Planctus* will be following a long meditative instrumental piece in *g* mode. Although the vielle part in Example 7.9 below was clearly composed in advance, the nature of the music is meant to be somewhat "fluid," meaning it would not have to be played exactly the same each time, especially in terms of rhythm and gesture. You will notice a recurrent use of the stepwise third *filii* motive, as well as the *ploratione* motive; and in the vielle part on verse 3, the *abbreviatio* of the *Clangam filii* motive as shown previously in Example 7.4.

Example 7.9 shows just a few of the endless possibilities for incorporating some of the rhetorical motives of the *Planctus* into a pre-planned but fluid arrangement. On the other hand, you may wish to experiment with a more improvisatory approach. For example, one could imagine a performance in which a long improvised instrumental based on the *Planctus* would be presented either just before or just after the sung version of it, as a related yet separate piece. As an exercise in preparation for that, I would suggest isolating individual patterns and motives from the piece and then experimenting in a practice session with the many ways in which the motives could be varied using the rhetorical figures in treatises such as the *Poetria Nova*. Example 7.10 shows one possibility, using the *alitis cygni* motive from verse 2a of the *Planctus cygni*.

Example 7.9: *Planctus cygni*, sample arrangement of first three verses

Practice 7.1 below narrates in stepwise fashion the process of using rhetorical analysis as an approach to the improvisation and arrangement of a medieval piece.

PLAYING POETRY: MELODIC *INVENTIO*

The title of this chapter, "Playing Poetry," comes from a story that the fiddler and medieval vielle virtuoso Shira Kammen related in the course of a 1998 radio interview for the early music radio program Harmonia.[15]

---

15. Shira Kammen, from the author's interview with Shira and the late John Fleagle for the radio program *Harmonia*, 1998. Like Shira, I am also indebted to Barbara Thornton, who planted the seeds of this chapter during several iterations of the same Vancouver Mediaeval Programme.

PLAYING POETRY (175)

Example 7.10: Rhetorical variations of "Alitis cygni" motive

Practice 7.1
RHETORICAL ANALYSIS

This practice is most effective when the object of the exercise is a piece that you are already planning to perform. You may use a score, neumed lyrics, or just a set of lyrics if you have committed the piece to memory already.

PRELIMINARY ANALYSIS

Step 1. If the piece is not in your native language, obtain an excellent translation of the text. This is of utmost importance; know the meaning of each individual word, whether your role in the performance will be vocal or instrumental. It is at this point that decisions must also be made about historical pronunciation; even Latin varied greatly in regional pronunciation.

Step 2. If you have not already done so, set an intention from the very beginning to memorize the piece: the melody, the text, and the figures and patterns from which you will draw. Instrumentalists should also memorize the words as much as possible, or at least know from memory the gist of what is being sung.

Step 3. Begin with a basic analysis of the structure and grammar of the poem: number of lines, number of syllables per line, rhyme scheme, and patterns of accent or length. It is not necessary to have extensive knowledge of the grammar of the original language to do this; even if you do not know what iambic meter is, for example, you would be able to recognize that the meter of a Latin poem was short-long, short-long, short-long (or, in an accented language such as English, accented-unaccented). Determine where rhymes occur, and how many syllables are in each line.

Step 4. Note whether or not the melodic phrases, cadence points, repeated melodic patterns, and other characteristics appear to be determined by the structure of the text. (This may not always be the case.)

Step 5. Analyze the poem in terms of the rhetorical divisions of *inventio* outlined above. Is there a clear *exordium*, or introduction? Where does the main *narratio* begin? A lyric text can have a *narratio* as well as a text that contains a narrative storyline. Is there a clear *conclusio*? Is this the type of text that might contain some aspects of *divisio, confirmatio,* or *confutatio*?

Step 6. Examine whether your decisions about the rhetorical *inventio* of your piece are based on the text alone, or if the music changes also.

Step 7. Find a resource, such as Geoffrey of Vinsauf's *Poetria Nova*, that explains the different kinds of rhetorical ornaments (amplification, repetition, abbreviation, comparison, opposition, and so forth). Analyze the musical content of your piece for melodic motives and figures, and look for ways in which they have been amplified, abbreviated, repeated, decorated, elaborated, shortened, or otherwise manipulated. Write them down; compare them and analyze them.

NOW YOU WILL APPLY YOUR RHETORICAL ANALYSIS TO PERFORMANCE:

Step 8. If your chosen piece is very simple and strophic, more of the rhetorical content may be reflected in the text than in the melody. A simple melody need not hamper the expression of the rhetorical power of the text; this is part of the singer's art.[16] Inquire into the musical elements that are not on the page, but would serve the rhetoric and expression of the text, and might therefore create an engaging

---

16. A chart of Quintilian's "tones of voice" and the characteristics of delivery that he prescribes for delivering specific emotions can be found in Judy Tarling, *The Weapons of Rhetoric* (St. Albans, UK: Corda Music, 2005), 111.

> performance: dynamics, tempo, gesture, or even judicious ornamentation or variation of the simple melody. If you are playing an instrument, consider melodic figures or gestures that would express the rhetoric without interfering with the performance of the text.
>
> Step 9. Consider whether you will play/sing the melody, add preludes, interludes, transitional passages, and so forth. Decisions made in the previous step may be helpful if you are inventing an instrumental accompaniment.
>
> Step 10. By now you have the elements of a predetermined musical plan or structure. Which aspects will be variable from one performance to another, and how much will consist of "fluid composition" or outright improvisation? If you are going to include variable material (improvisation), it is advisable to memorize a set of figures and patterns from which you will draw and to know exactly at what point in the piece you may utilize them. This will prevent you from meandering randomly if you lose your focus for any reason in performance.

Years before the interview, Shira had attended a medieval music workshop taught by the ensemble Sequentia at Vancouver Early Music's Mediaeval Programme, where the instrumentalists and instructors were engaged in a discussion of strategies for accompanying singers. Barbara Thornton had presented the instrumentalists with the text of a poem—no notation was offered—and, after a discourse about the poem's prominent characteristics, had asked Shira to "play the poem." This event, Shira said, "completely changed" the way she approached the accompaniment of medieval song.

On first hearing, the instruction "play the poem" sounds a bit like a koan, the Zen term for one of those infamous mind puzzles such as "What is the sound of one hand clapping?" A directive like "play the poem" has very much the same intent; it forces our mind to jump outside the box. Above all, it forces the instrumentalist to engage with the poem's meter, structure, rhyme, and meaning, instead of jumping directly to playing the melody. The responsibility for the musical interpretation of the text is thus shared by both the singer and the instrumentalist, facilitating a unified approach to the piece and a vastly more integrated final performance. It is far more effective, and far more satisfying for the instrumentalist than being relegated to modal meandering, playing phrases that have nothing to do with the singer's phrasing, making lovely flourishes on unimportant words, and in general feeling like a hindrance instead of a help. The "play the poem" method develops and informs both our process of "oral composition" and our process of creating a performance of a medieval song that already has an extant melody.

There are a number of medieval lyric poems that do not have an extant melody, even though it is quite probable that they were sung—a veritable invitation to *inventio*. It is, of course, possible to simply choose a mode or key and some melodic formulas and throw together a melody to which one could fit the syllables of the text. But if we are willing to engage closely with the text, internalize its meaning, explore what our own personal relation or reaction to it might be, and ultimately memorize it, I suggest that our performance ultimately will be more convincing. It will result in more direct communication between the performer and the audience. It will be—dare I say—more authentically *our* music.

A number of medieval music performers have created new melodies for medieval lyric. By way of example, I will relate my own process of setting "Cum polo Phoebus" (see Table 7.3), a Latin poem, or *metra*, from Boethius's *Consolation of Philosophy*, a work that was well known in the Middle Ages and one of the first books to be translated from Latin into Middle English (by Chaucer). Most of the Boethian *metra* from the *Consolation* can be found in medieval sources with added neumes; indeed, these neumed *metra* are the subject of a scholarly *tour de force* by Sam Barrett of the University of Cambridge.[17] "Cum polo Phoebus" is one of the few Boethian *metra* for which a neumed version has not been found.[18]

Assuming that one does not speak conversational Latin on a daily basis, how then to engage with this text? Here is a suggested set of exercises that incorporate processes that will help a performer come up with a melody for the poem but, more importantly, engage the memory not just through repetition but through exploring sound, structure, grammar, rhetoric, and meaning, and facilitate the process of memorization. This process is delineated in Practice 7.2, which for the purposes of this exercise I have broken into several separate parts with added commentary.

You may need a Latin dictionary for some of the above steps; most translations are not word for word. It is not completely necessary to understand all the declensions and conjugations; you are looking for images, meanings, emotions. The verbs in our Boethius poem include *spargere* (scatter, spread), *coeperit* (begin), *inrubit* (redden), *spiret* (breathe, blow), *radiat* (radiate), *concitat* (stir up), *crede* (believe). The nouns include *quadrigis* (chariot), *lucem* (light), *stella* (star), *zephyr* (breeze), *spinis* (thorn), *mare* (sea), and *aquilo* (north wind).

---

17. See Sam Barrett, *The Melodic Tradition of Boethius' De consolation philosophiae in the Middle Ages*, 2 vols., Monumenta Monodica Medii Aevi, Subsidia, 7 (Kassel, Germany: Bärenreiter, 2013). Barrett has also collaborated with Benjamin Bagby and Sequentia, who have engaged with the Boethian *metra* as part of their Lost Songs Project. It is worth noting that it was Benjamin Bagby's setting of the Boethian *metrum Felix qui potuit* on Sequentia's CD *Lost Songs of a Rhineland Harper* (Deutsche Harmonia Mundi 58939, 2004) that inspired me to try my hand at setting "Cum polo Phoebus," a few years before Barrett's work was published. Reading Barrett's work after going through the process of setting "Cum polo Phoebus" myself was revelatory, and provided additional invaluable insights regarding poetics, structure, and performance.

18. I quite consciously attempted to find a poem that to my knowledge had not been set to music or recorded previously, in an attempt to make sure that I was not unconsciously remembering someone else's melody. (This is also part of the reason why the *incipit* of my melody, as we will see, stays very close to the Hypodorian "Secundum autem" Latin formula; I am quite sure I did not invent that!)

Table 7.3. "CUM POLO PHOEBUS"

Latin Text and syllable count	Translation [a]
Cum polo Phoebus roseis quadrigis (11)	When Phoebus from his roseate car
Lucem spargere coeperit, (8)	Begins to spread his light across the sky
Pallet albentes hebetate vultus (11)	His overwhelming fires
Flammis stella prementibus. (8)	Dim the white faces of the paling stars.
Cum nemus flatu zephyr tepentis (10)	Warmed by the west wind's gentle breath
Vernis inrubit rosis, (7)	The groves blush pink with roses in the spring;
Spiret insanum nebulosus auster: (11)	Let but the stormy south wind madly blow
Iam spinis abeat decus. (8)	And the thorns are stripped of their loveliness.
Saepe tranquillo radiat sereno (11)	Sometimes the sea gleams calm, serene,
Immotis mare fluctibus, (8)	unruffled;
Saepe ferventes aquilo procellas (11)	Sometimes the north wind whips up raging storms
Verso concitat aequore. (8)	And overturns the sea.
Rara si constat sua forma mundo, (11)	Earth's beauty seldom stays,
Si tantas variat vices, (8)	But ever changes.
Crede fortunis hominum caducis, (11)	Go on, then: trust in the passing fortunes,
Bonis crede fugacibus. (8)	The fleeting pleasures of men!
Constat aeterna positumque lege est (12)	It is decreed by firm, eternal law
Ut constet genitum nihil. (8)	Nothing that comes to be can firm remain.

[a] Text and translation from Boethius, *Tractates and The Consolation of Philosophy*, Loeb Classical Library 74, trans. H. F. Stewart, E. K. Rand, and S. J. Tester (Cambridge, MA: Harvard University Press, 1973).

Practice 7.2a

PLAYING POETRY

Step 1. Recite aloud both the original text of the poem and its translation. This is best undertaken as a contemplative exercise, with mindful attention given to the meaning of each word. It is very important at this stage for both singers and instrumentalists to know or find out the exact pronunciation of the text, so that both know where to place emphasis, length, and stability in each line.

Step 2. Grammatical analysis:
  a. How many lines are in the poem? Does it have a symmetrical structure?
  b. How many syllables per line does it have?
  c. What is the poetic meter? Even if you don't know the technical names for the different meters, you can find patterns of accent, emphasis, and length.
  d. Do the lines rhyme? What poetic devices do you find: assonance, alliteration, metaphor?
  e. Identify the verbs, and then the nouns. Are there words that create a particularly vivid image or feeling?

The syllable count in "Cum polo Phoebus" alternates, mostly 11/8/11/8. This is a combination of two classical meters: Sapphic (eleven syllables) and Glyconic (eight syllables).[19] These meters are also associated with patterns of long and short syllables. In general, Sapphic meter has the following arrangement of long and short syllables:

long short   long short   long short short   long short   long short

Glyconic meter has eight syllables, arranged in the following way:

long   long   long   long short short   long short

"Cum polo Phoebus" is also a *stichic poem*, meaning that it is not divided into stanzas. If this had been a notated *metrum*, the neumes would have given us clues about the way in which the poetry had been rendered musically, but we do not have that information. However, if we take a look at the meaning and syntax of the text, as we will see in the following analysis, we will notice that the eighteen lines seem to suggest groupings of four lines, resulting in the pattern 4–4–4–4–2. Each group of four lines gives an example of the constantly changing state of both nature and fortune. In fact, the imagery in each group even matches up with the four elements: 1–4, fire; 5–8, air; 9–12, water; and 13–16, earth, with the last two lines acting as a general platitude that can be drawn from the examples given. In the process that follows, the above information is combined with a deeper contemplation of the text's meaning and rhetorical structure to guide us to a musical realization of the poem.

Practice 7.2b

Step 3. Put the poem in your own, idiomatic words, in whatever native language is most comfortable for you. Do not try to match the translation exactly; do this for meaning and feeling, not literal duplication of each word. Then read your own version of the text aloud.

Reading aloud slowly and meditatively helps one internalize the meaning of a poem or any text; in fact, this was the basis for the medieval monastic technique of *lectio divina*, in which a scriptural text would be learned and internalized

---

19. The first line of "Cum polo Phoebus" is somewhat anomalous. Barrett says, "The opening Sapphic line of ["Cum polo Phoebus"] is implausibly divided even for a metre that resists parsing." Barrett, *Melodic Tradition*, 1:100.

through a four-step process of reading aloud meditation, prayer, and contemplation (*lectio, meditatio, oratio, contemplatio*). In the field of contemplative education, this "deep reading" process has also been secularized in various ways.[20] In the case of our practice exercise, we might read the text aloud, sit in silence, internally inquire into our experience of the text's effect and meaning, and then slowly do the exercise cited above, putting the song into our own idiomatic words. By way of example, here is the "Cum polo Phoebus" text in my own words.

> When the sun god in his rosy chariot
>   Starts to spread the light of day across the sky,
> The light of that overwhelming fire
>   dims the light of the star-faces.
> The western breezes blow, and warm
>   The spring groves, and pink roses bloom;
> But when the storms blow in from the south,
>   The lovely blooms are stripped off the thorns.
> Sometimes the sea shines
>   Calm and peaceful and undisturbed;
> Sometimes storms rise up with the north wind
>   And churn up the waves.
> The beauty of the earth is impermanent.
>   And it is always changing.
> You may believe in passing fortune,
>   And in the transient pleasures humans value;
> But the law of karma says
>   Nothing that arises is permanent.

Do not hesitate to make it personal. Boethius said nothing about "karma," but since that word is part of my own everyday lexicon, it helps me remember the meaning of the poem's punch line.

Practice 7.2c

Step 4. Having put the poem into your own words, try to manipulate your own words to match the structure of the poem (syllable count, vowel sound, rhyme, or any combination of the above).

Read it aloud.

---

20. See "Lectio Divina" on the website of the Association for Contemplative Mind in Higher Education, http://www.contemplativemind.org/practices/tree/lectiodivina, accessed August 1, 2015. See also their "Tree of Contemplative Practices." Many are applicable to musical study and performance.

The above step allows us to deeper engage with the poem's meaning and combine our words with elements of the poem's own grammatical characteristics. It does not have to be great poetry; this is a tool for memory enhancement, and also for feeling the "music" of the poem:

When the sun god in his rosy chariot (11 syllables)
   Spreads daylight all across the sky, (8)
The light spreading from that overwhelming fire (11)
   dims the light of the star-faces. (8)
The gentle breath of the western breezes warms (11)
   The spring groves, and pink roses bloom; (8)
But when the storms blow madly in from the south, (11)
   Lovely blooms are stripped off the thorns. (8)
Sometimes the sea shines calm, serene, and peaceful (11)
   And undisturbed; but then sometimes (8)
The north wind causes raging storms to arise, (11)
   Whipping and churning up the waves. (8)
The beauty of the earth is impermanent, (11)
   And always in a state of change. (8)
You may think that you can trust fortune, and the (11)
   Transient pleasure humans value; (8)
Nothing that arises remains permanent. (11)
   The law of karma thus decrees. (8)

Practice 7.2d

Step 5. The next step is to identify rhetorical elements in the original poem. Is there a clear *exordium*, or introduction? Where does the main *narratio* begin? Is there a clear *conclusio*? *Divisio, confirmatio,* or *confutatio*? Look for rhetorical ornaments: amplification, repetition, abbreviation, comparison, opposition, and so forth. (Note that this is the same as Practice 7.1, Step 5.)

Boethius presents this poem in the context of a larger work, *The Consolation of Philosophy*, that contains a number of poems as well as a long dialogue between Philosophy (Wisdom, Sophia) and Boethius himself. In a sense, the *exordium* takes place in the prose that precedes the poem; alternately, one could consider the first verse as a kind of *exordium* that sets up the pattern of contrasting images that will follow in all the subsequent verses.

Cum polo Phoebus roseis quadrigis
   Lucem spargere coeperit,

> Pallet albentes hebetate vultus
> > Flammis stella prementibus.

Philosophy strengthens the argument by narrating (*narratio*) two more examples. This can also be viewed as a *confirmatio*, since she is building the argument with additional corroboration:

> Cum nemus flatu zephyr tepentis
> > Vernis inrubit rosis,
> Spiret insanum nebulosus auster:
> > Iam spinis abeat decus.
> Saepe tranquillo radiat sereno
> > Immotis mare fluctibus,
> Saepe ferventes aquilo procellas
> > Verso concitat aequore.

She then refutes all possible arguments (*confutatio*):

> Rara si constat sua forma mundo,
> > Si tantas variat vices,
> Crede fortunis hominum caducis,
> > Bonis crede fugacibus.

"Go ahead," says Philosophy, "believe in fortune and fleeing pleasures of men; I have just given three examples that prove that earth's beauty seldom stays, but ever changes." The punch line comes with the conclusion: not only is it true that "nothing that comes to be can firm remain," but it is in fact an eternal law.

> Constat aeterna positumque lege est
> > Ut constet genitum nihil.

In a sense, the end is both conclusion and thesis, and is the underlying message of each example from nature that he cites (sky, wind, seas, earth).

The progression from rhetorical analysis to the construction of a melody is next, the steps are summarized below in the continuation of Practice 7.2 below and then discussed in more detail, using as a model the process of creating a melody for "Cum polo Phoebus."

As poetic and rhetorical structure suggests possibilities for musical structure, we note once again that our analysis of "Cum polo Phoebus" reveals four sections encompassing four lines, with a final concluding statement containing two lines, yielding eighteen lines in all. It is indeed very different from the previous example of the *Planctus cygni*; the music of a planctus follows sequence form (A BB CC DD, as in Table 7.1). A sequence typically does not have the same number of syllables in each verse, and the line length of the

> ### Practice 7.2e
>
> Step 6. Determine a structure for the melody. The structure of many medieval song forms and genres is defined by their poetic structure.
>
> Step 7. Choose a mode. In your work with the mode models, you may have developed your own subjective reactions to the sound and color of each mode; if so, it is perfectly acceptable to factor that into your choice.
>
> Step 8. Having chosen a mode, review its modal formulas and patterns (chapter 4). It is useful to alternate the singing or playing of the modal formulas with the recitation of your chosen text. Progress from reciting your chosen text to intoning it, trying different possibilities and avoiding the urge to edit as you go. Note if there are specific modal patterns that seem to "work" with your text, and consider how you might vary them.
>
> Step 9. It should now be possible to begin inventing the actual melody to which you will set your chosen text.

successive versicles often follows a pattern, with the verses getting gradually longer or following an arc-pattern with the longest verses in the middle. In contrast, Boethius's poem is very regular in terms of its structure and syllable count. That regularity is reflected in the text meaning, with each group of four lines embodying a metaphor for the concept of impermanence. The characteristics of the text therefore present a strong argument for setting "Cum polo Phoebus" as a strophic song. The last two lines, which cite an eternal law governing the phenomenon of impermanence, would therefore serve very well as a refrain, since it is relevant to each individual strophe.

Having determined a basic structure for the melody, the next step is to choose a mode. This is a subjective process. While it is true that multiple treatises in the Middle Ages and the Renaissance make reference to certain qualities associated with specific modes, we must exercise caution in making definitive claims for modal "affects." While personal observation suggests that there seem to have been preferences for certain modes when setting texts of a particular character, there is no consistency; a completely reliable scheme of associations is lacking; and among theorists there is no universal consensus.[21]

---

21. For an excellent and comprehensive discussion of the topic of modal affect and the association of different qualities to different modes, albeit focusing on a slightly later time period, see the chapter "Mode" in Anne Smith, *The Performance of 16th Century Music: Learning from the Theorists* (New York: Oxford University Press, 2011), 88–101.

In some cases, theorists were ascribing affects to specific modes on the basis of Greek treatises that attributed the names Dorian, Phrygian, Lydian, and Mixolydian to modes that had entirely different notes than the corresponding medieval church modes. On the other hand, if you as a practitioner of melodic *inventio* find certain modes to be evocative of specific feelings, follow your instinct; your personal reaction simply constitutes one more aspect of your own creative process.

This subjective process led me to use mode 2, Hypodorian, in creating the melody for "Cum polo Phoebus." I experience mode 2 melodies as having a certain amount of gravitas, as do the texts of many chants in mode 2; and the poem, while full of beautiful imagery, is a weighty text. Eternal truths such as "nothing is permanent" may help us to approach life's trials with some equanimity, but they are not easy truths. As a result, I felt that in singing Boethius's text in this mode would express the feeling I wished to convey. Example 7.11 shows the intonation formula, *neuma*, and Latin formula for mode 2:

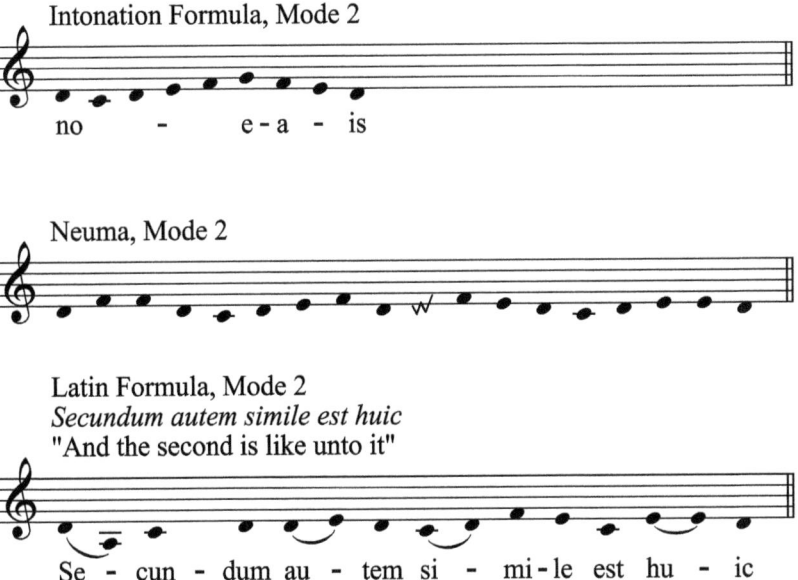

Example 7.11: Mode 2 formulas

It is not necessary when setting a medieval text to copy an intonation or Latin formula exactly, but it occurred to me that "Secundum autem" and "Cum polo Phoebus" have the same syllable count and accent pattern. Approximating that formula yielded the result shown below in Example 7.12:

Example 7.12: "Cum polo Phoebus," incipit

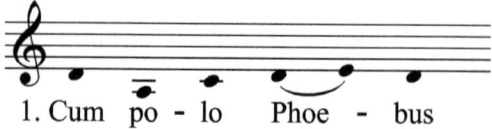

The above phrase seemed to work nicely with the beginning of all the "verses." Continuing, I kept in mind the cadential pattern E to D, and also the interplay between C and E that often characterizes a move toward the d in both modes 1 and 2. Beyond this, I admit that the creative process was somewhat instinctive; I sang the formulas to myself a few times, spoke the text a few times, and improvised in mode 2 using the syllables of the text, keeping in mind the word emphasis. The result is given below in Example 7.13.

Example 7.13: "Cum polo Phoebus," verse 1

For the refrain, I sought something that would set it off melodically from the rest—a strong rhetorical statement that would still feel integrated with the rest of the melody. Since it is not always required that a medieval song stay strictly within the confines of the theoretical ambitus, or range, of a mode, I decided to play with the A-C-D motive and begin the refrain with it, only up an octave. For the second line of the refrain, I would match the melody

I would create for the second line of the verse, but with a different cadence, as in Example 7.14.

Example 7.14: "Cum polo Phoebus," refrain

The following score (Example 7.15) is the final result. A more accurate representation that conveyed more information about phrasing, word accent, and stable and unstable gestures would be written in medieval *neumes*; however, for the sake of making this example accessible to as many readers as possible, I chose to use the "notehead" method that has become a widely-accepted way of conveying medieval non-metered notation. In an ideal world, I would teach it to another performer either in person or via a recording, so that he or she could learn it by ear.

From here, the individual performer must make a number of decisions in order to create their own unique performance: instruments, no instruments, added preludes or interludes or none, rhythmic variations, and so forth.

Many of the processes described in this chapter entail the creation of new music, either in the setting of the text or in the creation of an invented arrangement that will be either played exactly as written or used as a framework for fluid composition. There is absolutely no arguing the fact that "Cum polo Phoebus" is Boethius's poem set to my music. What, then, is "medieval" about any of this? For one thing, both texts used in this chapter are undeniably medieval, as is the melody of the *Planctus cygni* (although the rhythm and meter are not notated and therefore must be invented). We can add to that the conscious application of processes, formulas, and structures known to have been relevant to medieval music—rhetoric, mode, Latin language, poetry, formulaic melody—and, depending on the resources available to us, perhaps reproductions of historical instruments. That is what makes it medieval performance practice. Is a performance of the *Planctus cygni* that might arise from our process

Example 7.15: "Cum polo Phoebus," score

(continued)

Example 7.15: (*continued*)

Example 7.15: (*continued*)

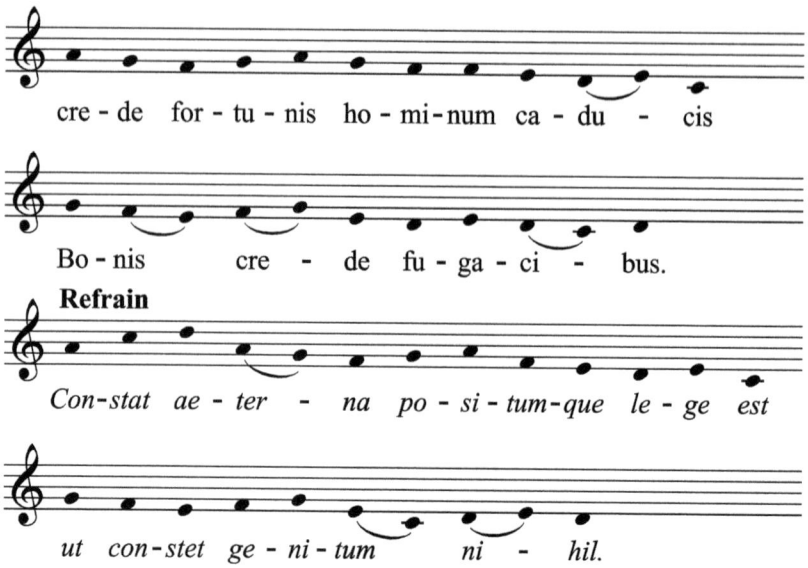

going to sound "the way it sounded" in the Middle Ages? We do not know; we have let go of that goal. Instead, we seek in "medieval performance practice" to create performances that contain specific medieval textual and/or musical content, employing processes and procedures deemed through research to be analogous in some way to the processes followed by the musicians who performed it in the Middle Ages. Those processes created new music in their time, and it also creates new music in our time: our music, created with historical imagination.

CHAPTER 8

The Long Memory

A Reflection on Teaching Medieval Music

Before the advent of recording technology, music was truly an impermanent and ephemeral art. It is difficult even to imagine how music was perceived and valued before it could be captured for repeated listening. No performance could ever be saved; after the last note, it was gone faster than a leaf in the wind. Unless you had a young Mozart scribbling down every note of your improvisation, it was gone as soon as you played it. Furthermore, Wolfgang's notes would only be "readable" to the select few who knew how to decipher them, and would only record a small part of the entire event. Even with the now-unimaginable memory capacity of our forebears, it would be impossible to "save to disk" an entire musical performance, complete with every nuance.

Thus, while we can hold in our hands an art object that was created in 500 BCE or gaze at a fresco painted by Giotto, in truth we have no idea what actual sequence of tones or intervals a twelfth-century vielle player may have sounded while accompanying a song. However, if we did not believe that we could to some extent learn to employ in our performances various aspects of the musical language extant at the time of the original poem or musical work, there would be no point in calling our activity "medieval performance practice." In that case, the arrangement and performance of medieval song would become another respected tributary of the equally valid and venerable stream of orally transmitted folk music, in which old material is incorporated into newly created music without the additional intention—additional baggage, some might say—of following some real or imagined historical process. Indeed, this would be a more straightforward task, by several orders of magnitude. So why do we engage with medieval performance practice, not to mention the additional challenge of trying to teach it? I believe that we do so because it speaks to us, because we still find it relevant and powerful, and because engaging with medieval music through an examination of the processes of its transmission and invention transforms how that music is regarded, heard, and understood within the "long memory" of the history of Western music.

THE OLD MODEL

The evolutionary model used for many years in the teaching of Western music history was not kind to medieval music. I vividly recall sitting in a classroom with some of my medieval music colleagues, preparing to play for a class of college freshmen while their professor gave them an introductory lecture about the "primitive beginnings of Western music." Fortunately, that paradigm of Western music history is no longer found in contemporary textbooks and certainly is not reflected in musical scholarship.

In decades of teaching music history and communicating with classical radio listeners via a syndicated early music program, however, I have found that the notion that Western music somehow evolved directly from "one line of chant melody" to Schoenberg, with various mutations along the way, is more prevalent than one might suppose. It is a misunderstanding that is strongly influenced, in my view, by received value judgments based on the presence or absence of functional harmony and the subsequent conscious rejection thereof. It is also a relic of a postcolonial equation of "orality" with the unsophisticated or rudimentary—an equation happily rejected by our contemporary standards, but which nevertheless implicitly and explicitly contributed long ago to the cultural gap between "classical" and vernacular musics that became embedded in Western culture. (For example, we still use terms such as "serious" music or "art" music to imply "not popular or vernacular music," as if popular and vernacular music were not serious and not art.)

It is no surprise, therefore, that it has only been in recent decades that we have come to appreciate that an understanding of the oral, aural, inventive, and improvisatory processes of medieval music leads to a more reasoned assessment of the musical sophistication of our ancient forebears, a better comprehension of their musical and rhetorical values, and a more accurate understanding of the place of medieval music in the continuum—the long memory—of both classical and vernacular Western music practice.

IMPLICATIONS FOR TEACHING

Embedded cultural value judgements that privilege one repertoire over another also influenced the development of music education in an earlier era. The paradigm that prevails in both conservatory and university music education still leans heavily toward classical music, despite the obvious fact that a parallel stream of orally transmitted music has always existed in the West. While ethnomusicology and now musicology both embrace oral and vernacular traditions, differing in methodology but frequently sharing subject areas, performance degree programs—with the exception of the jazz programs added in the last thirty years or so—still tend to emphasize and require the study and knowledge of music from the Western classical Baroque and common practice period forward.

Operating within this older paradigm, we have twentieth- and twenty-first-century music students and their teachers who grew up immersed in commercial music that favors vernacular and popular repertoire by a huge factor. The memory storehouse of the average young musician attending the aforementioned educational programs contains equal amounts of popular/vernacular and classical/"literate" music. Thus we can easily relate to the aspects of medieval music performance that involve invention, oral transmission, memory, and so on, but in the classroom that is not usually emphasized. Selected pieces of medieval music are instead presented in the context of later classical music, and often presented only in the first few weeks of the first semester of a music history sequence. Thus we not only give short shrift to five hundred plus years of repertoire but also present it in a vacuum separate from the process that was used to create it.

I suggest that it is completely reasonable and possible to present medieval music to students in a music history curriculum in a way that emphasizes process, just as we teach it to students of early music performance. Music history students can easily comprehend that the dearth of extant medieval instrumental music does not indicate that instruments were not used very often, or that the presence of four extant variants of a troubadour song does not imply that only one of them is "correct." Students can imagine two trouvères at a *puys*, a musical event that featured, among other things, contests to see who could spontaneously compose a better song. They can understand that in order for these trouvères to compete "on command" in this way, they must have completely internalized a virtual encyclopedia of idiomatic conventions of music and rhyme so well that they could compose spontaneously—in other words, so well that they could improvise, remember the fruits of their improvisations, and use the same basic melody, perhaps with minor variations, for the subsequent strophes, employing invention and memory at the same time. Examples of musical processes employed in the medieval era are not limited to monophonic music; as we have seen, even polyphonic pieces such as organum may have been composed in the memory and taught through a method of transmission that is quite different from the written method utilized by Western classical music today.[1]

All of this has ultimately led me to the view that many medieval music repertoires have more in common with vernacular musics than with later classical music. I use *vernacular* here in the context of music that has a process-oriented rather than an object-oriented conception of performance. The term has been most commonly associated with popular, folk, traditional, and world musics, in part because a majority of the world's vernacular music employs a process-oriented conception of performance and aesthetics that value the responsivity and immediacy such a conception makes possible. In contrast, later Western classical music has come to be characterized by an object-oriented conception of performance in which the "work" is presumed to be a fixed, static object, unchanging and unchangeable, requiring only "proper execution" by performers in order to be complete. Such a conception of music as a fixed, static object is alien to most of the world's vernacular traditions and, I have come to believe, to medieval music as well. In terms of the process of spontaneous invention, our two competing trouvères have much more in common with hip-hop musicians than with composers of romantic German *Lieder*.

This commonality with vernacular music has enormous implications for the way in which medieval music is taught. I advocate a pedagogical model that involves modes of oral transmission and mnemonic elements, in keeping with the mode of teaching as employed in the Middle Ages and, as we have seen, in many parallel world traditions. Many such pedagogical methods have been employed in medieval music workshops and in the course of private study ever since the revival of medieval music in the mid-twentieth century. However, an aural approach to learning and understanding medieval music is almost never brought into the realm of academic classrooms or university ensembles. This may be partly because musicians accustomed to Western learning paradigms must accept significantly contrasting teaching and learning styles in order to learn improvisation, which in turn constitutes a cognitive challenge (as we witness, for example, when Westerners decide to study an Eastern musical repertoire and are told that the first ten lessons will consist of sitting in front of the teacher and watching him play).

I have observed that students of both music history and performance practice are intrigued by the idea that most medieval instrumental music was "transmitted orally and understood aurally," that it tended to be the product of mostly non-literate musicians, and that a very high degree of musical skill

---

1. Berger, *Medieval Music and the Art of Memory*, 253–54.

and prodigious memory is present in the performance of many unwritten repertoires.[2] Indeed, a great deal of the rock, folk, jazz, and traditional music that they listen to on a daily basis falls into the same category. Placing medieval music into this context not only gives students a more accurate idea of its place in the long memory of music history but also allows for increased agency on the part of the performer, leads to an enhanced engagement in different learning paradigms, and increases motivation to include medieval music in their own performance repertoires.

PRACTICAL CONSIDERATIONS: THE CHALLENGE

I end this book, therefore, with a challenge for teachers of medieval music and a suggestion for further study and development. How can we devise teaching methods that are "in keeping with the mode of teaching as employed in the Middle Ages" and compatible with the restrictions placed on us by the prevailing academic paradigm? How do we persuade students to work from memory when both they and we ourselves are to some degree completely dependent on the written word (or score)? How do we "assess" students who are learning to improvise using data from their storehouse of memory when improvisation is, to some extent, incompatible with Westernized, standardized pedagogical models that require one "correct" answer? How do we deal with the inevitable time-management issue, since teaching via oral transmission and the demonstration-imitation-critique model also requires a lot of time?

The answers to the above questions will include more than just the synthesis of a series of methods such as I have offered here. It will be necessary to clearly describe and articulate our model to both academic colleagues and students. It is difficult, for example, to introduce an alternate teaching style into an established pedagogical paradigm unless one is prepared to explain the new paradigm and make persuasive arguments to colleagues and curriculum committees. Also, a new paradigm can be confusing to students; therefore, it is crucial that we go through a process similar to the one required by many academic institutions that require professors to articulate clearly the expected outcomes and methods of assessment for each class that they teach.

If we propose to incorporate aural learning, mnemonic techniques, and improvisatory processes into the teaching of medieval music, we will also need to come up with new and useful models for assessment. We must decide

---

2. For the phrase "transmitted orally and understood aurally," I am indebted to J. Peter Burkholder. It is a particularly useful construction, because "oral transmission" alone focuses on the person doing the transmitting, while "transmitted orally and understood aurally" includes the receiver in the process. Both are critical to the demonstration-imitation-critique paradigm described in chapter 2.

in concrete terms how much we can expect a student to absorb through demonstration-imitation and ear learning in two hours per week over the course of a sixteen-week semester (or a two-week workshop). We must decide, in an educational paradigm that assesses progress on the basis of increased technical skill and mandates the conferral of grades, how we will assess "invention" and improvisation, and how we will convey this assessment to a student in a way that does not arrest the creative process in its tracks. If the notion of "grading an improvisation" is repugnant, we must come up with a different model for assessment that can coexist within a paradigm that demands a graded system. If we can rise to this challenge, I believe that we may completely change the way medieval music is perceived and experienced by the average music student: not as something that is arcane and inaccessible, but as a vehicle for their own creativity, musical inventiveness, and historical imagination. To quote Bruce Haynes, "In striving for Authenticity, we are creating something of our own, modern through and through."[3] Barbara Thornton of Sequentia once put it this way:

> It is very *un*authentic to perform from the point of view which says, "I am now going to perform someone else's music from long, long ago, not my music." As an audience member I would want to say something like, "Well, go home and find out what your music is and then come back."[4]

Ultimately, the challenge I set for myself in the teaching of medieval music is to convey to students that a musical repertoire does not exist in a vacuum separate from the process used to create it; that understanding the processes used in the creation of medieval music is crucial to the long memory of Western music history; that the tools that the medieval performer used were integral to the repertoire that he or she performed; and that it is possible to explore the contents of the medieval musical storehouse and *add them to one's own*. Medieval music must be performed with a sense of ownership acquired through the process of its performance, rather than with the sense that we are in a museum looking into a glass case labeled "authenticity," something that we do not understand and are not allowed to touch. Yes, the resulting music is both old and new; it has arisen through the process of invention, and thus it has become ours.

---

3. Bruce Haynes, *The End of Early Music* (Oxford University Press, 2007), 227.
4. Thornton and Rosenwald, "Poetics as Technique," 287.

APPENDIX

Mode Models

(198) Appendix

MODE MODEL 1 (DORIAN)

Intonation Formula, Mode 1

no - a - no - e - a - ne

Neuma, Mode 1

Latin Formula, Mode 1
Primum quaerite regnum dei
"First seek ye the kingdom of God"

Pri - mum quae - ri - te reg - num de - i

Psalm tone, mode 1

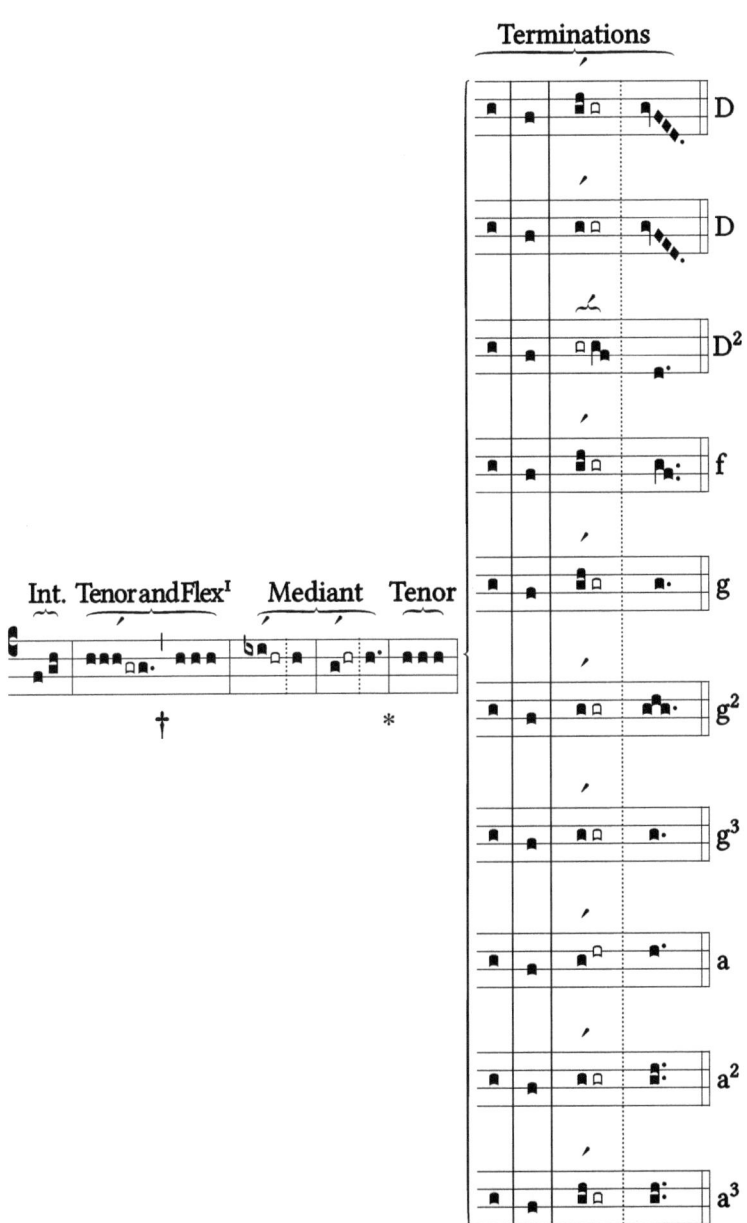

(200) *Appendix*

Example of plainchant in mode 1

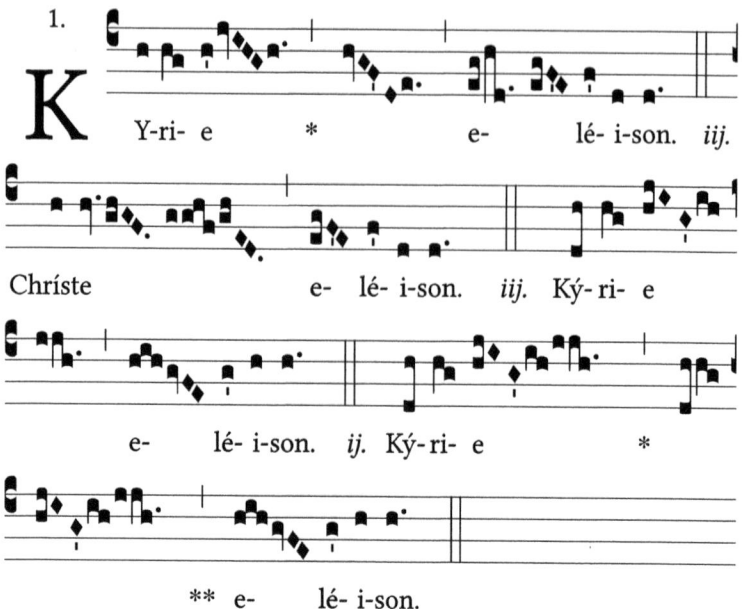

Appendix (201)

MODE MODEL 2 (HYPODORIAN)

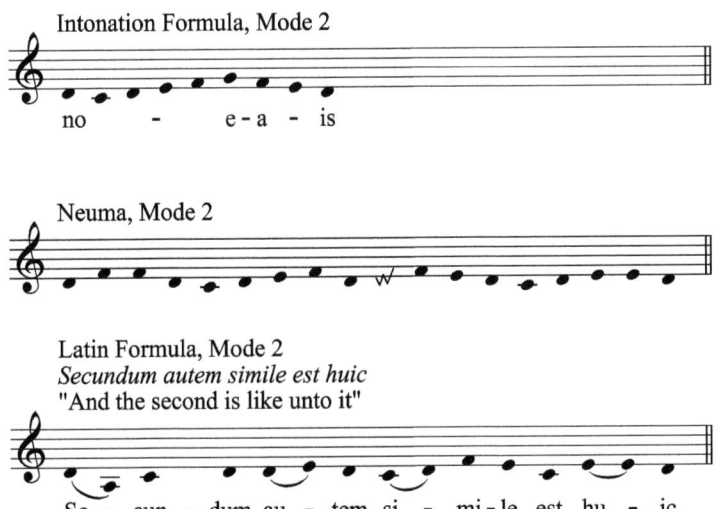

Intonation Formula, Mode 2

no — e-a — is

Neuma, Mode 2

Latin Formula, Mode 2
Secundum autem simile est huic
"And the second is like unto it"

Se - cun - dum au - tem si - mi - le est hu - ic

Psalm tone, mode 2

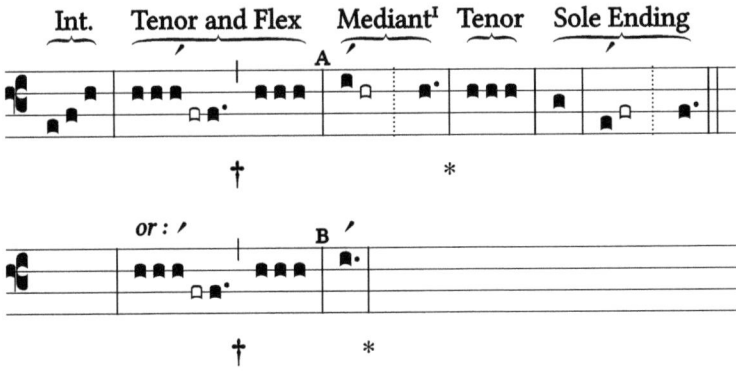

Example of plainchant in mode 2

Appendix (203)

MODE MODEL 3 (PHRYGIAN)

Intonation Formula, Mode 3

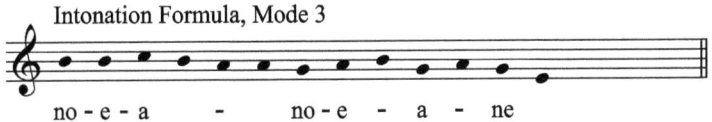

no - e - a   -   no - e - a - ne

Neuma, Mode 3

Latin Formula, Mode 3
Tertia dies est quod haec facta sunt
"Today is the third day since these things were done"

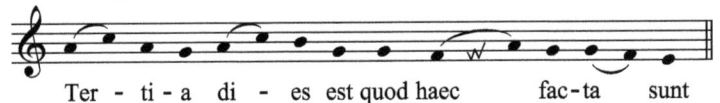

Ter - ti - a di - es est quod haec   fac-ta   sunt

Psalm tone, mode 3

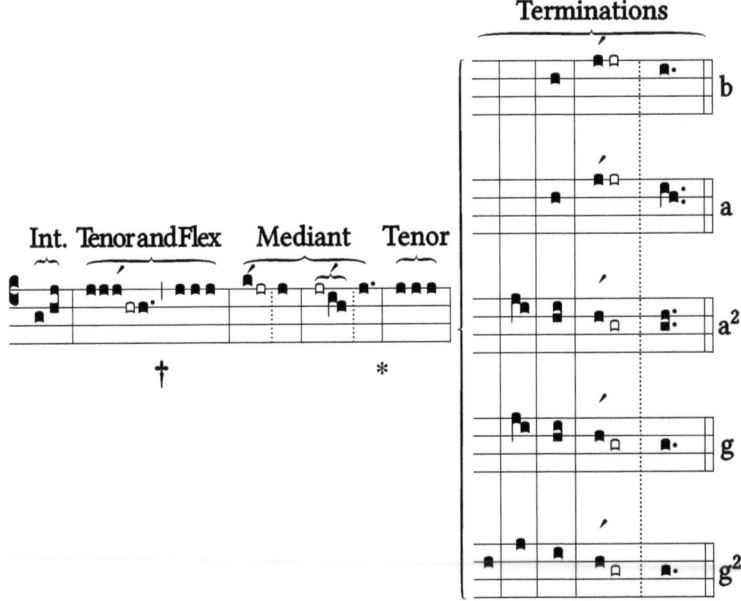

(204) Appendix

Example of plainchant in mode 3

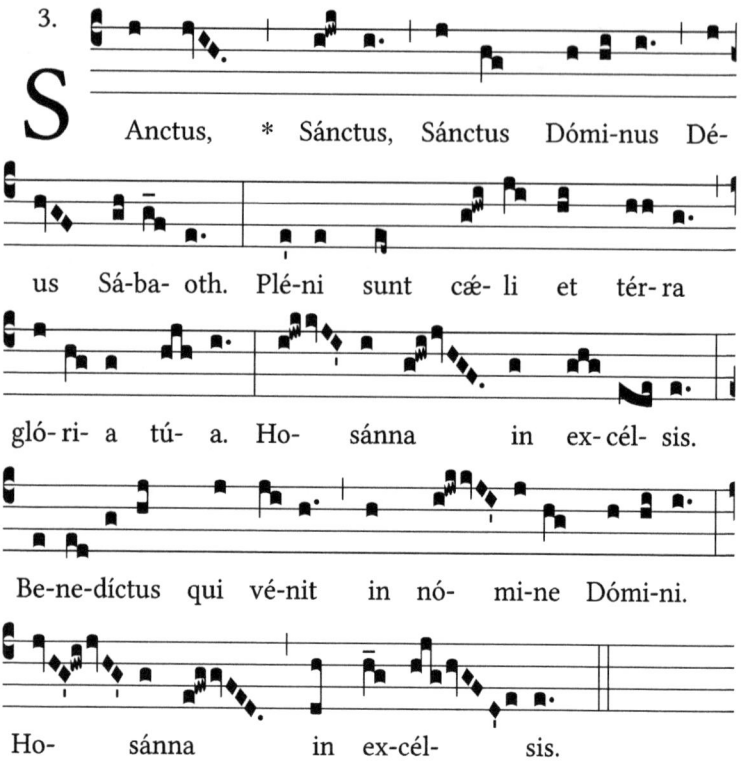

Appendix (205)

MODE MODEL 4 (HYPOPHRYGIAN)

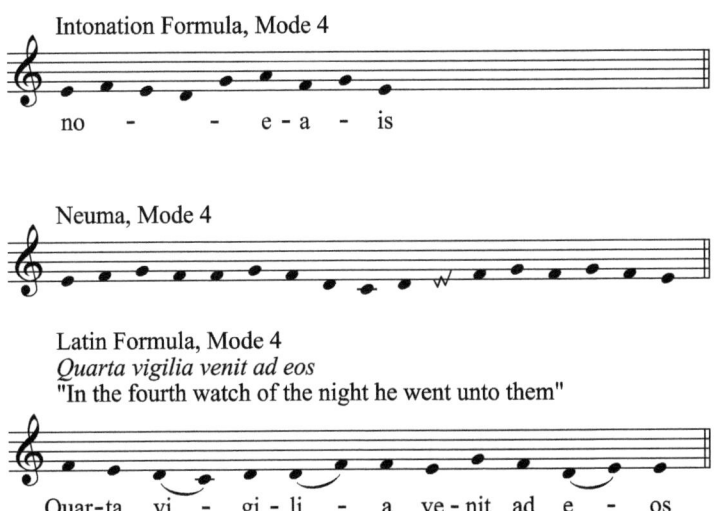

Intonation Formula, Mode 4

no - - e - a - is

Neuma, Mode 4

Latin Formula, Mode 4
Quarta vigilia venit ad eos
"In the fourth watch of the night he went unto them"

Quar-ta vi - gi - li - a ve - nit ad e - os

Psalm tone, mode 4

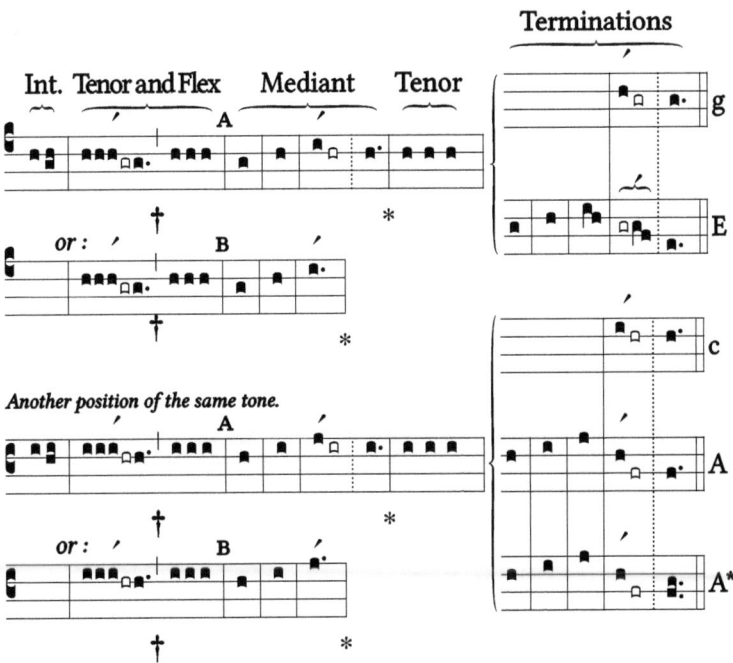

Another position of the same tone.

Example of plainchant in mode 4

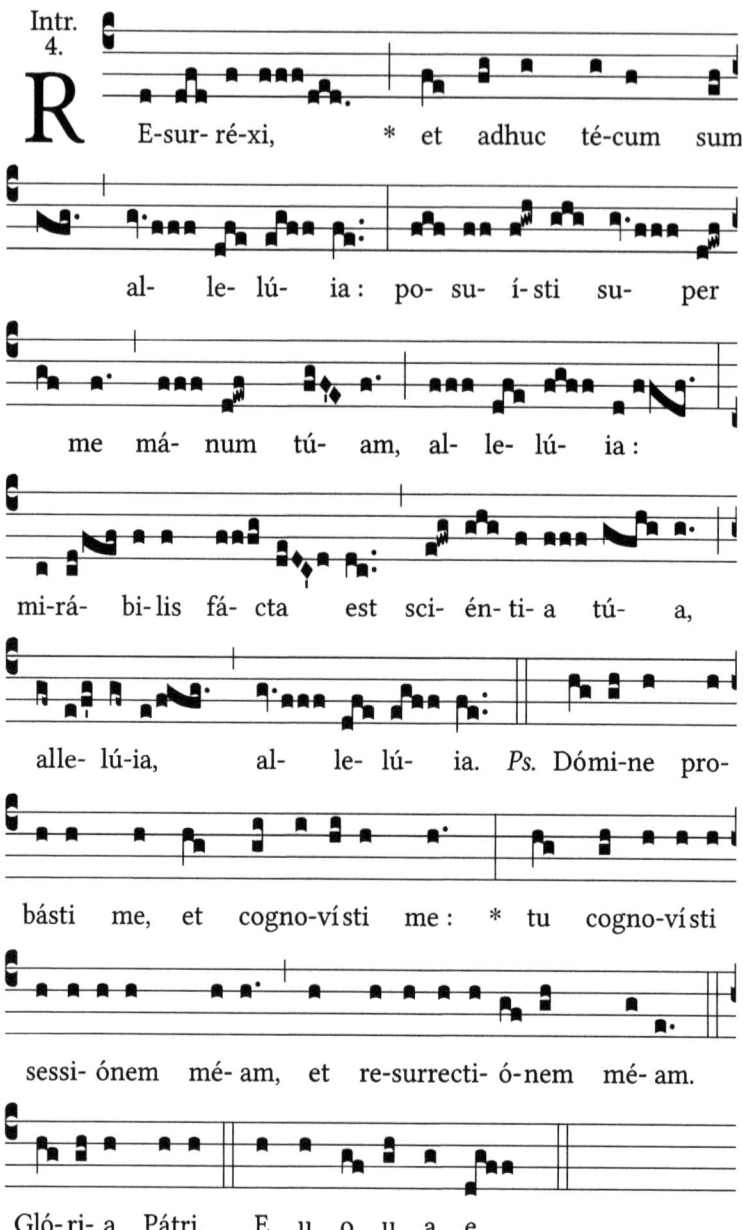

Appendix (207)

MODE MODEL 5 (LYDIAN)

Intonation formula and *neuma*, mode 5

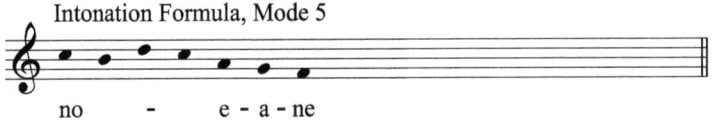

Intonation Formula, Mode 5

no - e - a - ne

Neuma, Mode 5

Latin Formula, Mode 5
Quinque prudentes intraverunt ad nuptias
"And the five wise ones went to the wedding"

Quin-que pru-den - tes in-tra-ve-runt ad nup-ti - as

Psalm tone, mode 5

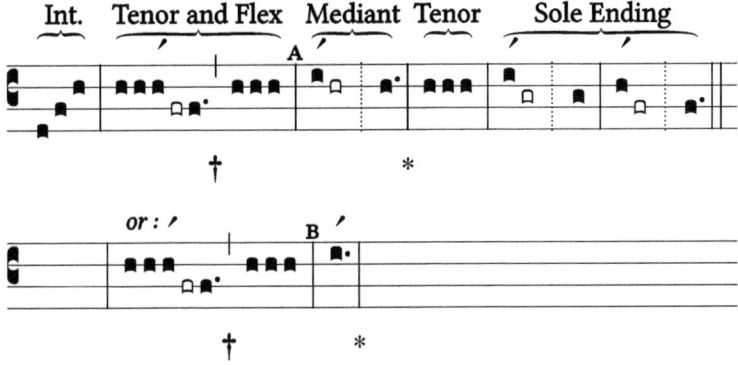

Example of plainchant in mode 5

Appendix (209)

MODE MODEL 6 (HYPOLYDIAN)

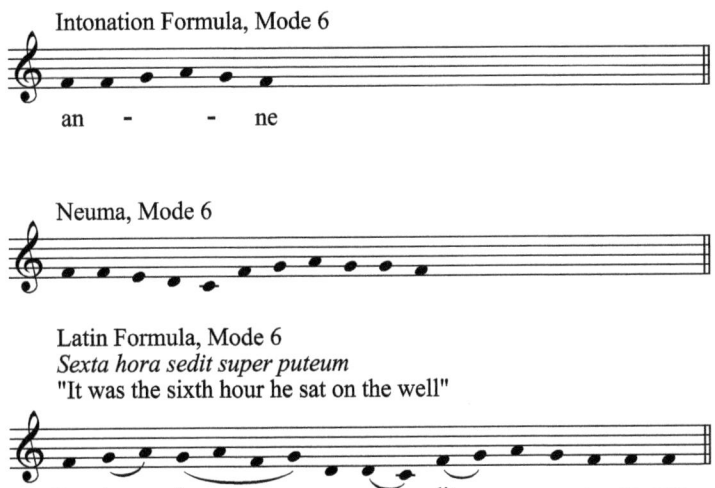

Intonation Formula, Mode 6

an - - ne

Neuma, Mode 6

Latin Formula, Mode 6
Sexta hora sedit super puteum
"It was the sixth hour he sat on the well"

Sex-ta ho - ra se - dit su-per pu-te-um

Psalm tone, mode 6

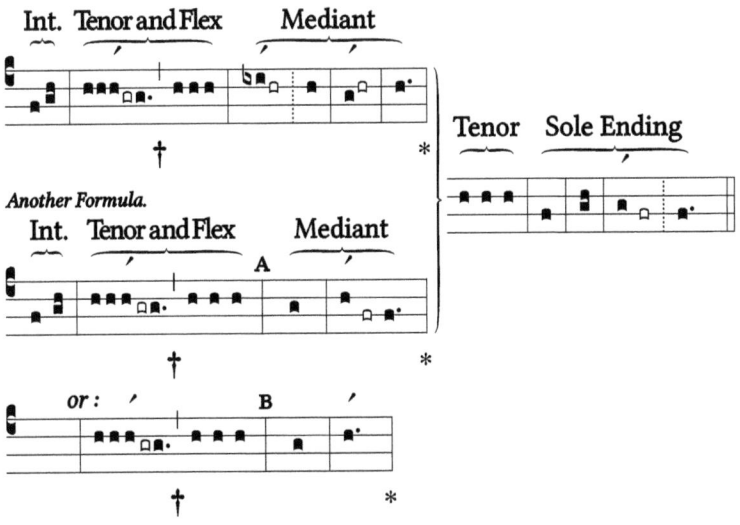

(210) Appendix

Example of plainchant in mode 6

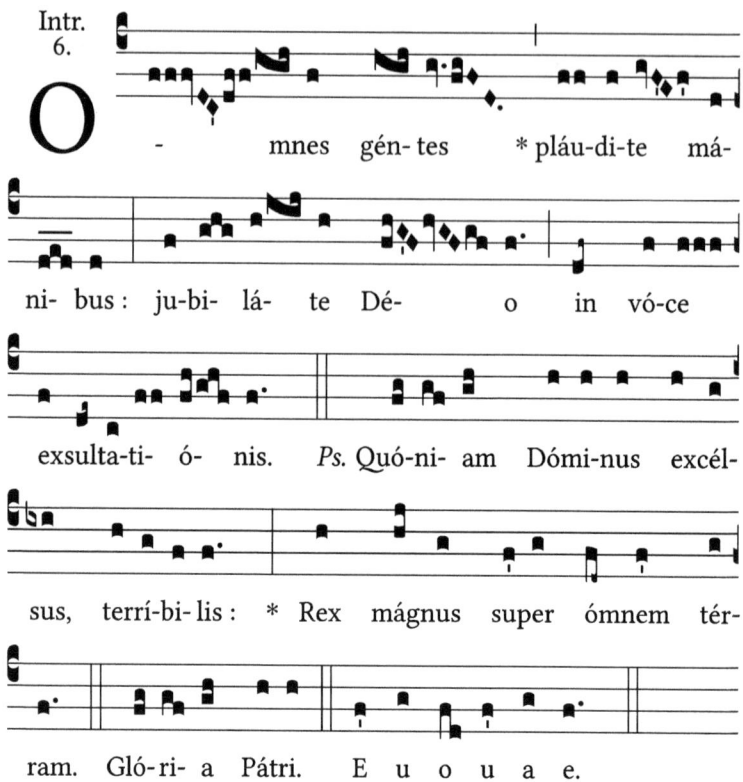

Appendix (211)

MODE MODEL 7 (MIXOLYDIAN)

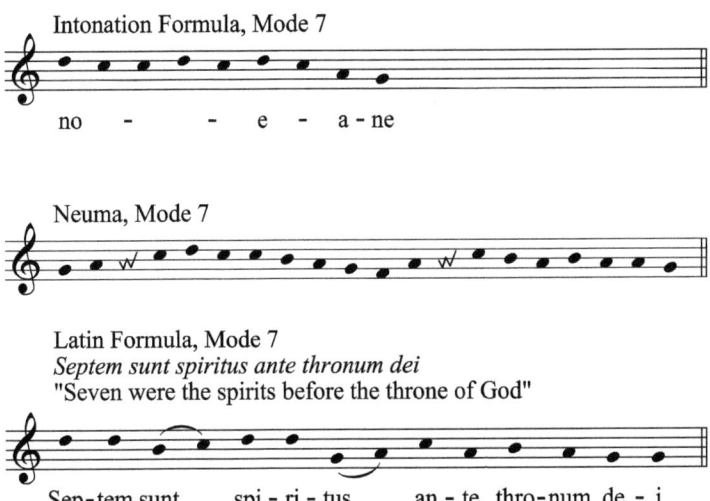

Intonation Formula, Mode 7

no - - e - a - ne

Neuma, Mode 7

Latin Formula, Mode 7
Septem sunt spiritus ante thronum dei
"Seven were the spirits before the throne of God"

Sep - tem sunt spi - ri - tus an - te thro - num de - i

Psalm tone, mode 7

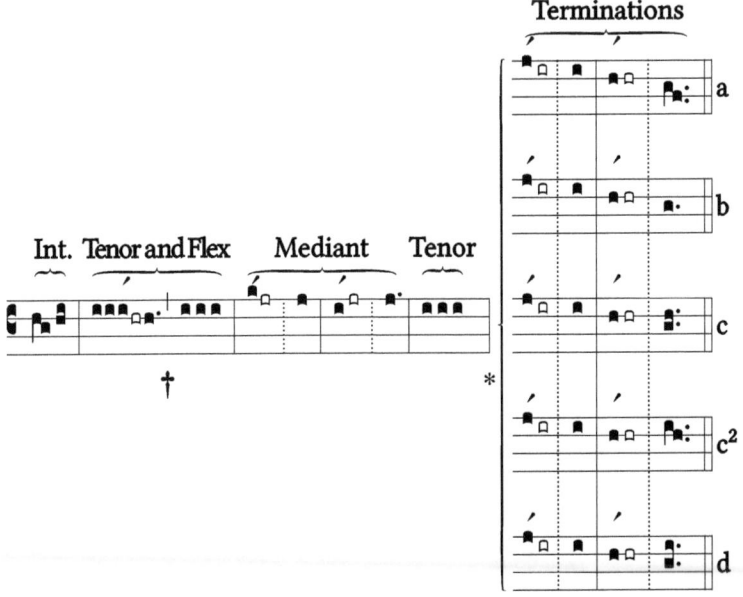

Example of plainchant in mode 7

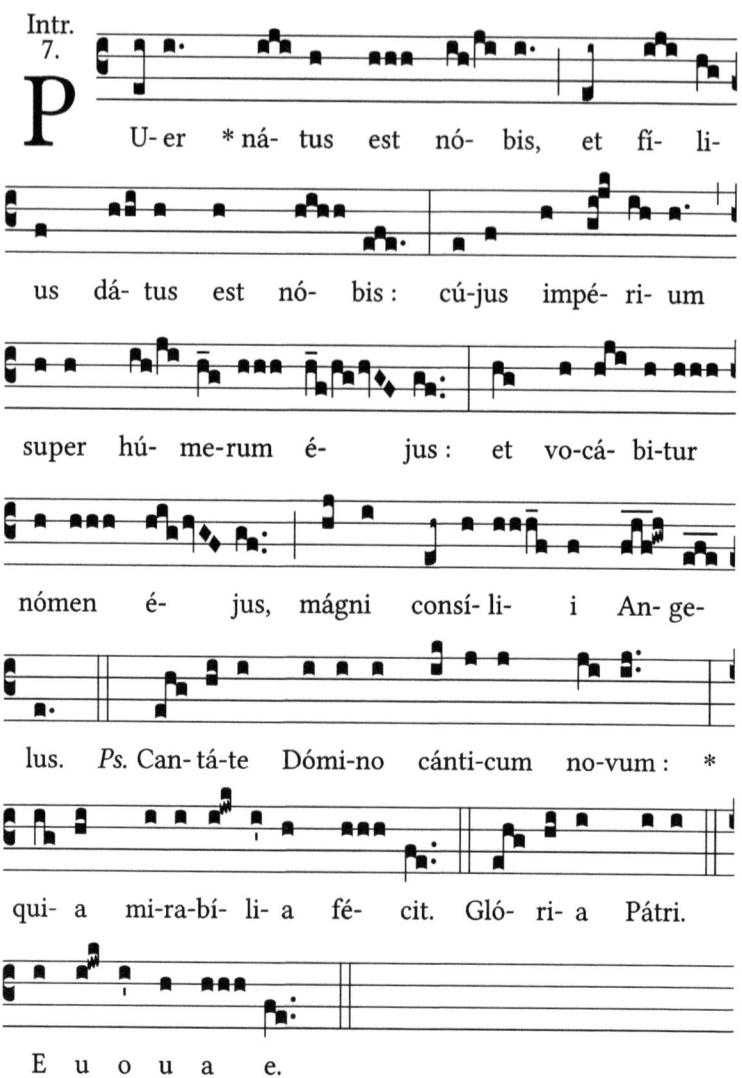

Appendix (213)

MODE MODEL 8 (HYPOMIXOLYDIAN)

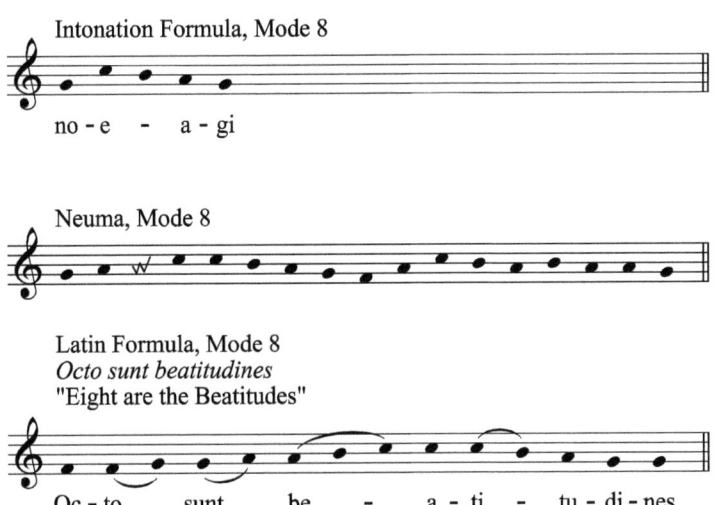

Psalm tone, mode 8

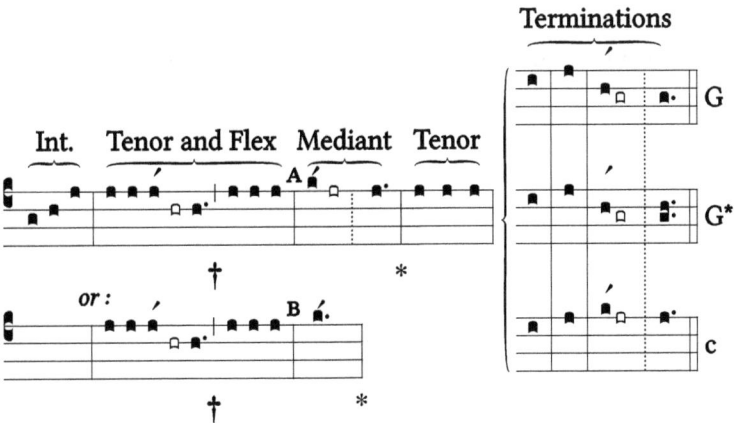

(214) *Appendix*

Example of plainchant in mode 8

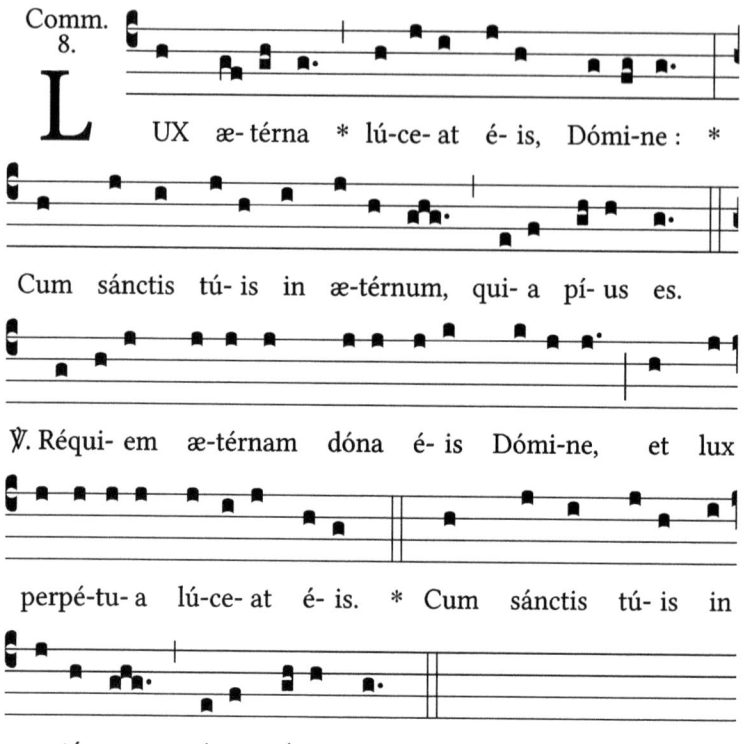

SELECTED BIBLIOGRAPHY

Altramar Medieval Music Ensemble. *Celtic Wanderers*. Albany, NY: Dorian Recordings DOR-93213, 2000.
Atkinson, Charles. *The Critical Nexus: Tone-System, Mode, and Notation in Early Medieval Music*. Oxford: Oxford University Press, 2009.
Aubrey, Elizabeth. *The Music of the Troubadours*. Bloomington: Indiana University Press, 1996.
———. *Poets and Singers: On Latin and Vernacular Monophonic Song*. Burlington, VT: Ashgate, 2009.
Bagby, Benjamin. "Imagining the Early Medieval Harp." In *A Performer's Guide to Medieval Music*, edited by Ross Duffin, 336–44. Bloomington: Indiana University Press, 2000.
———. "Reconstructing Medieval Instruments." Sequentia website, http://www.sequentia.org/writings/medieval_instruments.html.
———. "Reflections on the Image of Musical Roots." Sequentia website, http://www.sequentia.org/writings/musical_roots.html.
———. "Searching for the Lost Voice of My Germanic Ancestors." Sequentia website, http://www.sequentia.org/writings/lost_voice.html.
———. "What Is the Sound of Medieval Song?" Sequentia website, http://www.sequentia.org/writings/medieval_song.html.
Bailey, Terence, ed. and trans. *Commemoratio brevis de tonis st psalmis modulandis*. Ottawa: University of Ottawa Press, 1979.
———. *The Intonation Formulas of Western Chant*. Toronto: Pontifical Institute of Mediaeval Studies, 1974.
Baltzer, Rebecca, T. Cable, and J. Wimsatt, eds. *The Union of Words and Music in Medieval Poetry*. Austin: University of Texas Press, 1991.
Barrett, Sam. *The Melodic Traditions of Boethius' De consolation philosophiae in the Middle Ages*. 2 vols. Monumenta Monodica Medii Aevi, Subsidia, 7. Kassel, Germany: Bärenreiter, 2013.
Benedictines of Solesmes, eds. *Liber Usualis*. Tournai, Belgium: Desclée & Cie, 1952.
Bent, Margaret. "Grammar and Rhetoric in Late Medieval Polyphony." In *Rhetoric Beyond Words*, edited by Mary Carruthers, 52–71. Cambridge, UK: Cambridge University Press, 2010.
———. "Isorhythm." In *Grove Music Online*, http://www.oxfordmusiconline.com/subscriber/article/grove/music/13950 accessed August 12, 2011.
Berger, Anna Maria Busse. *Medieval Music and the Art of Memory*. Berkeley: University of California Press, 2005.
———. "Mnemotechnics and Notre Dame Polyphony." *Journal of Musicology* 14, no. 3 (Summer, 1996): 263–98.

Binkley, Thomas. "The Work Is Not the Performance." In *Companion to Medieval and Renaissance Music*, edited by Tess Knighton and David Fallows, 36–43. New York: Schirmer, 1992.

———. "Zur Aufführungspraxis der einstimmigen Musik des Mittelaters." *Basler Jahrbuch für historische Musikpraxis* 1 (1977): 19–76.

Bower, Calvin, ed. and trans. *Anicium Manlius Severinus Boethius: Fundamentals of Music*. Music Theory Translation Series. New Haven, CT: Yale University Press, 1989.

Burkholder, J. Peter, Donald Jay Grout, and Claude Palisca. *A History of Western Music*. New York: W. W. Norton, 2014.

Caplan, Harry, trans. *De Ratione Dicendi (Rhetorica ad Herennium)*. Cambridge, MA: Harvard University Press, 1964.

Cardine, Eugene, ed. *Graduel Neumé*. Solesmes, France: Abbaye Saint-Pierre de Solesmes, 1966.

Carruthers, Mary. *The Book of Memory: A Study of Memory in Medieval Culture*. Cambridge, UK: Cambridge University Press, 1990.

———. *The Craft of Thought: Meditation, Rhetoric, and the Making of Images, 400–1200*. Cambridge, UK: Cambridge University Press, 1998.

———. "The Poet as Master Builder." *New Literary History* 24 (1993): 881–904.

Chancey, Tina. "Contextual Improvisation, or Why Swat Flies with a Frisbee?" *Early Music America Magazine* 17, no. 2 (Summer 2011): 32–35 and 58–59.

Christensen, Thomas, ed. *The Cambridge History of Western Music Theory*. Cambridge, UK: Cambridge University Press, 2002.

Cohen, David E. "Notes, Scales, and Modes in the Earlier Middle Ages." In *The Cambridge History of Western Music Theory*, edited by Thomas Christensen, 307–63. Cambridge, UK: Cambridge University Press, 2006.

Cosart, Jann, Angela Mariani, Chris Smith, and David Stattelman. "Reconstructing the Music of Medieval Ireland: Altramar's Crossroads of the Celts." *Early Music* 28, no. 2 (May 2000): 270–81.

Duffin, Ross, ed. *A Performer's Guide to Medieval Music*. Bloomington: Indiana University Press, 2000.

Ensemble Alcatraz with Kitka. *Cantigas de Amigo (Songs for a Friend)*. Albany, NY: Dorian Recordings B00004UDER, 2000.

Ferreira, Manuel Pedro. *O Som de Martin Codax*. Lisbon: Impresa Nacional—Casa de Moeda, 1986.

Floros, Constantin. *Introduction to Early Medieval Notation*. Translated by Neil K. Moran. Warren, MI: Harmonie Park, 2005.

Godt, Irving, and Benito Rivera. "The Vatican Organum Treatise—A Colour-Reproduction, Transcription, and Translation." In *Gordon Athol Anderson, in Memoriam*, edited by Irving Godt and Hans Tischler, 2:264–345. Ottawa: Institute of Medieval Music, 1984.

Grymes, James A., and John Allemeir. "Making Students Make Music: Integrating Composition and Improvisation into the Early Music Classroom." *Journal of Music History Pedagogy* 4, no. 2 (2014): 231–54.

Haines, John. "The Arabic Style of Performing Medieval Music." *Early Music* 29, no. 3 (August 2001): 369–78.

Hildegard von Bingen. *Lieder: Faksimile; Riesencodex (Hs. 2) der Hessichen Landesbibliothek Wiesbaden, fol. 466–481v*. Edited by Lorenz Welker. Wiesbaden, Germany: Ludwig Reichert Verlag, 1998.

———. *Symphonia harmoniae caelestium revelationum: Dendermonde, St.-Pieters & Paulusabdij, Ms. Cod. 9*. Edited by Peter van Poucke. Peer, Belgium: Alamire, 1991.

Huot, Sylvia. "Voices and Instruments in Medieval French Secular Music: On the Use of Literary Texts as Evidence for Performance Practice." *Musica Disciplina* 43 (1989): 63–113.
Immel, Steven C. "The Vatican Organum Treatise Re-examined." *Early Music History* 20 (2001): 121–72.
Jeffery, Peter. *Re-envisioning Past Musical Cultures: Ethnomusicology in the Study of Gregorian Chant.* Chicago: University of Chicago Press, 1995.
Johannes de Grocheio. *Ars Musice.* Edited and translated by Constant J. Mews, John N. Crossley, Catherine Jeffreys, Leigh McKinnon, and Carol J. Williams. Kalamazoo, MI: Medieval Publications, 2011.
Johannes de Grocheo. *Concerning Music (De Musica).* Translated by Albert Seay. Colorado Springs: Colorado College of Music Press, 1973.
Kelly, Thomas Forrest. *Capturing Music: The Story of Notation.* New York: W. W. Norton, 2014.
Larson, Steve. "Composition versus Improvisation?" *Journal of Music Theory* 49, no. 2 (Fall 2005): 241–75.
Leech-Wilkinson, Daniel. *The Modern Invention of Medieval Music.* Cambridge, UK: Cambridge University Press, 2007.
Lewis, George E., and Benjamin Piekut, eds. *Oxford Handbook of Critical Improvisation Studies,* vol. 1. New York: Oxford University Press, 2016.
Mahrt, William P. "Gamut, Solmization, and Modes." In *A Performer's Guide to Medieval Music,* edited by Ross Duffin, 482–95. Bloomington: Indiana University Press, 2000.
Mariani, Angela. "'By Ear and in the Memory': Vernacular Music Processes and the Pedagogy of Medieval Music." *Journal of the Vernacular Music Center* 1, no. 1 (Fall 2015): 1–10.
Mattes, Ralf. "Ornamentation and Improvisation after 1300." In *A Performer's Guide to Medieval Music,* edited by Ross Duffin, 470–81. Bloomington: Indiana University Press, 2000.
McGee, Timothy J., ed. *Improvisation in the Arts of the Middle Ages and Renaissance.* Kalamazoo: Medieval Institute Publications, 2003.
———, ed. *Instruments and their Music in the Middle Ages.* Burlington, VT: Ashgate, 2009.
———. *Medieval Instrumental Dances.* Bloomington: Indiana University Press, 1989.
———. *The Sound of Medieval Song: Ornamentation and Vocal Style According to the Treatises.* Oxford: Clarendon, 1998.
McGee, Timothy J., A. G. Rigg, and David Klausner, eds. *Singing Early Music: The Pronunciation of European Languages in the Late Middle Ages and Renaissance.* Bloomington: Indiana University Press, 1996.
Mullaly, Robert. *The Carole: A Study of a Medieval Dance.* Abingdon, UK: Routledge, 2011.
Nims, Margaret F., trans. *Poetria Nova of Geoffrey of Vinsauf.* Toronto: Pontifical Institute of Medieval Studies, 1967.
Page, Christopher. "Jerome of Moravia on the Rubeba and Viella." *Galpin Society Journal* 32 (1979): 77–98.
———, ed. and trans. *The "Summa Musice": A Thirteenth-Century Manual for Singers.* Cambridge Musical Texts and Monographs. Cambridge, UK: Cambridge University Press, 1991.
———. *Voices and Instruments of the Middle Ages: Instrumental Practice and Songs in France, 1100–1300.* Berkeley: University of California Press, 1987.
Palisca, Claude V., ed. *Hucbald, Guido and John on Music: Three Medieval Treatises.* Translated by Warren Babb. New Haven, CT: Yale University Press, 1978.

Quintilian. *The Orator's Education, Books 1–2*. Translated by Donald A. Russell. Cambridge, MA: Harvard University Press, 2001.

Rastall, Richard. *The Notation of Western Music: An Introduction*. London: Travis & Emery, 1998.

Reckow, Fritz. *Der Musiktraktat des Anonymous 4*. Wiesbaden, Germany: Steiner, 1967.

Sarath, Edward W. *Improvisation, Creativity, and Consciousness: Jazz as Integral Template for Music, Education, and Society*. Albany: State University of New York Press, 2013.

Sequentia Ensemble for Medieval Music. *Edda: Myths from Medieval Iceland*. Freiburg, Germany: Deutsche Harmonia Mundi DHM 05472-77381-2, 1999.

Sequentia Ensemble for Medieval Music. *Lost Songs of a Rhineland Harper*. Freiburg, Germany: Deustche Harmonia Mundi DHM 05472-77378-2, 2004.

Shull, Jonathan. "Locating the Past in the Present: Living Traditions and the Performance of Early Music." *Ethnomusicology Forum* 15, no. 1 (June, 2006): 87–111.

Smith, Anne. *The Performance of 16th-Century Music*. Oxford: Oxford University Press, 2011.

Smith, Christopher. "The Old Ways: Access, Advocacy, Inclusivity in the (Post)/(Multi)-Literate Music Classroom." Paper presented at the Spring Conference of the Southwest Chapter of the American Musicological Society, Austin Texas, April 16, 2011.

Stäblein, Bruno. "Die Schwanenklage, Zum Problem Lai-Planctus-Sequenz." In *Festschrift Karl Gustav Fellerer: Zum sechzigsten Geburtstag am 7. Juli 1962*, edited by Heinrich Hüschen, 491–502. Regensburg, Germany: Gustav Bosse Verlag, 1962.

Stevens, John. *Words and Music in the Middle Ages: Song, Narrative, Dance, and Drama, 1050–1350*. Cambridge, UK: Cambridge University Press, 1986.

Studio der Frühen Musik. *L'Agonie du Languedoc*. London: EMI Reflexe 7243 8 26500 2 7, 1976.

Tarling, Judy. *The Weapons of Rhetoric: A Guide for Musicians and Audiences*. St. Albans, UK: Corda Music, 2005.

Taruskin, Richard. *The Oxford History of Western Music*. Vol. 1, *The Earliest Notations to the Sixteenth Century*. Oxford: Oxford University Press, 2005.

Taruskin, Richard, Daniel Leech-Wilkinson, Nicholas Temperley, and Robert Winter. "The Limits of Authenticity: A Discussion." *Early Music* 12 (1984): 3–26.

Thornton, Barbara, and Larry Rosenwald. "Poetics as Technique." In *A Performer's Guide to Medieval Music*, edited by Ross Duffin, 264–92. Bloomington: Indiana University Press, 2000.

Tindemans, Margriet. "Improvisation and Accompaniment before 1300." In *A Performer's Guide to Medieval Music*, edited by Ross Duffin, 454–69. Bloomington: Indiana University Press, 2000.

Treitler, Leo. "Homer and Gregory: The Transmission of Epic Poetry and Plainchant." *Musical Quarterly* 60 (1974): 333–72.

———. "Medieval Improvisation." *World of Music* 33, no. 3 (1991): 66–91.

———. *Music and the Historical Imagination*. Cambridge, MA: Harvard University Press, 1989.

———. "Oral, Written and Literate Process in the Transmission of Medieval Music." *Speculum* 56, no. 3 (July 1981): 471–91.

———. *With Voice and Pen: Coming to Know Medieval Song and How It Was Made*. Oxford: Oxford University Press, 2007.

van der Werf, Hendrik. *The Extant Troubadour Melodies: Transcriptions and Essays for Performers and Scholars*. Rochester, NY: published by author, 1984.
Wright, Craig. *Music and Ceremony at Notre Dame of Paris, 500–1550*. Cambridge, UK: Cambridge University Press, 1989.
Yates, Frances A. *The Art of Memory*. Harmondsworth, UK: Penguin, 1966.
Yri, Kirsten. "Thomas Binkley and the Studio der Frühen Musik: Challenging 'The Myth of Westernness.'" *Early Music* 38, no. 2 (2010): 273–80.
Ziolkowski, Jan, ed. and trans. *The Cambridge Songs (Carmina Cantabrigiensia)*. Garland Library of Medieval Literature 66. New York: Garland, 1994.
Zuckerman, Kenneth. "Improvisation in Medieval Music." In *Improvisation II: Internationale Tagung für Improvisation*, edited by Walter Fähndrich, 134–42. Lucerne, Switzerland: Amadeus, 1993.

INDEX

Page references for examples are indicated by *e*, for figures by *f*, for practices by *p*, and for tables by *t*.

abbreviatio (abbreviation), 132*p*
   Geoffrey of Vinsauf, 168n12
   Planctus cygni, 167–170, 167*e*,
      169*e*, 170*e*
adagio, 161
Adémar de Chabannes, 79
agent images, 52
Alia Musica, 62
ambitus, 68
amplificatio (amplification), 132*p*, 158
   Geoffrey of Vinsauf, *Poetria Nova*, 167
   Machaut-style, 111, 111*e*
   Planctus cygni, 167–168, 167*e*, 168*e*, 171
Anonymous IV, 45, 145n17
antiphon, 70, 70*e*
   melodic phrase or *neuma*, 92
   mode, 76
   psalm tone, 76
aperto, 118
Aquitanian polyphony, 139
Aribo, 37
ars antiqua motet, 155*p*
Ars Musice (Johannes de Grocheio), 92
artificial memory, 49
Art of Memory, The (Yates), 44–45, 49
Aubrey, Elizabeth, 103–104, 103n13
Aurelian of Réôme, 37
authentic mode, 61–62, 64
authentic sound, 8–9

Bach, Johann Sebastian, 134, 155–156
Bagby, Benjamin, 11, 11n13, 21

Bailey, Terence, 65n8, 76, 80, 80*p*
Barrett, Sam, 178, 178n17
Bent, Margaret, 8–9, 48
Bernard de Ventadorn, 104–108, 105*e*–108*e*, 109*p*–110*p*
Binkley, Thomas, 17–20, 18–20nn4–9, 90–91, 94n8
Boethius, 62
   Consolation of Philosophy, 178, 182
brevis, 152, 152*t*
Burkholder, J. Peter, 68, 195n2
Busse Berger, Anna Maria, 5, 5n5, 30, 135, 140, 146

Cambridge History of Western Music Theory, The (Cohen), 61
canso, 160
cantigas de amigo, 38
   "Ondas do mar de Vigo" (Codax), 38–41, 39*f* (*see also* Codax, Martin, "Ondas do mar de Vigo")
Cantigas de Santa Maria, 100
cantus coronatus, 92–93
"Can vei la lauzeta mover" (Bernard de Ventadorn), 104–108, 105*e*–108*e*, 109*p*–110*p*
Capturing Music: The Story of Notation (Kelly), 31n4
Cardine, Don Eugène, 37
Carolingian reforms, 83–84
Carruthers, Mary, 2–3, 30, 50, 52–53
Chansonnier du Roi, 118, 120*e*–125*e*
chiuso, 118
Cicero, 48, 49–50, 160
Codax, Martin, 38–41, 39*f*

(221)

Codax, Martin, "Ondas do mar de Vigo," 38–44
  architectural techniques, 53, 53f
  charting what is and is not on page, 41–43, 44p
  data, 38–41, 39f
  invention, 41–43, 44p
  rhythm, 39f, 39–40, 39–40n17
Cohen, David, 51n31, 61
Commemoratio brevis, 72, 73e–74e, 76, 77f
comparative approach, 10–11
composition, 2
  associative procedure, recollection, 53
  definition, 4
  high speed, 6
  improvisation, 4–7
  medieval process, 30
  memory, 3–4
  oral, 5, 6, 6n6
  performance, 134–135
  written and oral, 135
compositional thumbprints, 56–57
conclusio, 95, 160, 161
confirmatio, 160, 161
confutatio, 159, 160, 161
  "Cum polo Phoebus," 183
Consolation of Philosophy (Boethius), 178, 182
contemplatio, 181
copula, 140n8
Craft of Thought, The (Carruthers), 2
"Cum polo Phoebus," 178–190
  confutatio, 183
  exordium, 182–183
  line groupings, 180
  meter, 180, 180n19
  narratio, 183
  origins, 178
  "playing poetry," 174, 175e, 177–179
  practice, "playing poetry," 179–190, 179p–182p, 184p, 185e–190e
  text and translation, 179t

dances, inventing, 116–133. *See also* estampie
  estampie, 127–133, 128t–129t, 130e–131e, 132p–133p
  estampie, case study, 118–127, 119t, 120e–125e, 126p–127p
  form, structure, and rhythm, 117
  instrumentation or tempo, 117
  repertoire, surviving, 116–117
data, charting different and absent, 41–44
  practice, what is and is not on the page, 41–42, 42p
  practice applications, what is and is not on the page, 41–43, 42p–44p
De harmonica institutione (Hucbald), 61, 62
De inventione (Cicero), 49
demonstration-imitation-critique model, 15, 16–17, 85
  discrimination and imitation skills, 22–27 (*see also* discrimination and imitation skills)
descriptive approach, 9–10
deuterus, 61, 62
difference (*differentia*), 71, 71e, 72
discant, 140–141
  creating, on plainchant tenor using VOT rules, 154, 154p–155p
  improvisation, 5
  melisma, 150, 151e
  "Viderunt omnes chant," 150–154, 151e, 154, 154e
discipline: location and image, 48–54
  Guidonian hand, 50–51, 51n31, 52f
  hexachord system, 50, 50n30, 51f
  locational memory system, 52
  memoria verborum and *memoria rerum,* 49
  memory cultivation, 48
  practice, "placement" as memory technique, 54p
  rhetoric and *Rhetorica ad Herennium,* 48–50
divisio, 160, 161
Dorian mode, 57t, 58–59, 58t, 59e, 62–66
  "diatonic" triads, 58–59, 58t
  intonation formula, 198e
  Latin formula, 198e
  neuma, 198e
  plainchant, 200e
  protus, authentic, 64–65, 65e, 65t
  psalm tone, 199e
drones, 97–100, 99e
ductia, 119, 126

echemata (intonation formulas), 61, 72–76, 73*e*–75*e*
   practice, Bailey's *Intonation Formulas*, 80, 80*p*
Edda: Myths from Medieval Iceland (Sequentia), 21
educated memory, 3
epic poetry, memorization and transmission, 6n7
estampie
   creating an estampie, 127–133, 128*t*–129*t*, 130*e*–131*e*, 132*p*–133*p*
   definition, 118
   French *vs.* Italian, 118–119, 119*t*
   "Istampitta Ghaetta," 118, 121*e*–125*e*
   "La Septime Estampie Real," 118, 120*e*
   practice, sequential steps, 132, 132*p*–133*p*
   as template for *inventio*, 118–133

ethnographic inquiry, 21
exordium
   "Cum polo Phoebus," 182–183
   Planctus cygni, 165–166, 166*e*, 172–173
   prelude (introduction), 94, 160, 161

Faenza Codex, 113, 114*e*–115*e*, 116*p*
Ferreira, Manual Pedro, 39, 39–40 n17
Fiala, David, 21–22
final, 61, 62, 68
final cadence, 71, 71*e*, 72
flex, 70*e*, 71, 71n17
florid organum, 140
Floros, Constantin, 37
flos harmonicus, 101
fluid composition, 29, 31, 41, 43, 48, 92, 172
   "Cum polo Phoebus," 187
   definition, 7, 92, 129n25
   Hildegard von Bingen, 36, 37
   internalizing genre/repertoire characteristics, 91
   Planctus cygni, 173
formula
   Bailey's *Intonation Formulas*, 65n8, 79, 80, 80*p*

intonation *(echemata)*, 61, 72–76, 73*e*–75*e*
Latin, 78–80, 78*e*–79*e*
melismatic, 143
melodies, 65–68, 65*e*–68*e*, 65n8
modal, 69–72, 70*e*, 71*e* (*see also specific modes*)
Fragments for the End of Time (Sequentia), 21–22

Geoffrey of Vinsauf, 94, 158, 160, 171
   abbreviatio, 168n12
   Poetria Nova, 167
gestures, 104, 104n15. *See also* ornamentation
   definition, 104n15
   mode, 21
   repertoire of melodic, 68, 68n12, 69, 76
   repertoire-specific, 110–112, 111*e*, 112*p*
"Ghaetta," 118, 121*e*–125*e*
Girault de Bornelh, 98, 98n11
Glareanus, 66n9
Glyconic meter, 180
graces, 102
Graduale Romanum, 45
Graduel Neumé, 45
Graduale Triplex, 45
Guido d'Arezzo, 33, 50, 51*f*
Guidonian hand, 50–51, 51n31, 52*f*
Guillaume de Machaut, melodic figure, 110–112, 111*e*, 112*p*

Haines, John, 11, 11n12, 18–19n5
Haynes, Bruce, 196
heterophony, 17, 17n3, 18, 117
hexachord system, 50, 50n30, 51*f*
History of Western Music, A (Burkholder), 68
"Homer and Gregory: The Transmission of Epic Poetry and Plainchant" (Treitler), 6n7
Hucbald of Saint-Amand, 61, 62
Hypodorian mode, 63–66
   intonation formula, 201*e*
   Latin formula, 201*e*
   neuma, 201*e*
   plainchant, 202*e*
   protus, plagal, 64–65, 65*e*, 65*t*
   psalm tone, 201*e*

Hypolydian mode, 63
  intonation formula, 209e
  Latin formula, 209e
  neuma, 209e
  plainchant, 210e
  psalm tone, 209e
  tritus, plagal, 66, 67e, 67t
Hypomixolydian mode, 63
  intonation formula, 213e
  Latin formula, 213e
  neuma, 213e
  plainchant, 214e
  psalm tone, 213e
  tetrardus, plagal, 66, 67t, 68e
Hypophrygian mode, 63
  deuterus plagal, 66, 66e, 66t
  intonation formula, 205e
  Latin formula, 205e
  neuma, 205e
  plainchant, 206e
  psalm tone, 205e

imitation of models, 22–27
  choosing models, 22–23
  living models and models of transmission, 23, 23f
  practice, discerning layers of modeling, 26, 26p
  practice, listening for "invention," 25, 25p–26p
  practice, models from vernacular and world music traditions, 23, 23p–24p
  practice, what is your musical lineage?, 24, 24p–25p
  skills and procedures, 22–23
imitation skills, 22–27. *See also* imitation of models
Immel, Steven, 142–145, 142t, 145n17
improvisation. *See also* ornamentation; *specific topics*
  Binkley, 17–18
  composition, 4–7
  definition, 4
  Faenza Codex, 113, 114e–115e, 116p
  indications, 27
  instruments, 89–90
  internalized musical data, 56
  memory, 3–4
  modal, 84–85, 86p

performance art, 5
performance practice, 11, 11n14
polyphonic organum and discant, 5
preplanning, 6–7
process, 11, 11n14
storage, 7
Improvisation, Creativity, and Consciousness (Sarath), 4, 7
"Improvisation in Medieval Music" (Zuckerman), 16
Institutio Oratoria (Quintilian), 48, 158–159
instruments
  choice, by piece, 92
  improvisation, 89–90
  invention, musical, 90–91
  "play what the instrument wants to play," 90–92, 91p–92p
  use, 88–89, 89n2
interludes, 92–94, 95, 96p–97p
intervals
  pattern, 63
  species, 63–64
intonation, 70e, 71, 71e
intonation formulas, 61, 72–76, 73e–75e
  Dorian mode, 198e
  Hypodorian mode, 201e
  Hypolydian mode, 209e
  Hypomixolydian mode, 213e
  Hypophrygian mode, 205e
  Lydian mode, 207e
  Mixolydian mode, 211e
  Phrygian mode, 203e
  practice, Bailey's *Intonation Formulas*, 80, 80p
Intonation Formulas of Western Chant, The (Bailey), 65n8, 79, 80, 80p
inventing melody, 88–133. *See also* melody, inventing
inventing organum, 134–156. *See also* organum, inventing
inventio (invention), 1–11, 2
  improvisation *vs.* composition, 4–7
  listening, 25, 25p–26p
  Martin Codax's "Ondas do Mar," 41–43, 44p
  melodic, 174, 175e, 177–179
  memoria, 2–4
  modal, 84–85, 86p
  models and processes, 9–11

necessity, 1
  as process, 43
  rhetoric, 2, 157–190 (*see also* rhetoric of invention)
  Rhetorica ad Herennium, 160–161
  six parts of discourse, 160–161
  storehouse, building, 55
istampitta. *See* estampie
"Istampitta Ghaetta," 118, 121*e*–125*e*

Jerome of Moravia, 9, 97, 98n10, 101–102
Johannes de Grocheio, 92, 119, 126
jusla, 17

Kelly, Thomas Forrest, 31n4
key, 68
Kyrie cunctipotens genitor, 113, 114*e*–115*e*

Lament of the Swan. *See Planctus cygni*
Larson, Steve, 6–7
"La Septime Estampie Real," 118, 120*e*
Latin formulas, 78–80, 78*e*–79*e*
  Dorian mode, 198*e*
  Hypodorian mode, 201*e*
  Hypolydian mode, 209*e*
  Hypomixolydian mode, 213*e*
  Hypophrygian mode, 205*e*
  Lydian mode, 207*e*
  Mixolydian mode, 211*e*
  Phrygian mode, 203*e*
lauda spirituale, 100
learning. *See also* teaching medieval music; *specific topics*
  passive, 3
  specific pieces, 28
learning process: mnemonic score building, 44–47
  Liber Usualis, 45–46, 46*f*
  memory as written, 44–45
  neume transcription, 45
  noteheads and neumes, 46, 46*f*
  text and neumes, 46–47, 46*f*
  Thornton transcription, 47, 47*f*
  working performance scores, 45
lectio divina, 180–181, 181n20
Leech-Wilkinson, Daniel, 8, 9
Liber Usualis
  incipit, 149*e*, 150
  marking of solo sections, 149n22
  mnemonic score building, 45–46, 46*f*
  mode, 69–71nn14–17, 69–72, 70*e*, 71*e*
  practice, modal model source, 80–81, 81*p*
lineage, musical, 24, 24*p*–25*p*
lineage-driven approach, 10
liquescence
  definition, 32–33
  example, 32*e*, 33
liquescent neumes, 1, 32–33, 32*e*, 32*f*, 36, 36*f*, 46, 46*f*
  quilisma, 36, 37*f*
listening
  "invention," 25, 25*p*–26*p*
  medieval music, 29–30
  passive, 3
literate culture, 44
living and "imagined" models, 15–27
  Binkley, Studio der frühen Musik, 17–20, 18–20nn4–9
  demonstration-imitation-critique model, 15, 16–17
  discrimination and imitation skills, 22–27 (*see also* discrimination and imitation skills)
  ethnographic inquiry, 21
  imagined models, 15, 16–17
  inventive, improvisatory, and compositional skill, 27
  layered musical lineage, 22
  living models, 16–20
  memory and transmission, 16
locational memory system, 52
loci, mental, 49
longa, 152, 152*t*
Lord, Albert, 6n7, 17
"Lux aeterna," 137, 137*e*
Lydian mode, 57*t*, 58*t*, 59, 59n1, 63
  intonation formula, 207*e*
  Latin formula, 207*e*
  neuma, 207*e*
  plainchant, 208*e*
  psalm tone, 207*e*
  tritus, authentic, 66, 67*e*, 67*t*

Machaut. *See* Guillaume de Machaut
major scale, construction, 63
McGee, Timothy, 33, 33nn6–8, 37, 102, 102n12, 126n23

mediation, 70e, 71, 71e
"Medieval Improvisation" (Treitler), 134–135
Medieval Instrumental Dances (McGee), 126n23
Medieval Music and the Art of Memory (Busse Berger), 5, 5n5, 30, 140
meditatio, 181
melisma
  discant, 150, 151e
  formulas, 143
  Notre Dame organum, 150
  "*Viderunt omnes* chant," 150, 151e, 153, 153e, 154e
melody, formulaic, 65–68, 65e–68e, 65n8
melody, inventing, 88–133
  dances, 116–133 (see also dances, inventing)
  drones, 97–100, 99e
  instrumentalist–singer collaborations, 88
  instruments, choice by piece, 92
  instruments, improvisation, 89–90
  instruments, musical invention, 90–91
  instruments, use, 88–89, 89n2
  interludes, 92–94, 95, 96p–97p
  ornamentation, 100–116 (see also ornamentation)
  "play what the instrument wants to play," 90–92, 91p–92p
  postludes, 92–96, 96p–97p
  preludes, 92–95, 96p–97p
melody, modal characteristics, 80–83, 81p–83p
  mode models as mental folder, 83
  practice, mode models, *Liber Usualis*, 80–81, 81p
  practice, mode models, 81, 82p–83p
memoria
  inventio, 2–4
  notation, 28–55 (see also notation, *memoria* and)
memoria rerum (Sententialiter), 49
memoria verborum, 49
memorization
  epic poetry, 6n7
  medieval repertoire, 6n7
memory
  architectural techniques, 53, 53f
  artificial, 49
  associative procedure of recollection, 52–53
  Cicero, 49–50
  cultivation, 48
  educated, 3
  events or ideas, 49
  Guidonian hand, 50–51, 51n31, 52f
  hexachord system, 50, 50n30, 51f
  locational memory system, 52
  natural, 49
  pedagogy, medieval, 5, 5n5
  reconstructive, 50
  rote, 50
  storehouse, 30
  structured, 2–3
  transmission, 5, 5n5, 16
  value, 3
  word-for-word memorization, 50
mental folder, 83
mental place, 49–50
metra (metrum), 178, 178n17, 180
Micrologus (d'Arezzo), 50, 51f
minor scale, construction, 63
Mixolydian mode, 57t, 58–59, 58t, 63
  intonation formula, 217e
  Latin formula, 217e
  neuma, 217e
  plainchant, 218e
  psalm tone, 217e
  tetrardus, authentic, 66, 67t, 68e
mnemonic score building, 44–47. See also learning process: mnemonic score building
"Mnemotechnics and Notre Dame Polyphony" (Berger), 135
mode, 56–87. See also specific types
  affect, 184n21
  altered scales, 58, 58t
  antiphon, 76
  authentic, 61–62, 64
  definition and concept, 57–60
  Dorian "diatonic" triads, 58–59, 58t
  eight, 61–68, 65e–68e
  formulas, 69–72, 70e, 71e (see also specific types)
  functional harmony context, 60
  hearing modal melody, 57
  historical background, 60–63
  improvisation and invention, 84–85, 86p (see also improvisation; *inventio* (invention))

intonation formulas, 61, 72–76, 73e–75e
Latin formulas, 78–80, 78e–79e
Liber Usualis, 69–71nn14–17, 69–72, 70e, 71e
melody, 60
melody, formulaic, 65–68, 65e–68e, 65n8
melody, modal characteristics, 80–83, 81p–83p (*see also* melody, modal characteristics)
models and secular/vernacular repertoire, 83–84, 85p
neumae, 69, 76, 77e, 80p–83p
Renaissance changes, 84n26
rhythmic, 152, 152n24, 152t
models, 9–11. *See also specific types*
discerning layers, 26, 26p
mode models, 198e–214e
  Dorian
    intonation formula, 198e
    Latin formula, 198e
    neuma, 198e
    plainchant, 200e
    psalm tone, 199e
  Hypodorian
    intonation formula, 201e
    Latin formula, 201e
    neuma, 201e
    plainchant, 202e
    psalm tone, 201e
  Hypolydian
    intonation formula, 209e
    Latin formula, 209e
    neuma, 209e
    plainchant, 210e
    psalm tone, 209e
  Hypomixolydian
    intonation formula, 213e
    Latin formula, 213e
    neuma, 213e
    plainchant, 214e
    psalm tone, 213e
  Hypophrygian
    intonation formula, 205e
    Latin formula, 205e
    neuma, 205e
    plainchant, 206e
    psalm tone, 205e
  Lydian
    intonation formula, 207e
    Latin formula, 207e
    neuma, 207e
    plainchant, 208e
    psalm tone, 207e
  mental folder, 83
  Mixolydian
    intonation formula, 211e
    Latin formula, 211e
    neuma, 211e
    plainchant, 212e
    psalm tone, 211e
  Phrygian
    intonation formula, 203e
    Latin formula, 203e
    neuma, 203e
    plainchant, 204e
    psalm tone, 203e
  practice, 81, 82p–83p
  secular/vernacular repertoire, 83–84, 85p
modern interpretation, 20–21n10
Modern Invention of Medieval Music, The (Leech-Wilkinson), 8, 9
modern Western music, 57–58, 57t, 58t
monophonic song melodies, variants, 104–108, 105e–108e, 109p–110p
Morocco, music, 18
motet, 154p–155p
music, rhetoric and, 48, 157–159. See also *Planctus cygni;* rhetoric
Musica Enchiriadis, 61, 136–139, 136e–138e, 139p
  "Lux aeterna," 137, 137e
  parallel organum, 136, 136e
  "Rex caeli domine," 138, 138e
musical-poetic forms, 17
Music and Ceremony at Notre Dame of Paris, 500–1550 (Wright), 140–141
Music of the Troubadours, The (Aubrey), 103–104, 103n13

names, modern usage, 57t
narratio, 160–161
  "Cum polo Phoebus," 183
  Planctus cygni, 166–167, 169
natural memory, 49
neumae, 69, 76, 77e, 80p
  Dorian mode, 198e
  Hypodorian mode, 201e
  Hypolydian mode, 209e
  Hypomixolydian mode, 213e

neumae (Cont.)
   Hypophrygian mode, 205*e*
   Lydian mode, 207*e*
   Mixolydian mode, 211*e*
   Phrygian mode, 203*e*
   practice, mode models, 82*p*–83*p*
neumes, 31–32n4
   German, early, 35*f*–36*f*, 35n11
   graphic, 32, 32*e*, 32n5
   Hildegard von Bingen, 35, 35*f*–36*f*, 35nn10–11
   liquescent, 1, 32–33, 32*f*
   liquescent *vs.* non-liquescent, 36, 36*f*
   meanings, exact, 36–37
   modern transcription, 45
   ornamental, 33
   quilisma, 36, 37*f*
   shapes, regional differences, 33, 33n8
   text, 46–47, 46*f*
   written above noteheads, 45, 46*f*
notation, *memoria* and, 28–55. *See also specific types*
   classical music background, 29
   data, missing *vs.* different, 31–34, 32*e*, 32*f*
   discipline: location and image, 48–54 (*see also* discipline: location and image)
   durational data, 32
   history, 31n4
   imagination, historical, 41
   improvisation background, 29
   internalized storehouse, musical language, 29
   learning process: mnemonic score building, 44–47 (*see also* learning process: mnemonic score building)
   listening, 29–30
   neumes, graphic, 32, 32*e*, 32n5
   neumes, liquescent, 1, 32–33, 32*f*
   neumes, regional shape differences, 33, 33n8
   non-prescriptive, 1
   performance implications, 31
   practice, charting different and absent data, 41–44
   preparation, performance, 28–30
   staff, standard five-line, 32n5
   storehouse of invention, building, 55
   symbols and meanings, 31
   working with different data, Hildegard von Bingen, "Spiritus sanctus vivificans vita," 34–38, 35*f*–37*f*, 35nn10–11, 42*t*
   working with different data, Martin Codax, "Ondas do mar de Vigo," 38–41, 39*f*
Notre Dame organum, 134–141
   brevis and *longa*, 152, 152*t*
   discant, 139–141
   improvisation, composition, and performance, 134–135
   melisma, 150
   polyphony, 135
   polyphony, early practice examples, 136–139, 136*e*–138*e*, 139*p*
   "*Viderunt omnes chant*," 149–150, 149*e*, 150*e*, 153, 153*e*, 154*e*

object-oriented performance, 194
Odington, Walter, 37
"Ondas do mar de Vigo" (Codax)
   architectural techniques, 53, 53*f*
   charting what is and is not on page, 41–43, 44*p*
   data, 38–41, 39*f*
   invention, 41–43, 44*p*
   rhythm, 39*f*, 39–40, 39–40 n17
oral composition, 6
oratio, 181
ordos, 153
Ordo Virtutum (von Bingen), 127–129, 128*t*–129*t*, 130*e*–131*e*
organum. *See also specific types*
   definition, 136
   duplum, 152
   florid, 140
   Musica Enchiriadis, 136–139, 136*e*–138*e*, 139*p*
organum, inventing, 134–156
   beginning before the beginning, 155–156
   Notre Dame, 134–141 (*see also* Notre Dame organum)
   Vatican Organum Treatise, 9, 141–155 (*see also* Vatican Organum Treatise)
oriscus, 33
ornamental neume, 33

ornamentation, 100–116
    definition and examples, 100
    descriptions, primary sources, 101–102
    monophonic song melodies, variants, 102–108, 105e–108e, 109p–110p
    original, reproduction, 100–101
    practice, medieval dance, 126, 127p
    repertoire-specific patterns and gestures, 110–112, 111e, 112p
    written descriptions, 100
    written manifestations, improvisatory practice, 112–113, 114e–115e
O Som de Martin Codax (Ferreira), 39, 39–40n17
outrigger strings, 98
ouvert, 118
Oxford History of Western Music, The (Taruskin), 31–32n4

Page, Christopher, 88, 97, 98n10
parallelism, 38
parallel organum, 136–137, 136e, 137e
passaggi, 102
patterns. *See also specific types*
    repertoire-specific, 110–112, 111e, 112p
perfection, 140
performance. *See also specific pieces and topics*
    authenticity, 8–9
    composition, 134–135
    medieval music, 8
    notation, 1, 28–30, 31
    object-oriented, 194
    performer, 7–8
    process-oriented, 194
    working scores, personal, 45
peroratio, 160
philosophy of mind, 2
Phrygian mode, 57t, 58t, 59, 63
    deuterus authentic, 66, 66e, 66t
    intonation formula, 203e
    Latin formula, 203e
    neuma, 203e
    plainchant, 204e
    psalm tone, 203e
plagal mode, 61–62, 64
plainchant
    Dorian mode, 200e
    Hypodorian mode, 202e
    Hypolydian mode, 210e
    Hypomixolydian mode, 214e
    Hypophrygian mode, 206e
    Lydian mode, 208e
    Mixolydian mode, 212e
    Phrygian mode, 204e
plainchant tenor, applying VOT rules, 147–154, 149e–151e, 148p–149p, 152t, 153e–154e
    discant, 154, 154p–155p
    organum, 150, 151p
Planctus cygni, performance issues, 173, 174e–175e
Planctus cygni, rhetorical analysis, 161–172
    abbreviatio, 167–170, 167e, 169e, 170e
    amplificatio, 167–168, 167e, 171
    exordium, 165–166, 166e, 172–173
    Latin text and translation, 164t–165t, 165
    ploratione motive, 169, 169e
    repetitio, 167–168, 167e, 171, 171e
    rhyme scheme and meter, 165
    scholarship, 161n8, 165n8
    sequence form, 165, 166t
    transcription example, 162e–163e
ploratione motive, 169, 169e
Poetria Nova (Geoffrey of Vinsauf), 94, 160, 171
poetry
    memorization, 6n7
    "playing," 174, 175e, 177–179
    "playing," practice, 179p–182p, 184p
    strophic, 38
    transmission, 6n7
polyphonic organum
    improvisation, 5
    Notre Dame, 135, 136–139, 136e–138e, 139p (*see also* Notre Dame organum)
polyphony
    Aquitanian, 139
    practice, early examples, 136–139, 136e–138e, 139p
postludes, 91–96, 97p
practice
    Bailey's *Intonation Formulas*, 80, 80p
    charting different and absent data, 41–44

practice *(Cont.)*
  improvised organum (VOT) "relay," 147, 148*p*–149*p*
  layers of modeling, discerning, 26, 26*p*
  Liber Usualis, modal model source, 80–81, 81*p*
  listening for "invention," 25, 25*p*–26*p*
  medieval dance, inventing new section, 126, 126*p*
  medieval dance, varying sections, 126–127, 127*p*
  melodic variants as "invitations" to improvisation, 108, 109*p*–110*p*
  modal improvisation, 85, 86*p*
  mode in secular/vernacular repertoire, 83–84, 85*p*
  mode models, 81, 82*p*–83*p*
  "placement" as memory technique, 54*p*
  plainchant tenor, using VOT rules to create on, discant, 154, 154*p*–155*p*
  plainchant tenor, using VOT rules to create on, organum, 150, 151*p*
  polyphonic, early examples, 136–139, 136*e*–138*e*, 139*p*
  preludes, interludes, postludes, 96, 97*p*
  vernacular and world music traditions models, 23, 23*p*, 24*f*
  vox organalis, medieval source as model, 138, 139*p*
  "What does the instrument 'want' to play?," 90–91, 92*p*
  What is your musical lineage?, 23–24, 25*p*
preludes, 92–95, 97*p*, 161
pressus, 33
process, 9–11. *See also specific types*
  improvisation, 11, 11n14
  teaching, 193–194
process-oriented performance, 194
proparoxytone rhythm, 165n9
protus, 61, 62
psalm tones, 69–72, 70–72nn15–18, 70*e*, 71*e*
  antiphon, 76
  Dorian mode, 199*e*
  Hypodorian mode, 201*e*
  Hypolydian mode, 207*e*
  Hypomixolydian mode, 213*e*
  Hypophrygian mode, 205*e*
  Lydian mode, 207*e*
  Mixolydian mode, 211*e*
  Phrygian mode, 203*e*
punctum (puncta), 118, 118n21
  French *vs.* Italian estampies, 118–119, 119*t*
  practice, inventing new section, 126, 126*p*
puys, 193

quilisma, 1, 33
  Hildegard von Bingen, 36, 37*f*
  interpretations, 37
  performance practice, Aribo's, 37
  symbols representing, 66, 66*e*
Quintilian, 48, 158–159

Rastall, Richard, 37
reciting tone (note), 62, 70*e*, 71, 71*e*, 72
reconstructive memory, 50
"Reis glorios" (de Bornelh), 98–99, 98n11, 99*e*
repertoire-specific patterns and gestures, 110–112, 111*e*, 112*p*
repetitio (repetition)
  Machaut-style, 110–111, 111*e*
  Planctus cygni, 167–168, 167*e*, 171, 171*e*
reverberatio, 102
"Rex caeli domine," 138, 138*e*
rhetoric, 92–93
  amplificatio, 158
  Institutio Oratoria (Quintilian), 48, 158–159
  medieval education, 158
  mental places (loci), 49–50
  music, 48, 157–159 (see also *Planctus cygni*)
  skill, universality, 158
Rhetorica ad Herennium, 48–50, 160–161
rhetoric of invention, 157–190
  "Cum polo Phoebus," 178–190 (see also "Cum polo Phoebus")
  melodic *inventio,* 174, 175*e*, 177–179
  performance: example, 173–174, 174*e*
  performance: voices, instruments, and arrangements, 172–173

Planctus cygni, analysis, 161–172
  (see also *Planctus cygni*, rhetorical analysis)
practice, *Planctus cygni*, analysis, 175p–177p
Rhetorica ad Herennium, 160–161
text and music, 157–158
rhythm (meter)
  "Ondas do mar de Vigo" (Martin Codax), 39f, 39–40, 39–40n17
  "Spiritus sanctus vivificans vita" (Hildegard von Bingen), 37
rhythmic modes, 152, 152n24, 152t
rímur, 21
Robertsbridge Codex, 113
Romance of Flamenca, 88
Roman de Horn, 93
rote memory, 50
rotta, 119

saltarello, 119
Sapphic meter, 180
Sarath, Ed, 4, 7
scale
  construction, 63
  tones and semitones, 63–64
Schola Enchiriadis, 61
secular/vernacular repertoire, 83–84, 85p
semitones, scale, 63–64
Sequentia Ensemble for Medieval Music
  Edda: Myths from Medieval Iceland, 21
  Fragments for the End of Time, 21–22
Singer of Tales, The (Lord), 6n7, 17
sole ending, 70, 70e, 70n15
solmisation hand, 51n31
Sound of Medieval Song, The (McGee), 33, 33nn6–8, 37, 102, 102n12
species, 63–64
"Spiritus sanctus vivificans vita" (Hildegard von Bingen)
  charting what is and what is not on page, 41–43, 42p, 42f
  data, working with, 34–38, 35f–37f, 35nn10–11, 41
  noteheads and neumes, 46, 46f
  rhythm (meter), 38
  text and neumes, 46–47, 47f
  Thornton transcription, 47, 47f
stantipes, 92

stichic poem, 180
storehouse of invention, building, 55
strophic poetry, 38
structured memory, 2–3
Studio der frühen Musik, 17–20, 18–19nn4–8
substitute clausulae, 155, 154p–155p

taqsim, 18
Taruskin, Richard, 5, 5–6n6, 31–32n4, 113
teaching medieval music, 191–196
  classical music leanings, 193
  implications, 193–195
  old model, 192
  orally transmitted arts, 191–192
  practical considerations, 195–196
tempora, 152
temporal discontinuity, 7
tempus, 140, 152
tenor, 70e, 71, 71e
termination, 71, 71e, 72, 72e,
tetrardus, 61, 62
text. *See also* rhetoric; *specific texts*
  music, 157–158
  neumes, 46–47, 46f
  performer engagement, 38, 38n15
text-driven approach, 9–10
Thornton, Barbara, 47, 47f, 157, 196
thumbprints, 57
  compositional, 56–57
Tindemans Margriet, 127n24
tonaries, 61, 69–72, 70e, 71e
tones, scale, 63–64
tornada, 161
Tractatus de Musica (Jerome of Moravia), 97, 98n10, 101–102
transmission
  epic poetry, 6n7
  medieval repertoire, 6n7
  memory and, 16
  models, 23–24, 24f
  oral, with aural understanding, 195, 195n2
Treitler, Leo, 31n3
  "Homer and Gregory: The Transmission of Epic Poetry and Plainchant," 6n7
  "Medieval Improvisation," 134–135
  With Voice and Pen, 6, 6n7, 31n3

tremula, 37
tritone, avoiding, 137–138, 137*e*
tritus, 61, 62
trotto, 119

unica, 102

Vatican Organum Treatise, 9, 141–155, 142*e,* 142*t,* 144*e*–145*e*
    mnemonic model, 146–147, 147*f*
    plainchant tenor, applying rules, 147–154, 149*e*–151*e,* 148*p*–149*p,* 151*p,* 152*t,* 153*e*–154*e,* 154*p*–155*p*
    practice, creating organum on plainchant tenor using VOT rules, 150, 151*p*
    practice, improvised organum "relay," 147, 148*p*–149*p*
    rhythmic modes, 152, 152n24, 152*t*
"Vatican Organum Treatise Re-examined, The" (Immel), 142–145, 142*t,* 145n17
vernacular music traditions
    definition, 194
    using models, 23–24, 23*p,* 24*f*
"*Viderunt omnes,*" 149–150, 149*e,* 150*e,* 153
    discant, 150–154, 151*e,* 154, 154*e*
    melisma, 150, 151*e,* 153, 153*e,* 154*e*
vielle, 90, 90n3
    drone, 96–99, 99*e*
virelai, 110
vocis sive soni, 101
Voices and Instruments of the Middle Ages (Page), 88, 97
von Bingen, Hildegard
    fluid composition, 37–38
    neumes, 35, 35*f*–36*f,* 35nn10–11

Ordo Virtutum, 127–129, 128*t*–129*t,* 130*e*–131*e*
von Bingen, Hildegard, "Spiritus sanctus vivificans vita"
    charting what is and what is not on page, 41–43, 42*p,* 42*t*
    data, working with, 34–38, 35*f*–37*f,* 35nn10–11, 41
    noteheads and neumes, 46, 46*f*
    rhythm (meter), 38
    text and neumes, 46–47, 46*f*
    Thornton transcription, 47, 47*f*
vox organalis, 136–138
    adding, medieval source as model, 138, 139*p*
vox principalis, 136–137

Well-Tempered Clavier (Bach), 134, 155–156
"What does the instrument "want" to play?," 90–91, 92*p*
What is your musical lineage?, 23–24, 25*p*
With Voice and Pen (Treitler), 6, 6n7, 31n3
word-for-word memorization, 50
world music traditions, using models, 23–24, 23*p,* 24*f*
Wright, Craig, 140–141, 145–146
written music, 31

Yates, Frances, 44–45, 49

zajal, 18
Zuckerman, Kenneth, 16, 29, 116–117
"Züh Aufführungspraxis der einstimmigen Musk des Mittelalters" (Binkley), 94n8

www.ingramcontent.com/pod-product-compliance
Ingram Content Group UK Ltd.
Pitfield, Milton Keynes, MK11 3LW, UK
UKHW021318180426
11947UKWH00015B/1302